JAGGER

JAGGER

Carey Schofield

BEAUFORT BOOKS

PUBLISHERS

New York

Copyright © 1985 by Carey Schofield

All rights reserved. No part of this publication may be reproduced or
transmitted in any form or by any means, electronic or mechanical, including
photocopy, recording, or any information storage and retrieval system now
known or to be invented, without permission in writing from the publisher,
except by a reviewer who wishes to quote brief passages in connection with a
review written for inclusion in a magazine, newspaper, or broadcast.

Library of Congress Cataloging in Publication Data

Schofield, Carey.
Jagger.

Bibliography: p.
Includes index.
1. Jagger, Mick. 2. Rock musicians—England
Biography. I. Title.
ML420.J22S34   1985   784.5′4′00924 [B]   84-24415
ISBN 0-8253-0262-5 (pbk.)

Published in the United States by Beaufort Books Publishers, New York.

Printed in the U.S.A.   First American Edition
10 9 8 7 6 5 4 3 2 1

List of Illustrations

Acknowledgements

The author would like to thank all the friends, enemies and colleagues of Mick Jagger who helped with the research for this book. Thanks are also due to Laurence King, to Caroline Dawnay and Michael Sissons, both of A.D. Peters, and to Christopher Falkus of Methuen. A particular debt of gratitude is owed to my long-suffering editor, Cathryn Game.

Song lyrics quoted are copyright as follows: 'Under My Thumb', 'High and Dry', 'Stupid Girl', 'Lady Jane', all © 1966 and 'In Another Land' © 1967 ABKCO Music Inc., USA and Essex Music International, London; 'Shattered' and 'Respectable' both © 1978 and 'Summer Romance' © 1980 Cansel Ltd; sub-published by EMI Music Publishing Ltd.

Quotes from Cecil Beaton's diaries are from *Self-Portrait with Friends: The Selected Diaries of Cecil Beaton, 1926–1974* (edited by Richard Buckle; Weidenfeld and Nicolson, 1979).

Chapter One

Jumping Jack Flash is now forty, a man of wealth and taste. He owns a small château in the Loire, a house in Cheyne Walk in Chelsea, a pretty brownstone house in New York's Riverside Drive and he is building a house on Mustique. He spends his time supervising the Rolling Stones empire and looking after its investments, which range from record-producing companies to a fish-processing plant in Japan. He travels endlessly, zipping around from one place to another, hardly ever staying in the same country for more than a few weeks. He reads a great deal, especially history and biography. During the last twenty years he has seduced some of the prettiest girls in Europe and America, and hundreds of others as well. He knows that he has access to almost anyone in the world that he wants to meet. He cooks marvellously, and will spend most of a day bicycling around New York buying the best possible ingredients for a Japanese meal. He is a devoted but stern father to his enchanting eleven-year-old daughter, and takes a keen interest in her expensive education at a New York day school. He nurtures his body and his mind. He seems to have created, as nearly as possible, a painfree existence, and he will avoid, whenever possible, taking any risk or exposing himself. Rather than dare write it himself, he will hire a ghost-writer to help with his autobiography. Although he admits that he would like to act again, and has flirted with several projects, he has never made a film since the disastrous *Ned Kelly*. It took him nearly ten years to start work on another film (Herzog's *Fitzcarraldo*), and even then he did not complete his part, for reasons that remain unclear. But his caution is understandable. No one in the world is as vulnerable as Jagger. Newspapers can announce with impunity that he is dead, having affairs with strangers or retiring. No matter how ludicrous the story, Mick Jagger is news. All stars are public property: it's the price they pay for the millions. But no other twentieth-century entertainer, with the possible exceptions of Garbo and Valentino, has been accorded anything like his mythological status.

Legends accrete around him. As with a holy man or a mass killer, it hardly matters whether or not they are true. The belief of early fans that he had leukaemia represented more than a medical untruth. He was a rebel, assaulting head on the powers that were, and he diverged from normal models of masculinity. The Establishment seemed so strong that by contrast he appeared fearfully vulnerable, and almost certainly doomed. In the same way, the Mars bar, the Satanic practices and the poodle roasting are all images whose validity is hardly connected to their historical accuracy. He is a symbol of sex: almost everyone under fifty seems to know someone who knows someone who has slept with him. Stories of encounters in limousines or on bathroom floors abound, retold endlessly with slight variations and different heroines. He has been a focus of fantasy for thousands of adolescents, to whom he has epitomised sexual promise and illicit excitement. There is the story of the ambitious groupie who began her career with the drummer in an unheard of local band, which she decided was 'OK, but not like sleeping with Mick Jagger'. Her next conquest was the bass player with a fairly successful band, followed by a famous lead guitarist. Both of these she also pronounced to be 'OK, but not like sleeping with Mick Jagger'. Finally, in the fullness of time, she managed to seduce the great man himself. But this, too, was 'OK, but not like sleeping with Mick Jagger,' she had to admit.

It may not be the case that if he had not existed we would have had to invent him, but he is certainly related to an archetype that we seem to find reassuring. The Byronic hero, the character that is the invention of Byron rather than a description of the poet himself, redeems the mediocrity of everyone else's life. The noble, turbulent soul breaks all the normal restraints of society, but he towers above his fellows and is justified by the strength of his passions. He strays into mad, bad and cruel ways out of the whimsicality of aristocratic despair. These excesses make him endlessly fascinating to the ordinary people he affects to despise; we need someone to explore decadence and amorality since most of us will not. It is not important that Mick Jagger has not done so either. He is seen to have travelled beyond the bounds of normality, and that is what we need him for. In the case of Jagger, as of Byron, the timing was absolutely right: in both the 1800s and the 1960s a romantic rebel was needed. But of course Mick Jagger's supreme achievement has been to keep his mythological status alive by shifting his image and managing to remain continually contemporary.

However aware we are that he is now forty, Jagger still seems to be the definitive rock and roll singer. It does not seem to be true that he is older than the newcomers – he is just more important. And however much his performance or his songwriting might be criticised, he remains incomparable. Elvis is dead – the Beatles are no more. It would be laughable to compare anyone else. The Who seem to be fossilised relics of an earlier age. Others have clung to a dehydrated, cosmeticised youth. Paul McCartney, always bland, has degenerated into anodyne niceness. Jagger looks slightly different each time we see him, but always quintessentially modern. And each of his new haircuts makes everyone who is still wearing the last one look just a little tired and dreary. And even through the spell in the seventies when the band was at its lowest ebb, Jagger

3

himself has remained relevant. He has epitomised successive ages. When young people were in revolt, Jagger was the most revolting of all. He seemed dirtier and more uncouth than anyone else. But just as it appeared that there was nothing shocking left for him to do, we began to see him in a new light – suddenly he was languidly, sardonically elegant. He couldn't be said to have given up the bad fight, he still set himself clearly outside the bounds of normality, but Jagger rebellion no longer entailed shocking the middle-aged by looking scruffy. Now he was exquisite, but his bizarre beauty somehow seemed more threatening than his sloven- liness, perhaps because he retained his characteristic air of play- ful vice. And just as soon as we had got used to the decandent dandy, suddenly he emerged newly-born once again, this time sportif and clean-living.

Mick Jagger grew up during the 1950s in Dartford, Kent. It was a decade when national pride was high, despite the underlying tur- bulence of the times. Britain was dismantling the greatest empire the world had ever seen, and recovering from a costly victory in a bloody war. There was fighting in Korea, there was the Suez de- bacle, and there was the fear of Reds and of the Bomb. But the drear austerity of the immediate post-war period finally appeared to be ending. The nation that had stood alone against Hitler was no longer having to send humiliating begging missions to Washington. Rationing was being phased out and consumer goodies that had not been seen since 1939 were finding their way back into the shops. The voice of the narrator of the Pathé news bulletins, watched by millions who went to the 'pictures' every week, sounded cheerful and optimistic, reflecting a general feeling that life was getting better again. In that age of innocence the opening of a council tower block or talk of building motorways seemed to herald a bright future. A succession of elderly, avuncular prime ministers governed. They were all Conservatives but in reality they were distinguishable from their political opponents only by the cut of their suits and the colour of their rosettes. The third of them was widely believed when he told the nation that they had never had it so good.

Life must have seemed particularly hopeful in the sprawling London suburbs. Dartford is a small town in Kent, part of the vast area of south-eastern England which has been virtually assimilated into London. Between the two World Wars four million new homes were built in England (sufficient to house a third of the nation) so that by the 1950s most English people lived in suburbia. Thousands of previously distinct towns and villages were being effectively linked together. Wilmington, where the Jaggers lived for most of Mick's childhood, slid into Dartford, which slid into Bexley, which slid into Eltham, which slid into Blackheath, which slid into the pullulating metropolis. This was a new world, without a real past and without memories, either traumatic or proud. For many of the first inhabitants, decanted from grimy London streets, it must have seemed like Paradise, with tree-lined streets, parks and access to the countryside. Without actually being in the country, which was known to be uncomfortable, muddy and full of homicidal bulls, the curving streets and the privet-hedged front gardens alluded to a dream of rural life. It was Merry England deodorised for the twentieth century, every yeoman with his plot of land and a fast train to Waterloo or Charing Cross. Despite the apparent similarity of the houses, they were in fact shrines to the Briton's right to his eccentricities. The names of the houses, the porches their owners built onto them, and the varied gates and garden ornaments were all wilful statements of their owners' individuality. Huns and other foreigners might live in identical flats or rows of indistinguishable houses, but an Englishman's castle defiantly proclaimed his own idiosyncratic tastes. This world of hollyhocks and sunflowers, leaded windows and crazy paving must have felt very safe to its children – it was a long way from the barbarity of the city. There was nothing much to be frightened of here. Evil needed deeper roots: and it was not yet fashionable to think that people did too. But this quiet atmosphere also seemed terribly stultifying . . . just

5

plain boring to an imaginative youth. Wherever things might be supposed to be happening – London, Paris, New York or Hollywood – there certainly was not much going on in Dartford. And beneath the gentility there was as much tension as anywhere else. The issues may have been less dire, but the passions were not.

The fear was not of grinding poverty, but of sinking to a lower social level than one's parents or grandparents, or of failing to consolidate one's own achievements. Many in the Kent suburbs felt themselves tenaciously clinging to middle-class membership. As living standards rose many bureaucrats or lower-ranking professionals found themselves living next door to affluent builders or tradesmen. The social boundaries that had preserved the self-respect of the clerical classes were being eroded. So it was constantly necessary to reinforce one's status. It was not only the material success of the family that was important, but also those thousand distinctions of style and language that other third-generation white collar wearers would recognise as separating one from the dreaded 'working class'.

Such considerations were of some importance to Mick's mother, Eva Scutts. She had been born in Australia, but had come to England with her family as a teenager. As a result she seems never to have escaped the feeling of being *deraciné*, neither English nor any longer Australian. Neighbours in Dartford found her highly sensitive about being Australian, and convinced that the English found all her compatriots loudmouthed rednecks. She and Basil ('Joe') Jagger were married at Holy Trinity Church in Dartford on 7 December 1940. He was a games teacher at a local school, and she worked as a hairdresser. Wartime rationing meant that almost everything was scarce – food, drink and clothing especially. So it was a subdued wedding, with only about fifty guests at the reception at the local Conybeare Hall. Eva wore a lavender blue silk dress, and was given away by her brother. Joe's brother, Albert, was the best man. As a young wife Eva seemed to over-compensate for her insecurity: she became more conventional than everybody else, more normal than is normal. Even in Dartford she was thought to be exceptionally concerned with the trappings of gentility. She seemed unnecessarily concerned that her house should be perfectly clean and that everything should be in its place. Mick was later to be very aware of his mother's insecurity, but was careful not to get involved with it himself. He would say bluntly, 'My mum is very working-class, my father bourgeois, because he had a reasonably good education, so I come from somewhere in between that. Neither one thing nor the other.' In fact it was not difficult for Eva to assimilate herself into English life. She was pretty, fun and liked by her neighbours.

Her first child was born on Monday, 26 July 1943, and named Michael Philip. That weekend Mussolini had resigned, and RAF Mosquitoes had dropped 2000 tons of high-explosives and incendiary bombs on Essen, following raids on Hamburg and Cologne. The Allied advance in Sicily was slowing down as troops came up against the enemy's prepared line of defence in the mountains. The war situation was grave, but not as bleak as it had been two years earlier. Although the war effort dominated everyone's life, in some ways Dartford seemed surprisingly calm. At the town's State Cinema the Abbott and Costello film, *Money for Jam*, was showing, while the Rialto had *The Last of the Mohicans* with Binnie Barnes, Randolph Scott and Henry Wilcoxon. The same week at Dartford Police Court two men pleaded guilty to stealing a couple of chickens and were fined £5 each. A 74-year-old man was fined 5/- for begging, and two men found guilty of stealing hosepipe worth 30/- were each fined £2. Eva's son was a large, placid baby, much admired for his happy smile. He was slow to learn to walk, but so obviously bright that no one worried about his progress. His brother, Christopher Edward, was born on 19 December 1947.

They were both healthy little boys, with an air of attractive wickedness and nice manners. Mike, as the family called the elder one, had an especially perky air that neighbours and teachers found endearing. He would never walk sedately along the pavement if he

7

could run, swing from a tree or climb along a wall. At Wentworth County Primary School he managed never to be overlooked, even in a class of thirty children all dressed identically. He is remembered as always being the first to volunteer for anything, or to announce that he had finished a set task. His was one of the first names that any new teacher learnt. His eagerness and energy made him popular with the staff, and although he was not outstanding academically, his teachers always considered him to be one of the clever children. During Jagger's time at the school this was vitally significant. In their final year at Wentworth the children would take the 11+ examination, which would determine the entire future course of their lives. For the lucky ones there was the grammar school, where an academic education, a disciplined environment and a feeling of ascendancy over the other yobs could open the door to university, the professions or the civil service. The tinselly prizes of suburbia, that would safeguard precious membership of the middle classes, would probably be yours for the asking if you could get through the 11+. Otherwise, you would simply be relegated to the dustbin of the secondary modern. There only a minority of pupils would even be entered for 'O' levels, and there would probably be no sixth form at all. The system was well-intentioned; it was meant to provide an appropriate education for everyone, and theoretically there was provision for anyone who later seemed likely to benefit from a grammar school education but had failed the 11+ to transfer from the secondary school at thirteen or sixteen. But in practice the children and their parents knew that the result of the 11+ was almost always irrevocable. And Dartford was not a place where the opportunity for social advancement or decline was taken lightly. So a boy who was lead to believe that he was likely to pass the crucial 11+ might feel a certain arrogance. It is not surprising that by the time he was eleven both his schoolfriends and adults who knew him were beginning to feel that Mike Jagger was getting cocky. Freud remarked that an eldest son who has known the undivided love of a doting mother will never entirely lose the

8

sense that he is a hero. And not only had Jagger had his mother to himself for four years before any sibling came along, but as he grew up that sibling did not seem to pose a very dramatic threat. Adults found him less attractive and he appeared to be less intelligent. Schoolmasters noticed that Chris seemed to be modelling himself on his elder brother, to the extent of consciously copying his mannerisms and taking up his enthusiasms. But both the boys knew that everything Chris ever did Mike had done first, usually years before.

But even for a doted-on darling, transferring to the grammar school after the safety and familiarity of the junior school was a trial. There were twice as many pupils in the grammar school, and many of them seemed to the first form to be like grown-up men, with deep voices and hairy bodies. Dartford Grammar School was started in the sixteenth century, and late in March every year the founders, Mr Vaughan and Mr D'Aeth, were commemorated during the Founders' Day celebrations. In the morning there would be a service of thanksgiving at a local church, and in the evening the school prizegiving would be held in the new school hall, built at the beginning of the war. The teachers wore academic dress for the occasion, and the boys wore their normal uniform of maroon and gold. A local worthy would be invited to give an address, reminding the boys of the long history of the school and its glorious achievements. The headmaster would then make a speech, reminding the parents and the local reporters who would inevitably be there of the past year's contribution to those achievements and making any complaints he might have, such as Kent Education Committee's delay in providing the school with the new canteen that it badly needed.

The principal concern of the headmaster, Mr Hudson, and his staff was to make the school as much like their idea of an English public school as possible. To this end the boys were divided into four houses for games, and a great effort was made to instil into them a sense of house loyalty. Prefects were given a lot of re-

9

sponsibility within the school for policing the younger boys and enforcing discipline. And the headmaster's greatest pride was the Combined Cadet Force, which every boy joined. Friday afternoons were spent square-bashing and practising arms drill. The idea was that after several years in the CCF boys might be offered a commission when they did National Service, which was still compulsory.

So Jagger settled down into the school routine: lots of games, compulsory rugby in winter and cricket in summer, and lots of homework. He was noticed by teachers as a hardworking boy, with an enquiring mind that made him a pleasure to teach because at his best he was responsive and enthusiastic, and at his worst mildly insubordinate. For the first couple of years he seemed, according to a former teacher, 'keen to do well'. 'When he was young he was eager and wanted to get to the top. But after that he changed. I always felt that he would have liked to be outstanding, but suddenly realised that he wasn't going to be.' When it suddenly dawned on him that there were boys in his class who would always be cleverer than he was, he began to make it clear by his manner that he was not competing with them anyway. Another former teacher recalls that Jagger's class was 'an absolutely cracking form, one of the brightest I ever taught'. Possibly if so many of the others had not been exceptionally talented, Jagger would not have cast himself as the rebel. As it was, 'Jagger and his friend Gorman stood out as the uncooperative ones', after the first two years. Certainly Mike played little part in the organised life of the school. He never contributed to the school magazine, never sang in the choir or took part in a school play, except once when he was pressed into helping with the scenery. Although he was difficult in school, some members of staff formed the impression that he wanted to please his father. But this did not lead him to take a significant part in school games, despite the fact that his father was a PE teacher. He rarely played in any team – he was in the House Second XI for a few rugby matches, but did not show much enthusiasm. He showed some interest in cricket, but was not very good at it. According to friends he 'always fancied his chances as a fast bowler', but two of his contemporaries, Peter Holland and Ken Russell, were excellent fast bowlers, and both ended up playing for Kent. So once again Mike withdrew from a competition he couldn't win. The only game he seemed to enjoy was basketball, for which he eventually became school captain.

As he was becoming more unpopular with the staff he was also arousing the hostility of some of his peers. 'The mouth was already in evidence. He always had plenty to say for himself, not all of it well reflected. He would treat the rest of us to accounts of his conquests with girls. He certainly wanted to give the impression that he could have his pick of them. He had a gang of friends, most of whom were interested in jazz, and they would always dominate any room. They were quite an aggressive bunch. They included Tony Gorman, Allan Etherington, Richard Condon, Dick Taylor and Clive Robson. There was also Bob Beckwith who was much quieter than the rest of them.'

According to other contemporaries, the atmosphere in the form as a whole was vicious and cut-throat. Because there were so many clever boys there was a great deal of rivalry, most of it nasty. Not everyone in the class took against Jagger. There were those who felt a sneaking admiration for him. Peter Keir, who was in the same form throughout the school, recalls, 'What he had that we didn't was a wider view of things. Most of us were only really concerned with working our way steadily through the syllabus. But Jagger gave the impression that he had mixed with a wider circle of acquaintances. I daresay that through the television series he had got acquainted with people outside the narrow world of Dartford.' Joe Jagger had been involved with the making of a television series, *Seeing Sport*, which was intended to encourage young people to take up new sports, especially the more adventurous ones. Despite his dislike of sports at school, Mike and some of his friends appeared in the programmes demonstrating the activities his father

11

was describing, such as canoeing or rock-climbing. So as a junior boy at the grammar school, Jagger experienced a *soupçon* of celebrity, which must have boosted his confidence at a time of intellectual uncertainty. Peter Keir: 'I recall that he was quite interested in history, but related it to broader issues, like communism and nuclear war. And his interpretation of school uniform was more liberal than most people's. It was the age of drainpipe trousers, and his were always an inch narrower than anyone else's, his hair just a bit longer. He didn't wear anything really outrageous, just an exaggerated version of what was allowable. It was before widespread youth rebellion, and slight variations like that constituted a challenge to authority.' Walter Bennett was Jagger's housemaster throughout his time at the school, and also his form master while he was in the fourth and fifth years. He confirms Peter Keir's memories of Jagger's overstated clothes. 'At that time,' he says, 'boys were expected to turn out to school functions in uniform. One little excess that I remember was Jagger turning up to Sports Day in a black jacket with silver threads, with several girls in tow.'

The principal concern of most of the inmates of Dartford Grammar School was the pursuit of sex. Although Mike could find girls to accompany him to Sports Day, it was very difficult to find any real action. But one had to maintain appearances – to have bemoaned, publicly, one's enforced celibacy would have outraged convention. During cross-country runs Mike, Clive Robson and Tony Gorman would escape the rest of the class by hiding among the sand dunes and hillocks on Dartford Heath. (This was before the motorway had been built across the heath.) They would spend a pleasant hour or so smoking the few cigarettes they had managed to pinch from their parents that morning, and regaling each other with increasingly lurid tales of their conquests. 'It was always perfectly obvious to the other two that whoever was talking was telling a pack of lies. But we never said so.' The three would usually manage to join the others towards the end of the run, by taking a short cut. Contact with real girls was not easy to arrange. No one in Mike's circle of friends had a sister who could have kept them supplied with her friends. There were dancing classes at the girls school, but these were tense, embarrassing and unfruitful. Mike and Clive Robson were, however, unceasing in their girl-hunt. They volunteered to help shift scenery for the girls school dramatic society, but found to their dismay that they were so severely policed that they hardly got to talk to any girls. They even joined the photographic society, because that way they were given a key to the school dark-room, which they hoped would come in useful during the annual school dances. But still, according to Clive, 'none of us got beyond the occasional groping'. The staff of the two schools competently conspired to keep their charges apart. Even when pupils from both establishments were taken to a special schools showing of the film of *Richard III* they were carefully segregated. To the chagrin of all, the girls had to sit in the stalls, while the boys were put in the balcony. So they could only communicate by catcalling, throwing empty crisp bags and other established courting rituals.

Even when Mike and his friends managed to make friends with a girl they seem to have been slow pouncers, whatever they told each other. Anne, who was a girlfriend of Jagger when she was about thirteen and he was about two years older, says that he never really tried to seduce her. Her principal memory is not of him but of his mother's marvellous box of make-up. Now that the boys were both at school Eva Jagger had got herself a part-time job. She had become an Avon lady – selling cosmetics from door to door. Anne says that the chest, crammed full of every sort of Avon lipstick, scent, bath salts, eye shadow and so on, seemed to her quite magical, and that the best thing about going to tea with Mike was being allowed to explore the Avon goodies, and try on a bit of this and that.

Like many adolescents of the time, Jagger was absorbed in fantasies of America. For him the United States provided the imagery of a world of excitement and glamour far removed from Dartford and his virtuous classmates. He later recalled, 'Everyone was dreamin' about America. That whole American dream was in vogue then.' America was vast – everyone had seen cowboy films, or the Lone Ranger on television riding across a plain that seemed to be bigger than the whole of Kent. Imported copies of *Mad* and other inspired comics, with their esoteric anarchistic humour, were a whole world away from sturdy English comedy of the time. A generation reared on the stirring patriotic derring-do of *Eagle* and *Hotspur* couldn't help but be seduced by tales of superhuman superheroes battling zoot-suited hoods in, among and over towering skyscrapers. And the cars – in a land where most middle-class families still did not own a car, and the lucky ones proudly polished their dapper little Morris Minor on Sundays, glimpses of American freeways in the movies seemed like a revelation of Paradise. The ostentatious magnificence of a Crown Imp Convertible, a '56 Oldsmobile or a Lincoln Continental dazzled English teenagers. Who could doubt the cultural superiority of a country where every young white male burned down a sunny road in a winged, fanged, finned extravaganza with his date beside him? The sharpest clothes, the hippest slang and the junkiest food (crisps, tomato ketchup and hamburgers) were all immigrants from the fabled land of plenty. And the image of the American dream purveyed by the movies was reinforced by parents, who remembered the brash bounty of the wartime GIs. And it was from the United States that the blueprint for conflict between the generations arrived.

The Wild One (1954), *Rebel Without a Cause* and *Blackboard Jungle* (both 1955) had introduced into popular culture the notion of disaffected youth. All three movies were hugely successful worldwide. *Blackboard Jungle* dealt specifically with juvenile anarchy in a Bronx high school. But even by 1958 little of all this stirring of adolescent uprising had filtered through to Dartford Grammar School: only a few wild boys in the fifth form seemed to have any awareness at all of their power to evade the mould of their parents' choice. The few sophisticates shared an interest in music. But although their contemporaries described it as jazz, it was in fact rhythm and blues that was increasingly preoccupying them. 'Trad' jazz was hugely popular in the fifties, with jazz clubs springing up in every town. It was a fundamentalist movement, faithful to the New Orleans roots of jazz, and inimical to modern, 'bebop', white faggotty jazz. The bands of Chris Barber, Kenny Ball, Acker Bilk and others filled the clubs and the airwaves. They wore waistcoats or braces and bowler hats, and played trumpet, clarinet, banjo and drums. Rhythm and blues was heard in Britain as a result of the skiffle craze that swept the country in the early fifties. Skiffle was a syncopated mixture of jazz, folk and blues, played on tea chests, washboards, tin cans and anything else out of which penniless sharecroppers in the southern states could wring a sound. The style had originated at emergency rent parties, held to raise enough money to keep the landlord at bay. The public enthusiasm for skiffle encouraged record companies to launch, tentatively, a few blues records in England. Initially they only released the gentler, mournful, rural blues sung by the likes of Big Bill Broonzy and Leadbelly. But very slowly the real R&B, raw, electric and urban, began to penetrate the UK. The converted frantically tried to persuade stores to import records for them, and then swopped their treasures among themselves. From Chicago came recordings produced by the legendary Chess company of Muddy Waters, Howlin' Wolf and Bo Diddley. These were the shrieking gut sounds that Jagger and his friends listened to, huddled round a single mono record-player. 'When I was around thirteen or fourteen I became interested in blues, firstly when I found out that it so much as existed. It was never played on the radio, and if it was, it was only by accident. Things that were hits in America, but never over here.' Jagger, Dick Taylor, Allen Etherington and Bob Beckwith would gather at one of their houses outside school hours and would painstakingly imitate the songs. Dick played drums, Bob guitar and Allen maraccas. Mike would sing. He had always been a remarkably good impersonator, and ever since he was a child he had been able to copy singers he had heard a few times. His first group, Little Boy Blue and the Blue Boys, as they called themselves, seems to have been mainly a vehicle for Jagger's adolescent narcissism, although a good time was presumably had by them all. But it sounds as though he was far more involved with his own performance than that of the Blue Boys as a whole. After a session he would closely question his friends about what he had sounded like, whether it was better than last time, and so on. But studying the giants of R&B so closely was an invaluable musical education – the only one he had, since he avoided musical activities at school, and didn't even learn to read music.

It had become clear that National Service was going to be phased out, and that Mike and his contemporaries would not be called up. This removed the principal excuse for the Combined Cadet Force, which so many of the boys hated and found oppressive. The headmaster continued to consider the Force an integral part of the school life, but it was not, strictly speaking, compulsory. Jagger, Richard Condon, Clive Robson and a couple of others spearheaded a mass defection from the CCF. They simply refused to take part in it any longer. There was nothing the headmaster could do. But he never forgave the mutiny, and seems to have held Jagger particularly responsible, although it does not appear to have been his idea. It was a group rebellion.

Although he was becoming ever more bolshie at school, Mike was working hard enough to get by. Walter Bennett recalls, 'I found that he worked, but somewhat grudgingly. In the fourth year his term marks for French made him thirteenth out of a class of twenty-five, while his exam mark, 65 per cent, made him fifth.' This pattern seems to have repeated itself in most other subjects; he was generally performed well when it was absolutely necessary, but was not so keen on the hard slog throughout the term. He got by. He passed seven 'O' levels, and stayed on to do 'A' level English literature, history and French.

Life in the sixth form was in many ways easier than it had been in the lower forms. There was more freedom and the boys were only doing the two or three subjects they had chosen to take at 'A' level, which were usually the ones they liked best. It became easier to escape school and spend time in the Carousel coffee bar in East Hill. Occasionally sixth formers would even venture into a pub, but it was a considerable risk. Clive Robson remembers going with Mike to the nearby Oddfellows pub for a drink one lunchtime at the end of one Christmas term. But they were seen coming out, and made to feel that they had disgraced the school by their heinous conduct. Sixth form boys were not turned out into the playground during every break and many of them enjoyed the status of being prefects. Since leading the CCF defection there was no question that Mike would be made a prefect, of course. Those who were prefects had their own room and certain privileges, such as being able to go straight to the top of the queue for lunch. But in any case the sixth form room was an improvement on most of the other classrooms. It was on the ground floor, and had a window over-looking the headmaster's garden. Through this window anyone who was out of favour, which frequently included Mike, was liable to be hurled. The atmosphere in this clever, violent class had not softened as they all grew up. And they did not only give each other a hard time: the English master was one of their favourite victims. He seems to have been a tempting target. According to Clive Robson, whenever the class was reading a play he would nab the plum part for himself. And during readings of *King Lear*, which was one of the set 'A' level texts, he would be so moved by his own performance that he would begin to weep. But he was mainly disliked because the boys had no confidence in his teaching. They began to worry that he was so incompetent that they might fail their examination. So Mike enrolled in a correspondence course in 'A' level English. The rest of the class joined in – Mike wrote the set essays (although he often neglected the work the school required) but his friends also read all the notes that he was sent, and the criticisms of his work. Mike seems to have gained quite a

17

lot of respect from his fellows through this piece of initiative, which helped everyone in the class to pass the exam. But of course the English master felt that the good results vindicated him. Clive Robson went to the school prizegiving, the year after he had left. It was the first time he had seen the teacher in question since they had obtained the exam results. 'You see,' he told Clive, 'I told you there was nothing wrong with my teaching, and I was right. You all passed.'

Although he failed French, Mike got into the London School of Economics, part of London University, to do a degree in economics. Dartford Grammar School was not sorry to see him go. The headmaster was especially glad to see the back of him. His dislike of Jagger had been well known within the school although no one suggests that he was unfair to him. Jagger had evolved a highly efficient system of baiting him enough to irritate him, but not quite badly enough to warrant serious punishment. He would niggle about anything he was asked to do, and argue with any public statement, making it clear that he was laughing at the school authorities, and the headmaster in particular. He would half-impersonate him, but would quickly revert to his normal manner when the headmaster was about to explode. Ian Harris, the young maths master, was one of the few members of staff who had a good word to say about him. Years later, in the late sixties, the school governors refused to allow a BBC film crew to interview Harris about Jagger inside the school buildings. And Harris' suggestion that the Rolling Stones should be persuaded to give a concert in aid of the school was met with howls of disgust. Even the prospect of a new swimming pool or extra classrooms could not persuade the governors to let the school's name be associated with that of Jagger any more than they could help.

Although he was going to continue to live at home, and travel up to London daily to attend lectures at the LSE, Jagger seems to have been excited by the idea of London. He took a holiday job, as he had frequently done before, to help pay for his clothes and his record habit. During Christmas vacations he had worked as a temporary postman, helping to deliver sackfuls of mail during the two weeks before Christmas. This time he had to settle for a less profitable job, as a porter in a local hospital. Tony Gorman's father was the secretary of Bexley Mental Hospital, and arranged for his son and several friends to work there during the summer holidays. They were paid £4 10/- a week each, which seemed a reasonable wage. It was a depressing place where, it seemed, most of the patients had just been dumped to die. 'There was no attempt to treat people, it was a purely custodial institution. Most of the nurses were illiterate Italian nymphomaniacs. And most of the female patients were better-looking nymphomaniacs, who we were warned to stay away from,' one of the friends who worked there with Mike says. But despite all that nymphomania he thinks it unlikely that Mike slept with any of the nurses or patients. Years later he told friends how he had been snooping around the hospital one day, and had come across a room full of boxes containing all the worldly goods of people who had died fifty or sixty years earlier – clothes, watches, false teeth, the occasional photograph, and the odd collections of trinkets that were all that remained of them. Mike quite enjoyed the job. It was not very hard work, and he managed to spend a considerable amount of time talking to the other porters, the gardener and anyone else who was around.

Like most arts students, Jagger seems to have gone up to university without any clear idea of what he wanted to do when he graduated. He talked idly of becoming a journalist, but does not seem to have done anything about the idea. But whatever his ambitions may have been in that summer of 1961, it seems highly unlikely that he seriously harboured any plan to sing professionally.

Chapter Two

When he left school Mike Jagger became Mick. His family had always called him Mike, and continued to do so, but his musical friends addressed him as Mick, and among his new London acquaintances the name stuck.

Despite the excitement of going to the London School of Economics, Mick continued to spend a lot of time with Little Boy Blue and the Blue Boys. The group had been revitalised by the recent arrival of Keith Richards. Like Mick, Keith had been born in Dartford, but the Richards family lived on the other side of town, on a modern council estate. He was the only child of an electrical engineer, and grew up spoilt by a bevy of doting aunts who all lived locally. Keith and Mick had been friends at their primary school, but they had lost touch since and had only met once in the intervening years, when Mick had been selling ice-creams outside the public library to earn some holiday money. Keith had recognised him and bought an ice-cream, but at that time they did not seem to have very much in common. Mick had been at the grammar school, and Keith at the technical school, which was lower, on the socio-intellectual scale, even than the secondary modern. It was intended to train those children who were unfit for an academic education of any sort with basic training in a trade or craft. Keith beat the system, however, and emerged at sixteen without any of the skills that the school had intended to instil. He was, however, already a talented guitarist and a passable painter, and he managed to get himself into Sidcup Art School. The principal advantage of the art school for Keith was that it provided him with an excuse for not taking a job, plenty of free time and like-minded friends. Among those with whom he entered into an alliance of indolence and music was Dick Taylor, who had arrived at art school from Dartford Grammar School, through motives broadly similar to Keith's. Dick was by now playing with several different bands. But although he flirted with folk and jazz, he remained emotionally faithful to rhythm and blues and was pleased to find a fellow fanatic in Keith. But although they became close friends, he did not introduce Keith to Jagger or the other members of the Blue Boys.

It was not until Mick and Keith met again, purely by chance, on a suburban train that they discovered their mutual obsession. Keith described the meeting in a 1971 interview for *Rolling Stone* Magazine:

> So I get on this train one morning, and there's Jagger and under his arm he has four or five albums. I haven't seen him since the time I bought an ice-cream off him, and we haven't hung around together since we were five, six, ten years. We recognised each other straight off. 'Hi, man,' I say. 'Where you going?' he says. And under his arm he's got Chuck Berry and Little Walter, Muddy Waters. 'You're into Chuck Berry, man, really?'

They were both amazed and delighted by the coincidence that they should share what was then such an unusual taste in music. Keith was particularly impressed by Mick's efficiency at writing to Chess records in Chicago and ordering records that were unobtainable in England. They quickly re-established the friendship that had lapsed for over ten years when they found out that, in Keith's words, 'I could play a little and he could sing a bit.' And when they found out that they both knew and played with Dick Taylor it became almost inevitable that Keith should begin to play guitar with the Blue Boys. As Jagger said later, 'It was a lot of coincidences seemingly falling into place.' Keith seems to have been a very much better musician at this time than any of the others, possibly because his life had been unencumbered by schoolwork. He seems to have boosted Mick's faith in the potential of the group – after the arrival of Keith he began to talk about the Blue Boys more, and to refer to the group as a whole, rather than just talking about his own singing. Mick and Keith became so close that the next summer, when Keith as usual went on holiday with his parents, Mick went too.

So it was that by the time Mick went to the LSE his life was busier and more exciting than it had been for some time. The group really seemed to be taking shape, and he was enthusiastic about his course at the LSE. The BSc economics course, for which Mick was enrolled, was not a soft option: especially for someone without maths 'A' level, mastering economics would have entailed a certain amount of work, so he must have had a genuine interest in the subject. With his 'A' levels it would have been easier for him to get into university to read history or English, and he would almost certainly have been able to get by on such a course with less work. His friends from the LSE confirm that he seemed absorbed in the course. Michael Densham, who was a year or two ahead of Jagger at the LSE, says that he was 'very bright and determined, and always very keen on business', although he did not ever suggest that he was thinking of going into business himself.

His school friends thought it odd that he had chosen to go to London University. They had all spent the last few years longing to get away from home. In their unending quest for sex they had all come to the conclusion that that commodity must be easier to come by anywhere other than Dartford. So it seemed strange that Mick, one of the most assiduous in the hunt, should go to a university so near that he could commute from home. But during the first Christmas vacation, when Mick and Clive Robson met by chance in Dartford, Clive decided that Mick had probably made a more sensible decision. He had gone up to Oxford, which far from being the 'cornucopia of female talent' that he had looked forward to, provided an even more monastic existence than Dartford Grammar School. Mick, however, seemed to have had some success, finally. He was seen around Dartford that Christmas with a girl called Bridget who had what Mick's friends described as a 'face like a pudding. She really was very ugly.' But Mick, even though he was slightly embarrassed by her, told the lads that he really loved her, and that he had 'found happiness with her'. Since Mick had hitherto been fussy about the girls he was seen with, his friends assumed enviously that she must be cooperative. And as Mick told his tales of London, describing it as a city full to overflowing with desirable, lustful women, they all began to regret their own dreary universities.

The London School of Economics was at that time an exhilarating place to be. Its alumni included a significant number of people who were visible, if not prominent, in the professions that seemed most exciting and innovatory. Cabinets might be full of people from Oxbridge, but television was increasingly full of past students of the LSE, including Bernard Levin, Robert Mackenzie, Michael Peacock and Mark Abrams. And in 1960 another, Paul Chambers, became chairman of the gigantic ICI (Imperial Chemical Industries). Lecturers included people of the calibre of Michael Oakeshott and Lord Robbins (himself a former student). Because of the current prestige of the establishment, and because of its convenient situation in the heart of London, it was easy to attract such people as Harold Wilson and Edward Heath to give the occasional lecture or take part in debates.

Student life centred around parties in peoples' flats in the evenings and particularly around the bar, called the Three Tuns, on the corner of Houghton Street. Every Friday evening there would be a bar social, at which everyone would get as drunk as possible. It was, according to someone who was there, a 'caricature of student life'. Since a great many undergraduates lived with parents or relations in the Home Counties, or in digs in the outlying parts of London, anyone who had a flat in the centre of town, or a car, was almost guaranteed popularity, and, in the case of a flat, almost as certainly denied any privacy. There would constantly be someone wanting to crash on their floor rather than catch the last train to Surbiton, Highbury or, indeed, Dartford. When he first arrived at the LSE, Mick seems to have kept a fairly low profile until he had worked out the relative power and prestige of different groups of people. 'Sometimes you could almost see him mapping out the structures that operated in the institution, wanting to be sure of himself before he got committed to relationships that might not be useful,' according to one contemporary. Not everyone thought that Mick was so Machiavellian. Others found him simply shy at first, and slightly unsure of himself. He seems in general to have been much more popular than he had been at school, although he did not make many close friends. 'For a while he seemed to be a drama society groupie, hanging round with the student actors, although he wasn't involved in plays himself. But then he moved on and made friends with another gang.' His contemporaries, both men and women, remember that he had a certain 'animal sexuality', although they say that he did not, at eighteen, look particularly nice. But some of those who have reason to know say that there was still more talk than action. A girl who was at the LSE with him recalls that Mick would always flirt with her and especially at parties, or whenever there was an audience, he would 'talk about sex, put his arms round me and endlessly proposition me. But whenever I was alone with him he didn't do anything about it, and the thing is, I rather liked the idea.'

His friends at the LSE were aware of his musical interests, although they did not take them very seriously. Michael Densham remembers being lured down to suburban clubs to see Mick play, but says that his performance in rounding up an audience was more successful than the show he put on once they got there. On stage, he says, Mick was 'not particularly impressive'. But he was struck even then by his faith in the band, and remembers Mick earnestly telling him that they were going to make it. 'One day, I'm going to be the biggest,' he used to tell his friends in expansive moments, good-natured even though they knew that he knew that they were unconvinced. But it was a time when many students felt confident of their ability to achieve great things. 'We would often talk late into the night about changing the face of music and of the cinema. We were very much into the idea that things were about to change, and that we had the power to alter them. But in fact I don't think we had any notion of what the sixties would bring.'

Mick's energy at this period simply seems to have expanded to enable him to do everything he wanted to do. At the same time that he was working harder than ever with the group, and attending lectures and producing reasonable essays, he was also going to music clubs in and around London, and picking up an idea of who was doing what, where.

From the way he talked about the group it was obvious that Mick was beginning to consider, even if tentatively, the possibility of becoming professional. Music offered the opportunity to shine that Mick had always craved. A successful singer would receive the adulation of his fans, whereas a businessman could hope only for the respect of his colleagues. But Mick's ambition, although intense, was never stronger than his shrewdness. There was no need for him to show his hand yet, and tell everybody that he was going to be professional, or to leave the LSE without good reason. Mick had always relied on a certain resourcefulness that enabled him to get the better of people who might be more talented. So he now explored the musical world and kept an eye out for the main chance.

This was a crucial time for rhythm and blues in England. In 1960 the first professional blues band in England had been started by Alexis Korner. Called Blues Incorporated, it was composed of several dissident jazz players who were tired of the intolerant, purist trad jazz convention, and wanted to play another form of black American music, one that was more emotional and less mannered. Alexis explained later that he did not consider himself to be a jazz player because 'to me setting moods was more important than improvising. And if the same phrase in the same place created the right effect, I was perfectly prepared to use it every time. I wasn't worried that I wasn't improvising.' Blues Incorporated's line-up varied constantly, as people with commitments elsewhere played with Alexis when they could. One way and another an extraordinary number of the significant musicians of the time passed through Alexis' band, including Ginger Baker, Eric Burdon, Long John Baldry and Paul Jones.

Alexis Korner was half Austrian, a quarter Greek and a quarter Turkish. After a nomadic childhood spent in France, Switzerland and North Africa, he came to England with his family in 1940. They had managed to leave France on one of the last boats to get away after the German invasion, and settled in Ealing. Alexis' father, a retired cavalry officer, tried to turn him into 'a virtuoso violinist who would never, of course, dream of becoming a professional. A brilliant nineteenth-century violinist was what he wanted.' But Alexis was being seduced by other ideas. 'It was in 1940 that I came across a record by Jimmy Yancey. I can't say how important that record is. From then on all I wanted to do was play blues. Blues and jazz pulled me away from what was left of my family.' And Alexis' infatuation with the blues survived. By the late 1940s he was playing professionally with Chris Barber's Jazz Band – at that time almost no one else distinguished between jazz and the blues. 'There were no blues players – you played one sort of jazz or another sort of jazz.' But Alexis knew better, and after years of surreptitiously loitering under the jazz umbrella, he broke away and created the self-proclaiming Blues Incorporated. And on St Patrick's Day (17 March) 1962 he opened a blues club in Ealing.

As soon as Mick read about Alexis in *Melody Maker* he wrote to him, and soon afterwards went with Keith to meet him. Discovering the existence of Alexis Korner was like finding Man Friday's footstep in the sand. It meant that Mick and his friends were not alone, and that someone had already succeeded in doing what they hardly dared to dream about – setting up a professional blues band. The Ealing club was a great success. Initially it attracted folk fans, who had never heard the blues, but were pleased to discover any alternative to trad jazz. They seem to have liked what they heard. The club could only hold 200 people, but by the end of the fourth week there were 800 members. That night the room was packed half an hour before the first band went on, but the crowd outside, some of whom had travelled down from Scotland, were not easily deterred, and many hung around until the end, desperately trying to bribe Alexis £1 a head to let them in just to hear the last number. The club was held in a room at the back of a bakery that was a trad club on the other nights of the week. The advertisements in *Melody Maker* revealed how undistinguished the premises were: 'Alexis Korner's Blues Incorporated. The most exciting event of the year. G Club. Ealing Broadway Station. Turn Left, cross at Zebra, and go down steps between ABC teashop and jewellers.' And it was no better inside. In a BBC television interview years later Mick recalled: 'I remember the Ealing club . . . it was dripping off the roof all the time, wasn't it? It was so wet that sometimes we had to put a thing up over the stage, a sort of horrible sheet which was revoltingly dirty, and we put it up over the bandstand so the condensation didn't drip directly on you, it just dripped through the sheet on you. It was very dangerous too, you see, 'cause all this electricity and all these microphones and that . . . it was incredibly

27

primitive, you know, all these rock 'n' roll groups were much more sort of up to date . . . they had all these amplifiers.'

But neither the squalor nor the wet did anything to dampen the enthusiasm of the fans. 'When we saw Blues Incorporated it was like suddenly being on the South Side of Chicago,' Dick Taylor said later. At first they were dazzled by Blues Incorporated, and convinced that they would never be as good. But after their second visit the boys from Dartford became more critical, and decided that what they were doing was closer to real rhythm and blues. But they were nevertheless delighted to discover that there was at least somewhere for an R&B band to play. And the Ealing club was luring other blues fanatics out of the woodwork.

Among the enthusiasts who flocked to Ealing was Brian Jones from Cheltenham. Brian had befriended Alexis Korner when he had played at a concert in Cheltenham Town Hall late in 1961. Like Jagger and his friends in Dartford, Brian had been converted to the blues years before, and was unaware that anyone else in England even knew that the music existed. Also like many others, Brian had been reduced to playing in trad jazz bands, because there were not enough like-minded musicians in his area. He had never been a permanent member of a trad band, but would sit in occasionally with several different ones. Brian was already known in the area for his extraordinary ability to play almost anything. His enthusiasm and knowledge were immediately evident, and after he had introduced himself to Korner backstage at the Town Hall they went across the road to the Patio Wine Bar and talked for some time about the blues. Korner told Brian about various musicians he had come across who were struggling to play the blues. They kept in touch, and Alexis invited Brian to come down to the Ealing club when it opened.

Although Brian's family background was not dissimilar to Mick's – his father was an aeronautical engineer – Cheltenham, where he grew up, was very different from Dartford. It was a Regency spa town about a hundred miles from London, outwardly calm and pretty. But people who grew up there were aware of the strict caste divisions that operated. Barry Miles, who was later to be the editor of the underground paper, *International Times*, described them: 'Before the war the Promenade was out of bounds to the working class, and many of my relatives recall that if ever they ventured there they were soon accosted by the police and escorted back to the nearby High Street. . . . Such was the snobbery in those days that Cheltenham had two telephone exchanges, one named after the town and the other, Imperial Exchange, for the Promenade area. The street signs in the Promenade and its neighbouring streets were lettered white on black, whereas the rest of the town made do with black on white.'

'It was a very diseased town in which to grow up, and if like Brian you came from an ordinary middle-class family you would be likely to end up with the proverbial chip on your shoulder,' according to another contemporary.

Brian had been educated at Cheltenham Grammar School, where he did well. But he had always been unpopular at school, and was much teased. Unlike Mick, he did not even have a circle of friends. The other boys' favourite tease was to call him a bear-killer. Because of the Welshness of Jones they decided that Brian's family really came from the Forest of Dean, about twenty miles from Cheltenham on the Welsh border. There is a local story that in the 1920s an enterprising man set up a travelling show, which included a dancing bear. But he made the mistake of taking his show into the forest, where the local people, who are supposed by the inhabitants of Cheltenham to be simple and not a little mad, took fright at the sight of the bear and killed it. The joke went on for a long time because it was a great success – Brian was quite unable to tolerate any joke against him, particularly one that implied that he was stupid and unsophisticated. He was also short and bad at games. While he was still at school his fourteen-year-old girlfriend became pregnant. The girl remained in Cheltenham, and eventually had the child adopted. But Brian's parents, teachers and even the other

29

boys were shocked by the affair. And just as he couldn't bear to be teased, he found it intolerable to be publicly disapproved of.

Barry Miles: 'He was scruffy, moody and not very well liked – partly because of his annoying habit of borrowing small sums of money and never paying them back, and partly because his friends and acquaintances could see that he was plainly wasting his time and rapidly becoming a layabout with a chip on his shoulder. Girls felt sorry for him because he always looked so lonely and depressed and he played this up to his fullest advantage. Maybe because he was so short or maybe just because no one took him very seriously, but he seemed to use girls to get his own back on a world that he imagined had somehow done him wrong. He loved to show visitors the sad bloody sheets from the visit of an unfortunate virgin the night before and enjoyed boasting about how many women he had had. He was a creep.'

After leaving school Brian simply seemed to drift around Cheltenham. His GCE results were good enough to have enabled him to go to university, but he was even turned down for art school. It must be assumed that the school had provided him with bad references. He took a variety of jobs, but none of them seemed to last. He worked for a while as a bus conductor, but had to give that up because he couldn't wake up early enough in the mornings. His parents subsidised him intermittently, and his jobs included working for an optician, in a local factory, in Syd Tong's record shop in Pitville Street in Cheltenham, and in the architectural department of Gloucestershire County Council. Possibly his most undignified job was as a coalman, unloading sacks of coal that were being delivered to people's houses. He was so ashamed of this job that he kept it secret from his parents, and after work each day he would go to a friend's house to wash off the coal dust. At one stage he set out with his guitar to hitch-hike around Scandinavia, but he returned after a few months to Cheltenham, and took another bum job. Jobs were simply a way to keep body and soul together while he lived his real life, his musical life. He began to spend less and less time at home, and eventually moved in with the married sister of one of his army of girlfriends, Pat Andrews. In October 1961 she too had a baby, whom she called Mark.

So by the time Mick and Keith met Brian in the spring of 1962 in Ealing he had two illegitimate children and a well-established bohemian existence. Mick had been a bad boy, and Keith even badder, but Brian was indisputably the baddest of them all. He was in quite a different league of wickedness from them, and the other two were deeply impressed. He was worldly, he was an extraordinarily skilled musician and he had an undeniable charm when he felt like exercising it. It was inevitable that the three of them would start playing together. In the small blues world, where so many of those in the audience were musicians themselves, almost every possible combination of people played together at some time, somewhere. Brian also began to play occasionally with Blues Incorporated. At first he would hitch up to London from Cheltenham with a friend, and he would usually end up sleeping on the floor of Alexis' flat in Moscow Road, Bayswater. Soon afterwards he moved into a flat in Weech Road, West Hampstead, where on Easter Sunday 1962 the determined Pat joined him, bringing the infant with her.

Brian's playing impressed Mick and Keith the first time they saw him at the Ealing club, even though the regulars included people of the calibre of Eric Clapton, Jack Bruce and Manfred Mann. Keith described it later: 'Suddenly it's Elmore James, this cat, man. And it's Brian, man, he's sittin' on this little . . . he's bent over . . . da-da-da, da-da-da . . . I said, what? What the fuck? Playing bar slide guitar. We get into Brian after he finishes "Dust my Blues". He's really fantastic and a gas. We speak to Brian . . . He was a good guitar player then. He had the touch and was just peaking. He was already into living on his own and trying to find a pad for his old lady. Whereas Mick and I were just kicking around in back rooms, still living at home.' It was only through meeting Brian that Mick and Keith were shown the possibility of breaking

31

away from home and dedicating themselves to music. Brian was hardly any older than they were, and came from the same sort of family as Mick, yet here he was living a dispossessed urban life that conjured up visions of their heroes in Chicago, mindful of nothing but their music. The disadvantages of Brian's life must have been immediately apparent to Mick, but so must its glamour.

Mick and Keith began to play occasionally at Ealing, and Alexis even invited Mick to sing with Blues Incorporated, although it seems that despite his enthusiasm he was still not very good. A musician habitué of the Ealing Club: 'Mick was really diabolical, much worse than most of Alexis' people. And everybody was pretty amateurish, especially the vocalists. It was exciting because the whole thing was just getting going, but you can't pretend standards were very high. But what you noticed about Mick was that he was really into performing: it was touching the way he so obviously loved being there, holding everyone's attention. And although he was so bad, he had some quality, presence I suppose you'd call it, that stopped you laughing at him.' Others who saw him in Ealing agree: 'Oddly, Mick moved very badly in those days, he just had no idea what to do with his legs or arms. The only thing that really worked was the odd rhythmic way he used to shake his head – that was powerful.' Mick knew that he was not much good: 'I couldn't ever get in key. That was the problem. I was quite often very drunk 'cause the first time I was really nervous.'

But Alexis had faith in Mick, and by the middle of May 1962 his position in Blues Incorporated was as official as anyone's. The club was attracting attention. By the fourth week Harold Pendleton, manager of the Marquee, a cellar club off Oxford Street, came round to have a look. Thursday night at the Marquee was always rather dreary, and nothing that he had tried before had brought in much of an audience. But it was obvious that Blues Incorporated had a large following, so he suggested to Alexis that he should play at the Marquee regularly on Thursday evening. Naturally Alexis seized the opportunity. At first attendances at the Marquee did not seem to be good – the hard-core followers from Ealing would turn up, but since the Marquee premises were considerably bigger, the place looked rather empty. 'But bit by bit it began to look encouraging, because the people who started coming in were young kids who didn't dig the trad jazz scene and who wanted the excitement of something pretty raw. And that's exactly what we provided.'

Perhaps encouraged by the success of Blues Incorporated, Brian Jones became determined to put together his own band, and advertised in *Jazz News* (there was nowhere else he could advertise) for musicians to join him. He managed to assemble a line-up that consisted of himself, Geoff Bradford and a singer called Andy Wren. Ian Stewart, always known as 'Stu', who was normally to be seen wearing black leather shorts and riding a bicycle, played piano. The band rehearsed a few times, and once or twice Mick joined in, soon replacing Andy Wren. Mick and Keith still played with Dick Taylor, although Allen Etherington and Bob Beckwith were by now much less keen. The obvious answer was to merge the two groups, uniting the skills and energy of both. Mick insisted that he would not join unless Keith was included, and Dick Taylor also joined up, to play bass. Geoff Bradford faded out of the picture quite soon. It was Brian who suggested the name, Rollin' Stones (at that time apostrophed thus) after an old Muddy Waters song, 'Rollin' Stone Blues'. He was at the time the most versatile musician, and the others were still impressed by his experience of Life and Troublemaking. But it seems inaccurate to describe it, as many people have, as 'Brian's band', as if it were solely his creation. Mick, Keith and Dick Taylor, with old bonds of loyalty, constituted half the band. But Brian seems to have wanted to feel that he was the 'leader', and he still exercised a strong influence over the others. Brian's entire life was dominated by music. Mick was still at the LSE, attending lectures and working reasonably hard. And like Keith he was still living in the security of his suburban home. Dick Taylor was enthusiastic, but was not as obsessed by music. Ian

33

Stewart had a regular job with ICI. But Brian had cut himself off from the safety of Cheltenham and his family a long time ago. The band rehearsed, and played a few times in out-of-the-way spots. But although all the members were frequent visitors to Ealing, Alexis Korner knew nothing about their band. But the big break for him was to be the first break for the Rollin' Stones.

On 12 July 1962 Alexis was invited to record a radio show. The band normally consisted of seven people, but the BBC refused to pay more than six of them, and the producer did not want to use Mick. Alexis was prepared to turn down the show altogether, but Mick persuaded him that he should go ahead and do it. According to Korner, Mick said: 'No, no, don't turn it down because if you do that broadcast we'll have twice as many people in next week.' 'That's what everybody thought, "Wow, a broadcast, they're going to be flocking in by the millions." So we decided to go ahead with the broadcast and Mick, Keith, Brian, Ian Stewart and a friend – I don't remember who – would get a group together to work the Marquee that night as support group; John Baldry would get together the lead band.' The Rollin' Stones performance at the Marquee was not remarkable – but it was at least a beginning. The evening seems to be remembered mainly because John Baldry's trousers burst open as he began to sing. He was rescued by a woman in the audience who handed him a pin, in reply to his plea for help. The Stones line-up for that first appearance was in fact Mick, Brian, Keith, Dick, Stu and Mike Avery on drums.

So by the end of Mick's first year at the London School of Economics he had become part of a new band, and that band had performed publicly. Keith left art school that summer, but made no real effort to get a job. He told his mother that he was going to look for a job with an advertising agency, but he does not seem to have done much about looking for one. Dick Taylor, who was going to the Royal College of Art in the autumn, left the band altogether at this time. Keith and Brian tried to persuade Mick to leave the LSE, but he had more to lose by total dedication than they had, and was therefore understandably more cautious. 'I think they wanted me to leave the LSE but there was no point until I saw which way the wind was blowing,' he said later, realistically. But by the start of the next academic year Mick had moved into a flat in London with Keith and Brian.

The flat where they lived, in Edith Grove, impressed everyone who visited it by its augean squalor. It was pretty disgusting when they moved in, and they made the worst of it. There were two rooms with broken-down furniture and dirty wallpaper partly ripped off the walls. The grimy lavatory was several flights up. Mick's university grant was the only regular source of income, after Brian got himself sacked from his latest job working in a department store for stealing from the till. Keith's mother subsidised him with small cash handouts, food parcels and clean shirts which she delivered to the flat every week. 'I worried about Keith because of that awful place in Edith Grove. They'd stay in bed all day because they had no money for the heater, food or anything,' she admitted in an interview years later. And Bill Wyman, who had begun to play with them by the autumn of 1962, recalls that every time he went there he would have to put money into the gas meter to warm the place up, and that any cigarettes or food he brought into the flat would immediately be torn away from him. Mick, Keith and Brian became adept at begging from the neighbours, and at night they would prowl around the building, looking for leftover food to steal, or empty bottles that they could take back to the off-licence in order to claim the 3d deposit per bottle. But despite the apparent poverty in the flat, at the LSE Mick did not seem to be particularly short of money. So presumably he was not in fact sharing his all with his friends in Edith Grove.

Life in the flat seems to have been not only tough physically. There also seems to have been a habit of viciousness, stronger than the nastiness that Mick and Keith had always extended to each other and to their friends. One of Brian's oldest friends, Richard Hattrell, was a frequent visitor to Edith Grove. But Brian was

35

anxious to emphasise how very much more sophisticated he was than Hattrell, and would intentionally humiliate him to prove it. Keith described the process afterwards: Richard Hattrell '. . . got eighty quid a year for being in the Territorial Army in England, which is where you go for two weeks on a camp with the rest of these guys. Sort of a civil defence thing. They all live in tents and get soakin' wet and get a cold, and at the end they learn how to shoot a rifle and they get eighty quid cash, depending on what rank you've managed to wangle yourself. This cat arrived in London with his eighty quid, fresh out of the hills, from his tent. And he wants to have a good time with Brian. And Brian took him for every penny, man. Got a new guitar, the whole lot . . .' On one occasion Brian made Hattrell give him his army overcoat, on a freezing cold day, and then made him give Keith his sweater. Then they all set off to a local hamburger joint, and Brian made Hattrell walk twenty yards behind himself and Keith. He then demanded that he should stay outside, but should give Brian money to pay for the hamburgers. And there was more to come. Keith: 'It was snowing outside. We came back to our pad, and he was in Brian's bed. Brian for some reason got very annoyed that he was in his bed asleep. We had all these cables lying around, and he pulled out this wire. "This end is plugged in, baby, and I'm coming after ya." This cat went screaming out of the pad in his underpants. "They're electrocuting me, they're electrocuting me." Somebody brought him in an hour later and he was blue.'

Yet Hattrell was one of the oldest acquaintances of Brian's who was still prepared to have anything to do with him. And he worked hard to help the Rollin' Stones in the beginning. He was their first road manager, unpaid, predictably. The job entailed, at the time, planning a free route to wherever they were playing, using public transport. 'All the gear used to be carted on the bus or tube. If we were going to a gig in the West End we used to take the number 11 bus up the Kings Road, and where it slows down to go round Trafalgar Square we used to jump off the bus, complete with kit!

We'd jump off before the conductor got the fare out of us.' Occasionally, of course, it was impossible to plot a cost-free route, and the worst would happen. Dick Hattrell recalled another occasion: 'It was in a new sports club, somewhere quite a way from the centre, out of town. So we went out there, got the gear up, nobody turned up! Nobody! Not one person. And the promoter said, "Well, I can't give you any money because we haven't taken any money." And we had to hitch-hike back into town with all the gear because we hadn't got any money for the fares.' After Hattrell could stand it no longer the job of road manager was inherited by Stu. He was in the unusual position of having a regular job which gave him access to a telephone, so he would organise rehearsal rooms and places for the group to play during working hours.

However sordid and violent Edith Grove might have been, it was a period of vital importance for Mick. Although he lived there in biting poverty for less than a year, he and the other Stones have often talked about it since. The image of themselves as penniless young musicians living in unbelievable squalor obviously appeals, although for Mick, especially, it was essentially a game. Not only did he have a comfortable home to which he could and did go whenever he wanted, but he spent every day at college.

Chapter Three

Whatever anyone might have thought on 31 December 1959, the 1960s really began sometime during 1962. There were indicators before that there was a new age dawning, but it was not until 1962 that the new decade really began to shape up. Of course the times took their time a-changing, and certain events which took place after 1962 really belong to the 1950s, such as the Profumo and Vassal scandals (it was entirely foreign to the spirit of the sixties that we should have any secrets to sell, or any sexual morals to outrage). The years 1962, '63 and '64 witnessed a startling Renaissance, especially in England, a sudden cheerful awakening of talent and spirit. In 1962 an American orbited the globe thrice, and the Beatles began rocketing to stardom with 'Love Me Do'. The English-speaking world twisted, then reeled in horror as it heard of the death of the quintessential fifties sex goddess, Marilyn Monroe. It was the year of Kubrick's *Lolita*, of Seattle's World's Fair and of Rachel Carson's *Silent Spring*. And that was only the beginning. The following year saw Warhol, Rauschenberg and Johns at the Guggenheim Museum in New York in the first 'Pop Art' exhibition, as well as Elizabeth Taylor in *Cleopatra*. Jocelyn Stevens'

Queen (in England) and Huntingdon Hartford's *Show* (in America) burst through the plodding confines of conventional magazine design. *Vogue* worthily followed where they had dared to go, conscientiously recording the explosion of creativity and attempting to define and refine fashion as it had always done. In July 1962 English *Vogue* went so far as to publish an article by Herman Schrijver deploring the quest for prettiness in which he said, 'Finally, I place even pretty girls and pretty boys on my list. I feel they are *choses vues*, that they belong to another moment in history, to Greuze, Romney and to kitsch.' An odd verdict, considering some of the fashionable faces of the time, but good news for the Rollin' Stones. London seemed to be a particular hotbed of talent. Mary Quant had gone wholesale and crossed the Atlantic, and Vidal Sassoon's short, angular haircut completed the startled, futuristic *ingenue* look. Sally Tuffin and Marion Foale had left the Royal College of Art and taken three floors of a house in a grimy backstreet. 'We suddenly didn't want to be chic, we wanted to be ridiculous,' they said. By 1963 Carnaby Street was full of 'boutiques'. Ernestine Carter declared 1963 the 'Year of the Leg', as hemlines rose and went on rising. Terence Stamp and Peter O'Toole and Davids Bailey and Hockney and Lenny Bruce were young. Even Princess Margaret was nearly young.

There was a guileless naivety about that speedy mod world. LSD was still English money, heroin an unalluring beatnik vice that one knew about through William Burroughs. English theatre flourished, and was suddenly vitalised by a new force. The Angry Ageing Young Men of the 1950s were still whining away, but suddenly a new weapon was being used by gangs of brilliant young guerrilla entertainers, most of them from Cambridge. Vice and folly were no longer matters for Anger – suddenly they were the material for Satire. *Beyond the Fringe* and *That Was The Week That Was* hit holy cows and made a lot of money. *Private Eye* was born and rapidly grew. Nothing was sacred. all was restlessness, irreverence, frivolity.

39

Giants no longer bestrode the earth – Roosevelt, Stalin and Churchill had handed the reins of power over to Kennedy, Kruschev and Macmillan. But this was the age of the superstar, beside whom a giant was a cumbersome and ungainly thing. And although most of the grandest old men had gone there were still enough of them around to make the world feel safe. Europe was still dominated by de Gaulle and Franco. In England the Labour Party was run by Hugh Gaitskell and the Liberal chief was Jo Grimond. Revolution was still an exciting process: undermining the old order had not yet landed England with Mr Wilson.

Even disasters seemed to change with the decade. In 1960 an ancient curse visited England: foot and mouth disease smote farm after farm, and any herd that included even one diseased animal had to be slaughtered, and the carcasses burnt. By 1963 a technological plague was beginning to be suspected in the number of badly deformed babies born to women who had taken the drug thalidomide. This man-made disaster provided more unpleasant images, with endless newspaper photographs of misconstructed infants, than the eschatological familiarity of the funeral pyre. And there was no cure for man's plague any more than for God's, although all sorts of gruesome plastic limbs were custom-built to deal with it.

But although things could go wrong in the new world, it was essentially an easy one in which to live. Idealism was easy, and vice so very uncomplicated. In America, segregation was obviously bad. It was easy to frown on New Orleans City Council for offering free one-way tickets to blacks moving north, and to cheer when the black army veteran James Meredith finally got himself admitted to the University of Mississippi, despite riots that 3000 Federal Troops and National Guard had trouble quelling.

In that dawn 'twas undoubtedly bliss to be alive, but to be a young student at the LSE with a sideline musical career that might just make you a star must have been very heaven. The winter of 1962–3 was the coldest for a hundred years in England, but that only added to the feeling of excitement. The country iced over, and the English talked to each other as never before since the Blitz. The flat in Edith Grove was freezing cold, but the inhabitants were cheerful. In the middle of January Charlie Watts finally decided to join the Rollin' Stones. He had played drums with Blues Incorporated for a long time, but the past few months the Stones had been trying to persuade him to join them. They had had various drummers, but none of them had been satisfactory. Brian had been keen to persuade Carlo Little, who played with Cyril Davies, to join them, mainly because he was impressed by his personal glamour, and thought that the group would be more likely to be successful if it included the dashing Little. But the others were convinced that Charlie was simply a better drummer, and he got along very well with Mick and Keith. Mick liked Charlie's sharp, jazzy image. He dressed carefully in a snazzy, ad-man way and had a good job as a graphic designer with an advertising agency. Until he met Alexis he had known almost nothing about the blues. He had been a jazz fanatic who loathed rock and roll. But he was prepared to be converted to rhythm and blues, although he did not relinquish his love of jazz.

The next great stroke of luck for the Rollin' Stones occurred at about this time. Giorgio Gomelsky had recently opened the Crawdaddy Blues Club at the Station Hotel, Richmond. To suburban boys the flamboyant, bearded Gomelski, with his thick accent, must have seemed an even more exotic figure than Alexis Korner. He was the son of a Russian doctor who had been born in the Caucasus but had practised in Moscow, and a French mother. He was variously described as an experimental film-maker or an impressario. He had hitch-hiked around the world, had organised the first Italian jazz festival, and had lived in Chicago, where he had discovered the blues in their natural habitat. He had started the Crawdaddy with only £5 capital, which he had borrowed from a friend, but as enthusiasm for the blues was growing, the club flourished. Brian Jones went down to Richmond to see him and Gomelsky agreed to help the Rollin' Stones, simply because he was pleased by Brian's enthusiasm. He didn't even bother to see them before deciding to give them a chance. 'It didn't matter if they were the worst band in the world. If someone was into R&B they needed to be helped.' In February 1963 his usual group, the Dave Wood Rhythm and Blues Band, failed to turn up one freezing cold Sunday when snow was lying thin and mushy on the ground. Gomelsky was livid, sensing insufficient commitment to Art. The next day he telephoned Stu to invite the Rollin' Stones to become the resident band in their place. Now that they had a regular place to play life was much more promising for the boys. They could build up a regular following – the fans would know where to find them – and they could concentrate on their music without worrying about where their next booking was to come from. Food remained a problem – they were unlikely to get rich from the Crawdaddy – but that was less important to them. Giorgio suggested that he should split the club takings with the band – they would each get half. But he also guaranteed every member of the band £1/10-, and since there were six of them, he needed to take £15 before he would actually get his half . . . and for the first few weeks he took less than that. But his enthusiasm matched theirs, and he would go out with them at night flyposting advertisements, and would spend hours at Edith Grove talking to them about the music they all loved. Even the world-travelled Giorgio was startled by the disgustingness of life at 102 Edith Grove. 'When we used to go out flyposting we used to buy glue and often we ended up with more than we needed so all that glue was put in the bathtub in the bathroom of the apartment.' Two weeks later the glue was emitting a stench noticeable even among the cacophony of mephitic odours that normally hung over the flat. Mick and Keith had been throwing cigarette ends, lavatory paper rolls and old socks into it. 'Everything was thrown in there, this glue was kind of growing out of the bathroom into the kitchen and everywhere, it was crazy.' But Giorgio was not a man to be put off people by their eccentric notions of domestic hygiene, and he took a strongly paternal interest in the group. He was at the time making a documentary film about rhythm and blues in England, in which he intended to use sequences of the Rollin' Stones, and wherever he went he would tell people about his marvellous new band and try to persuade them to come and listen for themselves.

Apparently Brian was keen that the Stones should have a written contract with Giorgio, whereby he should become their official manager, but such a move seemed unnecessary to the mysterious vagabond figure who had lived a life untrammelled by the bother of legal documents and small print. Both Mick and Ian Stewart have since tended to dismiss the importance of Giorgio Gomelsky in their careers. 'Giorgio was only trying to push something that was there already. He's a marvellous character, but we believed in the band. People just came to see the Rollin' Stones. Eventually it was going to happen,' according to Stu. And Mick went even further in an interview years afterwards: 'As soon as we played everybody loved us. We were all very dedicated, but as soon as it started getting crazy, you realised what entertaining was about. After all, it was our first effort at entertaining people. We had to entertain them. It was a big place with five hundred or more people.' It is true that big crowds were coming to Richmond to see the Stones, and the Crawdaddy was beginning to be fashionable in a way that the more earnest Ealing club had never been. Giorgio created an atmosphere of exictement in the club in which the Stones automatically seemed more potent than they had in the makeshift leaky bakery. He was brilliant at galvanising the audience so that they believed in and responded to the group that was playing. And this in its turn gave the Stones new confidence. The local paper, the *Richmond and Twickenham Times*, carried the first ever press story about the Stones on 13 April:

A musical magnet is drawing the jazz beatniks away from Eel Pie Island, Twickenham, to a new mecca in Richmond.

43

The attraction is the new Craw-daddy Rhythm and blues club at the Station Hotel, Kew Road – the first club of its kind in an area of flourishing modern and traditional jazz haunts.

Rhythm and blues, gaining more popularity every week, is replacing 'traddypop' all over the country, and even persuading the more sedate modernists to leave their plush clubs. The deep, earthy sound produced at the hotel on Sunday evenings is typical of the best of rhythm and blues that gives all who hear it an irresistible urge to 'stand up and move' . . .

Rhythm and blues can claim to provide a happy medium for young jazz fans. Modernists and 'traddies' can be seen side by side at the Station Hotel, listening to resident group, the Rollin' Stones.

From a meagre 50 or so on the club's first night, less than two months ago, attendances have rocketed by an average of more than fifty a week to last Sunday's record of 320. And the membership book lists more than 700 names of rhythm and blues devotees from all parts of London and West Surrey.

Club promoter, bearded Italian film director Giorgio Gomelsky is thrilled with the success of the club – but fears he may soon have to close the membership list if its popularity continues to rise . . .

The Rollin' Stones were formed just 10 months ago.

Since then they have played in more than a dozen London rhythm and blues clubs, as well as appearances at the West End Marquee Club.

Semi-professionals now, although the average age is only 20, the daytime occupations of its members are as varied as the instruments they play.

Driving force behind the group is London School of Economics student Mick Jagger, vocal and harmonica. He is backed by architect Brian Jones (guitar, harmonica, maracas), guitarist

Keith Richards, an art student, bass guitarist Bill Wyman, a representative, drummer Charlie Watts, a designer, and on piano Ian Stewart.

And so it went on. It was publicity, even if it was only in a local paper. Even more exciting, for the Stones, was a visit to the Crawdaddy by the Beatles, who were indisputably the phenomenon of the moment. They had just had their first number one hit with 'Please Please Me', and there was a strong feeling that they were the coming musical force. Giorgio had met them and persuaded them to come and see his band. On 21 April they came, and got on so well with Mick, Keith and Brian that they all went back to Edith Grove and talked long into the night. Musically there was not much common ground – the Beatles raved about Chuck Jackson, and were not very impressed by the treasured recordings of Jimmy Reed, quite unobtainable in England, which Mick had imported from America. But Mick and Brian were transfixed by John Lennon's stories of what it was like to be mobbed by frantic fans. The Beatles were to become close friends of the Stones, and at one stage John even suggested that he should move into Edith Grove. It seems likely that the remark was a gesture of affection more than a serious plan. He complained that he was tired of living in hotels, but to have wanted to move in with the Stones he would have had to be tired of life. The longer they lived in the flat the more revolting it became, despite the occasional attempts of Keith's mother and well-meaning friends to fumigate it. One visitor to Edith Grove reports that whenever the inhabitants were told that there were too many dirty plates lying around they would throw most of them out of the window. It was a brave man who would risk even opening the fridge, which was full of months-old bottles of milk curdled green and solid, with lumps of sinister fossilised food stuck to the floor.

Giorgio also lured pop journalist Peter Jones down to the Crawdaddy to hear the Stones. It was probably the dumbest thing he ever did. Instead of writing an adulatory piece about the group, as he was intended to do, or even an unpleasant one, Peter Jones told Andrew Oldham, an ambitious young hustler who had worked for the Beatles' manager, Brian Epstein, about the Rolling Stones. On 28 April, one week after the Beatles' visit, Andrew Oldham drove down to Richmond with his business partner, Eric Easton. Giorgio's father had just died, and he had flown to Switzerland to arrange the funeral and deal with various legal matters. By the time he returned to England the band for whom he had tried to do so much had signed a management contract with Oldham and Easton. And that, as far as the relationship between Gomelsky and the group was concerned, was that, although the Stones continued to play at the Crawdaddy for a few months more.

Andrew Oldham was then nineteen. He had tried to be a singer himself, under a variety of names that included Chancery Laine and Sandy Beach, but had met with not the slightest sign of success. He had worked for Mary Quant as a window-dresser and general assistant. While working for her he admitted to the wife of Archie McNair, one of her backers, that 'he could do any of our jobs standing on his head (Archie's included)', according to Mary Quant herself. Mrs McNair asked what he actually did. 'Well,' he said, 'When Mary's a bit tired, I design a few dresses for her; when Alexander is choosing stock, I chat up the press for him. I could do it just as well on my own. It's easy.' He had also worked as a doorman at Ronnie Scott's Jazz Club, as a press agent for singer Mark Wynter. But having had a glimpse of the real action through working for the Beatles, he was determined to find his own group and become his own Brian Epstein. And having seen the Rollin' Stones, he was certain that he had found six characters who were in need of a manager, even if they were not actively in search of one. He was already aware that 'in just a few months the country would need an opposite to what the Beatles were doing'. And he could see that, with a bit of careful packaging from him, the Stones could be that opposite. His boss, the theatrical agent Eric Easton, was not immediately convinced, and thought that even if they did take the band onto their books they should get rid of Mick, because he could not sing.

Exhilarated by the possibility of sudden stardom, Brian seems to have done quite a bit of negotiating with the Easton/Oldham partnership on his own behalf. It has been suggested that he was happy to go along with Easton, and sack Mick, although the band would almost certainly have fallen apart if he had tried to. He somehow managed to talk Easton into paying him £5 a week more than anyone else, on the assumption that he was the leader of the band: understandably the rest of the group were livid when they found out about that one. But perhaps the most peculiar of all was the way that he told Giorgio, when he returned from his father's funeral, that Andrew was an old school friend of his, and that that was how the Stones had got to know him. But Mick seems to have allowed Brian to do some of the talking to Oldham and Easton. He was just as keen as Brian to get good managers and a big recording contract. But there could be no harm in letting Brian reveal his desperation for stardom while himself maintaining a degree of reserve until it became clear how things were going to work out.

Oldham wasted no time. He got the Stones into a recording studio, he tried to polish up their performance, he restored the 'g' to Rollin' and he got Stu off the stage. 'It was very rigid, the set up the first time I saw them. They were very much into a sort of blues roots thing. There was no production to the act at all. Everyone sat on stools and played very comfortably and saying, "Just listen to what I'm playing." ' A week after the contract was signed the Stones recorded a Chuck Berry song, 'Come On', and Willie Dixon's 'I want to be loved' at the Olympic Studio in Barnes. Easton, Oldham and the members of the group formed a company to produce the Stones' records, which would then lease tapes of their songs to one of the established giants, rather than hand over the whole process. It meant that they would have greater control over the finished product, and would retain a greater proportion of

47

the profits. It was not a new idea. Phil Spector, the first 'tycoon of teen', had done the same thing in America, but it was most unusual in England. Neither Andrew nor any of the group knew anything about record production – they did not even know what most of the equipment in the studio was meant to be used for. They simply hired a recording engineer, Roger Savage, and did the best they could. But Andrew was so very uninformed that he did not even know what the process of mixing the tapes was, still less that it was the most vital part of the operation. So he left it to the studio engineer to mix the tape of Jagger's singing with the other three. Not surprisingly, the result was disastrous, and there had to be several more recording sessions before an acceptable tape was produced. Because they were only used to singing in clubs the boys took the numbers far too quickly, and they also had difficulty generating the excitement necessary to R&B without the interaction with a live audience. But finally they managed to lay down a tape that was passable, although it did not really do them justice.

The Stones had a contract with Decca even before they had made the tape. Eric Easton had managed to sell them to Dick Rowe, the man whose name has resounded through the years as the executive who turned down the Beatles. Obviously he was careful not to make the same mistake twice, and when George Harrison told him how impressed he was by the Stones, Rowe's decision was made for him. As soon as the Decca contract was signed, and he had made sure that he could return in a year or two if he wanted to, Mick Jagger threw caution to the winds and left the LSE. All year the others had been encouraging him to do so, and his mother had been uncomfortably aware that he was toying with the idea. He now took the plunge, and from that moment was seen to become friendlier with Andrew.

Oldham now proceeded to work his magic on the Rolling Stones. He was intensely aware of the power and importance of the media, and learnt to use it long before most people in the music business. Before the release of 'Come On' Andrew had started work on his plans to package the Stones properly. The axeing of Stu seems to have taken place without much protest from anyone, and without causing pain to anyone but the pianist himself. Stu agreed to continue to play on records, although not on stage, and also to carry on as road manager. Although Oldham knew that the Stones would be able to do very well out of being the dirty opposite of the nice, cheerful Beatles, he decided that he had to clean them up a bit before he could air them for the first time. He managed to get them onto the important television pop programme, *Thank Your Lucky Stars*, the week their single was released, and for the programme he insisted that they wear identical black and white houndstooth jackets with black velvet collars. 'There were a couple of compromises that had to be made at first. Someone even said we would have to get rid of the lead singer because he would never pass an audition . . . we compromised to the extent of wearing some sort of uniform. We knew we had to. "Come on" was no great melody, it was just a good riff. The TV people were used to dealing with groups like the Searchers and the Swinging Blue Jeans. If the Stones had dressed the way they wanted, they wouldn't have been allowed inside the building. So they all wore those checked jackets. But we got rid of them as soon as we could.' But trying to keep the Rolling Stones cleaned up was even beyond Andrew. Keith: 'Charlie'd leave his jacket in some dressing-room, and I'd pull mine out and there'd be whisky stains all over it, or chocolate pudding.'

And although it was only Andrew who really understood, in the beginning, about creating and promoting an image, the Stones were naturally gifted at projecting an immediately recognisable type. They were never seen to behave out of character, and Mick and Keith seem to have found that the masks Andrew encouraged them to wear provided a kind of liberation. It was easier for them both to deal with people they didn't know if they had a clearly defined role to play, and knew what was expected of them. Charlie also seems to have been quite happy hiding behind a corporate persona that in his case bore no relation to even a part of his own character and Bill could look right for the part. It was Brian who found it most difficult to cope, since although he wanted fame more desperately than the others, he was less happy to restrain most of his personality and show people only one cardboard self. And also Brian was less practised than Mick and Keith at this particular act. They had years of experience, from school, of giving coarse but nevertheless convincing portrayals of bad boys. They had been practising the slouch, the sneer, the stoop and the other necessary attributes of the slob for years, and they both associated the act with the pleasurable sensations of baiting schoolmasters. For both of them it was an old favourite pose that could, of course, be cast off at will. But for Brian the whole matter was more complicated. He had spent the best years of his life genuinely in disgrace in his home town and with his family. He had played hard not at being bad, but at trying to seem convincingly good and misunderstood. His most impressive performances had been gaining the confidence of young girls he wanted to seduce, or older people from whom he wanted something. So it was more difficult for him to relax into a part that he desperately did not want anyone to be taken in by.

Despite Andrew's coup in persuading the producers of *Thank Your Lucky Stars* to feature it, 'Come On' was not a roaring overnight success. The original, Chuck Berry version was an angry account of the frustrations that beset adolescent life. The Stones recording was a pale imitation of the original, substituting a peevish whine for Berry's anger. Critics described the Stones as 'a bluesy commercial group that should make the charts in a smallish way'. Their dates were no longer fixed by Stu on an ICI telephone during working hours. By now Oldham had taken a smart office in Regent Street, from where he coordinated the band's career. Even for an ace publicist such as Andrew it was difficult to get much coverage for a group that had failed to make it into the hit parade. They themselves knew that the record was not very good, and refused to perform it publicly, which made life even more difficult for

Oldham. But by the end of June 'Come On' had crept into the bottom of the Top Fifty. He managed to persuade a few journalists and photographers to come round to the office to interview them, and the interviews were a success. The boys did their stuff, snarling at the journalist who asked whether they shouldn't emulate the Beatles, 'If people don't like us as we are, well that's too bad. We're not thinking of changing, thanks very much. We've been the way we are for much too long to think of kowtowing to fancy folk who think we should start tarting ourselves up with mohair suits and short hair.' The Rolling Stones began to feature fairly regularly in the press, and it became clear that Oldham had been right – their loutishness was a necessary antidote to the saccharine charm of the Beatles. Mick was genuinely upset at first that the press were more interested in the badness of the band than in its music. But he was a quick learner, and since the nasty image was at least getting them coverage he certainly would not argue with it. He quickly learnt the ropes, and began to further his image on his own initiative. Nicky Haslam, the interior designer and sometime cowboy, was a friend at the time, and remembers having dinner with Mick at the Casserole in the Kings Road. 'A broken down old actor leant across aggressively and asked Mick, "Are you a man or a woman?" Mick said nothing, he just stood up and unzipped his trousers.' 'Come On' hovered around the lower reaches of the charts for some time – it made it to number 18, slipped back, climbed a little, and so on. But it never rose above 18. Still, that was fine for the first release of a new band, and Andrew, Mick and Brian immediately began to concentrate on the next release, and on the tour which Andrew was planning for the autumn.

The tour started on 29 September. There were sixty concerts scheduled to take place in thirty days. Southend, Guildford, Watford, Cardiff, Cheltenham, Worcester, Wolverhampton, Derby, Doncaster, Liverpool, Manchester and on round the country. The bill was headed by the Everly Brothers and one of the Stones' heroes, Bo Diddley. After only five days Little Richard was flown in from America in a frantic attempt to boost box-office receipts. It was exciting for the group to be playing with two blues giants, but the tour was not a huge success. Most of the country was just not ready for the Stones – despite Andrew's good work, people had not yet learnt how to respond to them. But despite the lukewarm reception they received, especially in the smaller towns, the group was not dispirited. Three days before the tour ended their second single was released – a Lennon and McCartney number, 'I wanna be your man'. It was a nifty move, and a good song. By November 1963 any Lennon/McCartney composition automatically generated interest, and would be practically guaranteed good enough sales to get into the hit parade. John and Paul offered Andrew Oldham the song just as he was beginning to get desperate about what the Stones should record next. They had already ransacked the Chess catalogue without finding anything that seemed right, and Decca were pressing him to come up with the next Stones record, to capitalise on the publicity the group had received at the time of 'Come On'. Eric Easton worked with the boys in the studio, and 'I wanna be your man' was taped in a single day.

So by the end of 1963 the Rolling Stones really seemed to be on the way to great things. They had had two hits – 'I wanna be your man' reached number 9 – and they had begun to write their own material. The 'B' side of their second single was the mainly instrumental 'Stoned', attributed to Nanker/Phelge. It was admittedly very derivative – Mick and Keith have never denied the debt it owed to Booker T and the MGs' 'Green Onions' – but the few lyrics were also characteristic: 'Stoned . . . Outta mah mind . . . Where am I at?'

Girl-wise things were also looking up for Mick. He now had a remarkably pretty girlfriend, Chrissie Shrimpton, who was the sister of Jean Shrimpton, the most successful model of the moment, who was the girlfriend of David Bailey, the most successful photographer of the moment. The flat in Edith Grove had finally been abandoned during the summer, and Mick and Keith had moved with Andrew Oldham into a flat in Mapesbury Road, Kilburn. Brian had gone to live with his new girlfriend and her family in Windsor. Nicky Haslam remembers people asking Chrissie how she could have anything to do with Mick – 'He's so hideous.' Chrissie's answer – 'You won't think so in a year's time' – was to prove surprisingly accurate.

Chapter Four

1964 began well.

The Rolling Stones' second national tour began on 6 January at Harrow Granada. This was home territory. In the early 1960s local musical loyalties were very important. The Beatles' success was built on a foundation of strong Liverpool support. The Rolling Stones were a London suburbs band and were therefore already familiar to many of those in the Harrow audience. Fans were often possessive about their favourite local groups, and would have mixed feelings about them becoming nationally famous. They would be proud of their success, but they would also be upset because they would then have to share their idols with a vast audience – they would no longer be their own special property. But by now the London fans were resigned to the success of the Rolling Stones and glad of the chance to see them play. There were two concerts at the Granada and both were packed. The Swinging Blue Jeans, Marty Wilde and the Wildcats, and the Ronettes were on the road with them, but this time the Stones headed the bill.

In the autumn Mick had been furious that Eric Easton had insisted on sending the Stones to provincial ballrooms and dancehalls where the audiences had never heard their kind of music. But Eric had insisted from the beginning that even if they didn't like it, it was essential for them to go out and give concerts all over the country. The present blues following was too small. If the Rolling Stones were to survive, they had to make new converts, and capitalise on the small success of their singles and the greater success of Andrew's publicity. In the London clubs where they usually played people were either reverential about the blues, or, at worst, unresponsive. But north of Watford the audience would become violent if they did not like what they had paid hard-earned money to hear. And a great many of them did not like at all these Rolling Stones, who didn't seem to know the songs that everybody liked dancing to, and who had such long hair. Violence was not unusual at concerts in those days. Chairs were often hurled around dancehalls or windows smashed as drunken rockers quarrelled over girls or over some supposed insult. 'It really was all very, "Don't you step on my blue suede shoes," ' an early Stones fan says of the atmosphere at concerts. And the Rolling Stones obviously elicited more trouble than other groups. Brian was repeatedly beaten up, spat upon or jeered during the first tour by men in the audience who did not like the combination of aggression and rapacious sexuality that he suggested on stage. Mick incurred less trouble. It was not that he was liked better, but he was able to defuse potentially violent situations, pulling back from the brink when the locals seemed likely to beat his brains out. He was more afraid of being beaten up than Brian was, and did not find the idea of violence thrilling. The menace that Mick projected on stage was meant to fuel sexual fantasies, not to put nastier ideas into people's heads, and he was learning to control the audience, to calm them down after he had whipped them up into a frenzy.

But although the hostile reception during the autumn tour was disheartening, it did not do Mick any harm. By the end of that tour he was acquiring the carnal stage manner that was to become his hallmark — a volatile blend of explicit innuendo and erotic narcissism. Although he was singing, almost exclusively, works by black American artists, he made no attempt to reproduce their specific mannerisms but effectively translated them into English. He was developing a powerful stage style, rhythmically fluid as well as forceful. Bo Diddley later claimed that he had taught Mick to move on stage during the first tour. He seems to have picked up more of his gestures from Brian, whose sinuous, directly sexual mannerisms had been perfected when Mick had still been just shaking his hair around. But Mick was able to interact with the audience in a way that Brian never was. 'Brian was incredibly exciting on stage, but you felt that he was doing it for his own sake in a way, he wasn't relating to the audience like Mick did,' according to an early fan. The group's performance still lacked polish, but it was developing a raw, brash power that was more important.

But there were other reasons why the Rolling Stones enjoyed their second tour more than the first. It was not only their audiences with whom they were getting on well. They liked the Ronettes, the black American girl trio who were on the bill with them. With their grotesque beehive hairdoes and unrestrained use of eye-liner, the girls were the very embodiment of one brand of American glamour. *New Musical Express*, covering the tour, found good copy in the combination of the overtly sexy Ronettes with the Rolling Stones:

'Those Ronettes just set us dead in our tracks,' smiles Stone No. 1, vocalist Mike Jagger. . . . Said Estelle, a quiet-spoken girl whose smile brought hard-bitten reporters flocking around in droves: 'We just love that number, "I Wanna Be Your Man". It's got real go.'

Said Nedra, smoothing down a crease in her tight-fitting dress: 'We just never guessed they'd be so informal.' She beamed mischievously as the group's young co-manager (and, some say, the Phil Spector of English pop) Andrew Oldham – now making discs himself – came into the room. '. . . In fact, we like them almost as much as their manager. And he's not only a real nice person, he makes good records too.'

The girls seem to have been the cause of some competition between the Stones. It is generally suggested that during the tour Keith ended up with the Ronette that Mick wanted, and he had to be content with a different one. But the situation seems to have been resolved without rancour. Before the tour ended the Rolling Stones' first EP was released. During the 1960s the EP (Extended Play) filled a highly lucrative middle ground between the single and the LP. Most EPs were either a device for milking extra sales out of successful singles or for grabbing a market out of those who couldn't or wouldn't afford to pay the full price for an LP. The Stones' EP contained cover versions of four American songs – 'Bye Bye Johnny', 'Poison Ivy', 'Money' and 'You Better Move on'. The most powerful was the Arthur Alexander number, 'You Better Move On'. 'Poison Ivy' (Leiber/Stoller) had very nearly been released as the group's second single, but it was rejected when Andrew Oldham was offered the Lennon/McCartney number. It is easy to see why – it lacks all the punch of the best early Stones' work. The EP also contained a sloppy version of a song that was already over-exposed – 'Money' (the Elliott and the Fenmen version had just slipped out of the charts, and it had been included on the *With the Beatles* LP released in November). But the EP did well, and immediately entered the charts at number 28.

On 21 February the third single, 'Not Fade Away'/'Little by Little', was released. It had been recorded during January at the Regent Sound Studios in what used to be known as 'Tin Pan Alley', Denmark Street. Phil Spector, the Ronettes' Svengali, had been invited by Andrew Oldham to attend the recording session. Mick was very keen to meet the 'first tycoon of teen', who was also married to the Ronette-in-chief, Ronnie. Spector was not, as is frequently reported, a millionaire at nineteen. He was at least twenty-one by the time he had made his first million dollars clear

57

profit out of producing records. By then anyone he touched seemed to turn out Gold Discs – the Crystals, Bob B. Soxx and the Blue Jeans, Darlene Love and other American teen idols. Spector seemed to have infallible antennae for singers who could be made into stars, ephemeral, pre-packaged stars perhaps, but profitable none-theless. Mick had become fascinated by the music business. It was obvious to him that the success of entertainers (especially their financial success) was largely dependent upon the business acumen of their managers. Two years at the London School of Economics would not have taught him much about the way industry actually runs and even less about the workings of show business. But it gave him a familiarity with the terminology of business, and a crude understanding of the basic principles of international trade. So he was better equipped than most musicians of his age to study the music industry and to interpret what he observed. So as he became more friendly with Andrew he was perpetually alert, watching him and learning everything possible about the way he operated. Although Andrew was so young, it was obvious that he had great insight into the way the business functioned, and an extraordinary flair for manipulating it. But however bright Andrew was, he did not compare with Phil Spector.

The recording session at Regent Sound was quite a party. Two of the Hollies (Allan Clarke and Graham Nash) were there, and Andrew also telephoned Gene Pitney and asked him to come. He handled Pitney's publicity, and two of his records had been produced by Phil Spector. He said of the Stones later, in a much-quoted remark, that 'the first time I met them I didn't know whether to shake hands or bark', a quip that was presumably arranged by Oldham for their mutual benefit. By the time Pitney arrived, bringing a supply of alcohol with him, the session was already underway. It had begun badly. Everybody was in a bad mood, tempers were getting frayed and they seemed to be getting nowhere. But by the time the whole crowd had assembled, and Pitney's liquor had been drunk, it worked out all right. Pitney: 'So we ended up with a hell of a session, and out of it came "Not Fade Away" and I played piano and Phil Spector played an empty cognac bottle with a half dollar clickin' in it and we played on the flip side which was "Little by Little".' Spector also picked up the maracas at one stage, and seems to have fired everyone present with a sense of urgency and energy. The Rolling Stones had never sounded better. Mick was thrilled by the presence of Spector and naturally made friends with him at once. Spector even wrote the 'B' side with Jagger, although it owed, admittedly, a great deal to Jimmy Reed. Andrew described the scene later: 'After we had done "Not Fade Away" Phil and Mike disappeared. Nobody noticed they had gone until about five minutes later when they returned, looking very pleased with themselves. They sat down, told me to listen, and played the number they had just written in the outside corridor. It was very good so we decided to use it as the "B" side. Mike took hold of his harmonica, Phil found the maracas again, and Gene Pitney and the Stones road manager, Ian Stewart, sat down at the same piano. It was a fantastic scene.'

> Can't see the Rolling Stones missing out with their latest Decca release – a quivering, pounding rhythmic opus titled 'Not Fade Away'. It's a solo voice showcase, but the backing beat is quite fantastic, with handclaps and wailing harmonica adding to the effect. That fascinating plaintive quality peculiar to all Norman Petty–Buddy Holly numbers is prominent, despite the raucous treatment. I would have preferred that the ending, like the title, did not fade away – but this minor detail won't prevent the boys from enjoying a big hit. Pungent, strident guitar work – ably assisted by Gene Pitney's tinkling piano – are showcased in Phil Spector's composition, 'Little by Little'. The melody is insignificant, but the sound's sensational. (*New Musical Express.*)

For the first time the reviewers predicted a big hit with 'Not Fade

Away', and they were proved right. It made it to number 3. It also entered the American charts, where it climbed to number 44. In France an EP was released ('Not Fade Away', 'Stoned', 'Poison Ivy' and 'Little by Little') which reached the top of the charts. By now Andrew's star-making machinery really had something to work on, and it whirled into action. For the next few months there was never a week without a Rolling Stones story in the music press, and there was almost always one in the national papers too. In March there was the famous 'Would You Let Your Daughter Go With A Rolling Stone?' headline in the *New Musical Express*. The *Daily Express* was talking about the Stones on 28 February: 'They look like boys whom any self-respecting Mum would lock in the bathroom! But the Rolling Stones – five tough young London-based music makers with doorstep mouths, pallid cheeks, and unkempt hair – are not worried what mums think!

'For now the Beatles have registered with all age groups, the Rolling Stones have taken over as the voice of the teens.' And the *Daily Mirror* reported on 22 April that: 'Mr Wallace Scowcroft, President of the National Federation of Hairdressers, offered a free haircut to the next number one group or soloist in the pop chart, adding: "The Rolling Stones are the worst. One of them looks as if he has got a feather duster on his head." ' The marvellous thing about Andrew's publicity was the way that it became self-generating. The more noise he could make for the Stones, the more their natural enemies would make for them.

For Oldham the benefits of publicity were obvious, and more quite simply equalled better. But for the Rolling Stones themselves it was more difficult. People who knew Mick at the time noticed that he was becoming absorbed in his professional personality and would seem to be practising it, even when he was alone with friends. And Chrissie reported afterwards that he would at this time spend ages gazing at himself in a mirror. It was as if he were trying out different variants of the personality that seemed to go down so well in public, trying to find a version of it that was comfortable for everyday wear. Other friends of the period have a completely different impression, and say that he seemed totally in control, ironically aware of the potency of his nationally notorious nasty self, but separate from it. Oddly, it was with his newer acquaintances that he seemed more able to distinguish between his selves. People who had met him recently knew a Jagger who was gentle and intelligent when he was off duty. With friends from Dartford, or from the Ealing club, he appeared to be exploring the practical applications of violence.

Whatever the truth of Mick's control over his image at this time, it certainly impinged upon other people's lives. Charlie Watts, the Rolling Stones drummer, wanted to marry his long-time girlfriend, Shirley Shepherd. But Mick and Andrew Oldham forbade the marriage, as sternly as any outraged father might. It was seen by Mick and Andrew to be quite contrary to the necessary bad image of the Stones. Bill Wyman was already married when he first met Keith, Brian and Mick. That was annoying, but not even Jagger and Oldham could demand that a man get divorced for the sake of the group's image. But they thought that it would be crucially bad publicity to have another Rolling Stones wedding now. Finally, in October 1964, Charlie and Shirley were married secretly, but only after long months during which poor Charlie was buffeted between Mick, who refused to allow it, and Shirley, who didn't see why Jagger should influence her life. For Charlie, who idolised Mick and adored Shirley, it was a delicate situation. And it was not made easier by an alliance between Chrissie and Shirley. Chrissie would encourage Shirley to stand up to Mick, and then berate him for being such a thug to poor Charlie.

Chrissie herself was becoming used to being hidden away from fans, pushed into doorways or made to walk along the other side of the road if she was out with Jagger in case the fans should get wind of the fact that he had a steady girlfriend. It was crucial to his image that he should be known to be available, so that every teenage girl in the country should be free to fantasise about him. It was already universally known that John Lennon was married, but wives were nevertheless believed to be, in general, handicaps to idols. And George Harrison's girlfriend, Patti Boyd, had actually been beaten up by frenzied girls. By the spring of 1964 she had had a year of this treatment, and although she was getting used to it, it was not becoming any easier.

Chrissie and Mick were now living in a rented basement flat in Bryanston Mews, near Montagu Square. Thea Porter, the decorator who later became a fashion designer, helped them to renovate and furnish it. 'I remember that I found a delicious little stripped pine dresser with little bits of red and blue glass on the top. It was very pretty, it was the time when stripped pine was first becoming fashionable. And they had a huge teddy bear sitting on the bed.'

Chrissie was one of the first Stones fans. Like so many others she had been converted to the blues by Alexis Korner. She became a regular visitor to the Ealing club, which was where she saw Mick perform for the first time. When the Rollin' Stones began to play dates of their own around London Chrissie often went along with friends. The regular Stones audience was so small that Jagger inevitably got to know her by sight fairly soon. But it was left to Chrissie to make the first move. One evening she went to see the Stones play at Maidenhead with a boyfriend who boasted about knowing Jagger, although Chrissie suspected that he hardly knew him. He told her that Jagger was so shy that he bet her 10/- that she couldn't even make him kiss her. After the Stones had finished playing Chrissie sauntered purposefully up to Jagger. 'Will you kiss me?' she asked. Jagger giggled nervously, but he leant over and kissed her on the lips. She put her left arm around his shoulder as he was kissing her, and extended her right hand behind her, palm up, demanding the 10/-. Mick asked her for a date, and they went to the cinema a few days later. Since then they had been 'constant companions'. Each got on well with the other's family, and at the end of 1963 they had told friends that they were going to get married. But since then, whenever anyone mentioned the wedding plans to him, Mick shied away from the subject, so that many of his acquaintances, including Chrissie herself, were beginning to suspect by the spring of 1964 that he was having second thoughts about it. After finishing her secretarial course Chrissie found herself a job working for Decca. But as the group became more successful, she began to be treated as a celebrity herself. She was now only asked to do work connected with the Rolling Stones, and was given lots of time off for concerts and tours. Without a proper job she began to get very bored. It was an absurd situation, and when Andrew set up the Rolling Stones office it seemed natural that she should go to work for him. She might at least work properly for the Stones, if she was not to be allowed to do anything else.

Neither Chrissie nor Andrew was even-tempered, and their proximity to each other did not make for peace in Mick's life. The welfare of each of them was tightly bound up with him. They were both possessive by nature, and both seem to have been unusually attracted to him. But although working together may have been uncomfortable for them, it was convenient for Mick. 'He was adept at playing off against each other people who wanted too much of him,' according to someone else who worked with him. 'He was close to both of them, but it helped that they should be aware of each other, and should be, in a way, fighting over him.'

But whatever storms were brewing on the domestic front, there was no time, in the spring of 1964, for Jagger to get too caught up in them. The third UK tour began on 8 February, and on 17 April the first LP was released. Andrew had fought Decca to be allowed to issue the album without a title, and he had won. The cover was simply a shadow-washed photograph of the Stones by David Bailey, with the catalogue number and the Decca logo. It was one of Andrew's cleverest strokes. It meant that the record could not be mentioned without further imprinting the name of the group on the brain of someone, somewhere. And by forcing the photograph to speak for itself he emphasised how much the image had already come to mean. It is an arresting picture. Brian, Keith and Charlie stare suspiciously into the camera. Bill, in the centre, stands out in the darkness with the air of a purposeful Machiavelli. A petulant, cherubic Mick gazes dreamily into the distance. Oddly, twenty years later Bailey's photograph does not seem to be at all dated, although most photographs of the time now seem to have a strong period flavour. Oldham wrote the cover notes for the album, which included the inspired line, 'The Rolling Stones are more than just a group. They are a way of life.'

The album had been recorded in ten days at Regent Sound, at around the time of the 'Not Fade Away' session. Like the single, it had been recorded on two-track Revox machinery, much simpler than the equipment that had so mystified Andrew during their very first recording session. Regent Sound was a particularly unsophisticated studio, insulated with egg-boxes stuck to the wall. Inevitably the album is flawed, but it exudes energy and shining sincerity. It is true that 'I Just Want to Make Love to You' is rushed, and has none of the dignity of the original. 'I Need You Baby (Mona)' is over-adorned and much of the album is humourless when compared with the original recordings. Rufus Thomas' sprightly 'Walking the Dog', for example, is treated far too seriously. But the whole is compulsive, pungent and throbbing with excitement. The crude studio was no disadvantage. The equipment was no more complex than that of the mid 1950s, and it therefore captured something of the raw, funky blues sound that the Stones had always wanted on their records. To achieve the right effect on one track Charlie even wrapped an overcoat round the drums. As a result the Rolling Stones came up with some of their best work yet during the Regent Sound sessions. The dearth of technological toys necessitated some invention. The LP went down well with the critics, although there was the occasional dissenting voice: 'A curious sidelight is shown by the one original tune on the album, "Tell Me". The Negroid mask slips away and both tune and lyric are second-hand Liverpool.'

But the record was extraordinarily successful and twenty years later could still be described as one of the finest rock albums ever produced. Within two weeks of its release it was the number 1 bestselling LP in Great Britain, dethroning the Beatles from the position they had held solidly for a year. It is true that *With the Beatles* was in any case reaching the end of its natural reign (it had been released in November) but it was still a tremendous accolade for the Stones to get to the top so quickly. It was also marvellous publicity ammunition ... it was now perfectly justifiable, indeed inevitable, to talk about the Stones in the same breath as the Beatles.

But there was still no time for the boys in the band to pause and enjoy their success. In May they were on the road again. And the Oldham publicity machine did not let up. Andrew had learnt a great deal from Brian Epstein, and knew that the best way to make things happen was to say that they had already taken place. 'Beatlemania' had been invented by English newspapers the year before, abetted and manipulated by Epstein. And Oldham saw no reason why he and the Stones should be outdone. At first, girls used to scream during Rolling Stones concerts. But encouraged by Oldham, newspapers began to talk of riots. And sure enough, in the fullness of time, the riots appeared. Girls began to faint, as well as scream, and others would push and shove their way to the front of the hall. In due course they even began to assault the band. At the Mod Ball in London in April Charlie Watts was pulled backwards off the stage three times and Keith was dragged down into the audience. The *New Musical Express* carried an article describing the chaos at a concert in May:

> Fifty police and a squad of first aid attendants were called in to deal with the crowds at East Ham Granada when the Rolling Stones appeared there on Monday. Many girls fainted and were treated. At the stage door over 300 fans gathered.
>
> From my third row seat I had to lip-read on many occasions

to find out what song was being performed! The screams from the audience completely drowned the Stones.

Charlie sat amid a huge battery of amplifiers which, in normal circumstances, would have enabled people in the pub across the road to hear. But on Saturday, customers in the stalls strained to hear the music.

The long-haired ones began with 'Beautiful Delilah' and were met with a torrent of gifts which plummeted on to the stage from all parts of the theatre. To their credit, the Stones carried on even though they were hit several times. Mick's dancing was grade one and served to incite fresh attacks of frenzy from the fans.

Even though 'You Better Move On' is a slow number, the screams continued, but you should have heard what happened during 'I'm Alright'. From the moment Mick picked up his maracas and the Stones burst into action it was a battle between them and the teenagers as to who could make the most noise. The five lads built up such a wall of excitement that in the end they won. . . .

After 'Not Fade Away' Mick called Charlie to the front to announce the next number. It was almost two minutes before the drummer could say, 'I Wanna Be Your Man', and it was over ten minutes after the act finished with that song before the fans stopped chanting, 'We want the Stones'.

'Not Fade Away' sold a quarter of a million copies, earning the Stones their first silver disc. In France four tracks from the album were released as an EP and went to number 1. But the Rolling Stones still had to conquer America. The other four still seemed stunned and ecstatic about the Stonemania that seemed to be gripping what they saw of England. But Mick was aware that if they were to become really successful, it was dollars that counted. 'Not Fade Away' had been released in March in America, but it had only managed to stagger up to number 44 in the charts. The

66

LP had also been released, although the American distributors felt that it was just too bold to release an untitled record, and had splashed 'England's Newest Hitmakers' across the cover. It had not done very well either.

As the Rolling Stones hit New York in June 1964, things looked hopeful for them in America. The May issue of American *Vogue* carried a David Bailey photograph of Mick and described him in terms far removed from the usual scorn and celebration of horribleness in the English press:

> To the inner group in London, the new spectacular is a solemn young man, Mick Jagger, one of the five Rolling Stones who set out to cross America by bandwagon in June . . . To women, Jagger looks fascinating, to men a scare . . . with, especially, 'Not Fade Away' the Rolling Stones pushed ahead of the Beatles, perhaps because their message and their music are a shade more gutsy. They are quite different from the Beatles, and more terrifying. 'The effect is sex,' wrote one observer, 'that isn't sex, which is the end of the road.'

American teenagers had already been seduced by the Beatles, and according to Andrew's law, that meant that they were now ready for the Stones. Phil Spector had told them in January that they would go down well in America, and he had made a lot of money through being right about what his young compatriots wanted. It was true that the famous New York City disc jockey, Murray the K, had told them that since they had not had a hit in America they could not expect much of a reception. John Lennon had introduced Mick to Murray the K earlier the same year when the disc jockey had visited London. Murray had practically hijacked the Beatles when they had first visited New York and regularly described himself as the 'Fifth Beatle'. He followed them around doggedly during their triumphant tour so that in the end it almost seemed as if he were organising it, and had secured a series of scoop interviews with the visiting Liverpudlians. The Rolling Stones were warned by him that there was not much hope for them in America because if Americans wanted the music of Chuck Berry and Muddy Waters they would listen to the original, and anyway white people most certainly did not want what was considered 'nigger music', and even commonly classified as 'race music'. And it would not be realistic to hope that black people would want to listen to young Englishmen playing the blues. Having delivered his warning, Murray the K did what he could to help, despite the possibility that Beatles fans might think him a turncoat. But he was to be proved right.

The American tour was a great disappointment to the Stones, although it seemed to begin quite well. About 500 fans were waiting for them at Kennedy Airport when they arrived – a pathetic gathering compared with the 10,000 who had been screaming with excitement when the Fab Four landed, but not a bad beginning for a new group. In San Bernardino, where they played first, the audience knew all their songs and liked the Stones' interpretation of them. But if parts of England had had difficulty knowing how to respond to the Stones, Middle America could not cope at all. In Omaha there were 637 people in an auditorium built to hold 15,000, and there were at least fifty policemen in the audience. And in San Antonio things were even worse. The *Daily Mirror* reported: 'Britain's Rolling Stones got "the bird" when they appeared in a show at San Antonio, Texas, last night. Local singers were cheered wildly. A tumbling act and a trained monkey were recalled to the stage for encores. But the long-haired Rolling Stones ... were booed. After the show, at the Teen Fair of Texas, one seventeen-year-old girl said: "All they've got that our own school groups haven't is hair". Only three thousand of the twenty thousand seats were filled. The Stones had to compete with several other attractions – including a rodeo show.' Keith admitted later that their reception had not been good: 'Some towns you went into on that first tour they'd look at you with a look that could kill. You could just tell they wanted to beat the shit out of you.' But the real low point of the tour, from the group's point of view, was the *Hollywood Palace* television show. Dean Martin, the 'host' of the programme, ridiculed the Rolling Stones throughout their appearance, and used them as the butt of his silly jokes. The show was taped in Los Angeles on 5 June, and televised a week later, by which time they were in Chicago. The full indignity of the show only became apparent to them as they watched it in their hotel rooms; the ghastly jokes about them not having long hair, just small foreheads and high eyebrows, and about their forthcoming hair-pulling contest with the Beatles. There was the simpering snidery, before the commercial break: 'Now don't go away, anybody. You wouldn't leave me with these Rolling Stones, would you?' And the final insult, as he introduced the next act, a man on a trampoline: 'This is the father of the Rolling Stones, he's been trying to kill himself ever since.' Keith and Brian had wanted to walk out during the show, but Mick had persuaded them to stay. Now, he reacted predictably. He telephoned Eric Easton and screamed at him for allowing the Stones to be exposed to such humiliating treatment and for sending them on a tour that was proving to be so unsuccessful. 'Mick was never one to shoulder the responsibility for his failures, and this was no time to start,' one observer of the situation back in London put it.

Chicago was not all traumatic for the Stones. Mick, Keith and Brian were delighted to be in the home of the urban blues, the city that had been a staple feature of their adolescent dreams. While they were there they visited the legendary Chess Studios, where so many of their heroes had made their greatest records. The Rolling Stones' own recording session at Chess had been arranged by Phil Spector. Through it they actually got to meet a great many of their idols. Willie Dixon visited them in the studio and so did Buddy Guy. The next day Chuck Berry and Muddy Waters stopped by to see them. For years these colourful names had been enough to spark off their fantasies of louche American life, and now they were meeting them in the flesh and being treated as serious musicians by them. Bill Wyman later described meeting Chuck Berry: 'We played one of his songs, "Reelin' and Rockin' ''. He really liked it. Most of the cover versions of his records didn't swing. Actually Chuck Berry walked in while we were recording "Down the Road Apiece", and he said to us, "Wow, you guys are really getting it on!" ' But even more important than the thrill of meeting the great men of R&B was the experience of working with the Chess engineers. Ron Malo, the engineer who had worked on all the Chuck Berry, Bo Diddley and Howlin' Wolf records, engineered the Stones' Chess recordings. As Bill said: 'He knew exactly what we wanted and he got it almost instantly.'

The tour finished in New York, where the Stones played Carnegie Hall. The Beatles, in February, had been the first pop group ever to play there. And by booking the Stones to play there so soon afterwards Eric Easton was again implanting in the public mind the notion that the Stones were to be compared with the Beatles, even if they were not yet in the same league. For a decade American singers had dominated the English hit parade. Now, the Yanks were being told, things had changed. The Carnegie Hall concerts were packed, and Murray the K kindly organised an Oldham-style publicity coup, organising little girls to persecute them, running after them with scissors, trying to capture a 'curl for a souvenir'.

So the Rolling Stones returned home, having visited the land of their dreams. Even if it had not received them with the screaming, rioting, ecstatic, flailing arms that they would have liked, the experience had been an important one. If nothing else, it had given them the opportunity to hear more of the blues than they could have done in a million man years in England at that time. For the first time they were able to saturate themselves in the music they revered, which was played all day on some radio stations. It was a welcome relief from huddling round some holy import on a record-player.

Their arrival was very nice. A hundred 'screamers', as the newspapers succinctly described them, were waiting at the airport, and during the screaming there was a small-scale riot in which policemen's helmets were knocked to the floor. Fans who had suffered the anguish of separation from them while they were in the States flocked to an all-night, 'Welcome Home Stones' concert at Alexandra Palace, three days after they returned. The concert was scheduled to coincide with the release of 'It's All Over Now' (B. and S. Womack)/'Good Times, Bad Times' (Jagger, Richard). Although the 'A' side was a cover version of a song originally recorded by the Valentinos, the Stones treated it in an entirely different manner. Mick injected a thumping invective instead of Bobby Womack's wan resignation. It had been recorded at Chess and the difference that Malo had made was immediately evident. It went straight into the Top Ten, and the following week it knocked the Animals' 'House of the Rising Sun' from the pinnacle. They had done it! For the first time they had actually hit the top of the singles chart. Even in America, where the record was released a week later, it made it to number 25 But Mick felt bound to make it clear that such success was not what really mattered to the Rolling Stones. As 'It's All Over Now' rocketed up the charts Mick's bravado increased. He said publicly: 'I don't care a damn if our new record has reached number 1. I reckon it will do half a million in this country and in others altogether, and I'd rather have a sale like that than sell five hundred and fifty thousand in Britain alone and have the number 1 thing. What's it matter, anyway? "It's All Over Now" has reached the top, that's great. But I can tell you none of us has been worrying about it.'

Things could not have been better for the group at this time. They had swept the board in the *Record Mirror*'s Pop Poll. In the British Vocal Group Section they came first, with 5301 votes. The Beatles were second, with 4089 votes. Mick was voted the most popular Individual Group Member, and in the World Male Vocal Group section they came second to the Beatles. Even in the Instrumental Section the Stones came fourth. That was particularly startling, since they had only recorded two instrumental tracks – 'Stoned' on the 'B' side of 'I Wanna Be Your Man', and 'Now I've Got a Witness' on their LP. Perhaps the most astonishing result of all was that Mick came sixth on the Best-dressed list. In the Best Disc of 1963 or 1964 Section, 'Not Fade Away' was placed second, after 'She Loves You' (Cilla Black's 'Anyone Who had a Heart' was third and Elvis Presley's 'Viva Las Vegas' fourth). The Pop Poll indicated the enormous following that the Stones had built up, even though they had so far only had one single and one LP that reached the top of the charts. One factor in the Stones' success was the fanaticism of their followers. It was possible to be a lukewarm Beatles enthusiast. But because the Rolling Stones image was so controversial, their fans had all the zeal of an enjoyably persecuted minority.

The Fan Club was now flourishing under the devoted care of Shirley Arnold, a seventeen-year-old fan who found herself landed with it by accident. One Sunday at the end of 1963 she had been talking to Andrew Oldham in Studio 51. 'What's happening to the Fan Club?' she asked, since she knew that one had been started but nothing much had been heard of it. Andrew was at once blessed with a stroke of inspiration. 'Oh! Do you want to run it?' he asked. The next day he handed over to her the postal orders that had been sent in as subscriptions and she was left to get on with running it. During the first few months of 1964 it snowballed, so that by the middle of the year there were 50,000 members and Shirley was working full-time as secretary. She handled the subscriptions and organised the club, but most of the work was done by volunteers who came into the office after school. As the newsletters were sent out every two months a Post Office van would come to the office especially to collect them. During 1964 the Fan Club moved to smart new premises in Argyll Street. Andrew and Eric both had offices in the same building. By this time, Shirley says, 'things were going crazy. The boys often used to be chased down the street by fans.' Much time and energy was expended on simply

72

keeping frantic fans out of the Stones' office premises. In the early publicity material and Fan Club newsletters the Stones had lied about their ages. Mick claimed to be a year younger than he actually was. Since most of the fans were still at school, Mick decided that nineteen was a better age for him than twenty. Shirley recalls Andrew telephoning her once when the boys were on tour to ask how old they were. 'But,' she says, 'what he meant was, "how old did we say they were in the newsletter?" ' It was a pity that Mick had lied about his age, because it meant that his twenty-first birthday celebrations in July had to be rather subdued – according to his own publicity he was only being twenty, so he could not make too much fuss about coming of age. But he did not have much time to worry about the wages of his fibbing. The Stones worked solidly throughout the summer.

On 5 July they were the guest jurors on the television programme *Juke Box Jury*, in which they had to assess the chart potential of newly released records, awarding them marks out of ten. The producers of the show had been persuaded that in order to keep the ravenous fans at bay the Stones should be brought onto the stage in an armoured car. It was the appearance of the Rolling Stones which interested the viewers, not the singles that were being aired. They were described the next day in newspapers as 'anthropoid', 'boorish' and 'charmless'. But as Mick put it, 'If the producer had wanted a sophisticated panel, he could have got a bunch of West End actresses.' Better and better. It seemed that there was almost nothing the Stones could do that would not arouse the righteous indignation of somebody. They only had to blink pugnaciously to hit the headlines of the national press. In the *News of the World* a few weeks later Alan Whittaker wrote:

There are few mothers who wouldn't welcome a Beatle into the family. The Beatles bubble with laughter. They make jokes, wear neat clothes, get along with royalty. Even long hair becomes acceptable after a time. But it's different with the

73

Stones. They leer rather than smile. They don't wear natty clothes. They glower. Nobody would accuse them of radiating charm. And the extraordinary thing is that more and more youngsters are turning towards the Stones. The Beatles have become too respectable. The five Stones – and their young manager, Andrew Oldham – are symbols of a rebellion against authority, against the clock, the clean-shirt-a-day routine. How true is this carefully nourished picture of five indolent morons? The Stones give one the feeling that they really enjoy wallowing in a swill-tub of their own repulsiveness.

On 24 July the Rolling Stones were involved in Britain's biggest ever rock riot. It was the end of the fortnight when Glaswegians traditionally flocked to Blackpool for their annual holiday. They were due to go home the next day so they were all roaring drunk. The Stones were playing to an audience of 5000 in the Empress Ballroom in the Winter Gardens. Gangs of Scots seem to have begun spitting at the Rolling Stones. And Keith was not going to put up with that. Tension had been building up anyway, and as he kicked back at the troublemakers all hell broke loose. A Steinway grand piano was pulled off the stage and smashed to pieces. The red velvet stage curtains were ripped to the ground, chandeliers were hauled down from the ceiling. Fifty rioters were taken to hospital after the battle had ended. According to Bill: 'Later that night, after the riot was over, Ian Stewart, our road manager, went back to get our equipment. He came into our hotel room with little pieces of wood and metal. "Here's your amp," he'd say, and gives us a chip. "Here's your guitar . . ." ' Four fans were later charged with assault and carrying offensive weapons. Blackpool's Deputy Chief Constable, Ronald Gregory, was remarkably calm in the circumstances. He said: 'We shall advise the Winter Gardens authorities that they must not have the Rolling Stones again.' Wherever the Stones played that summer little girls ran amok. A hundred girls fainted when they played in Manchester, and so did two policewomen. A concert in Belfast at the end of July had to be cancelled after twelve minutes due to the pandemonium in the hall and two girls had to be carried off in straitjackets. The *Daily Express* reported, of a concert at the Tower Ballroom, New Brighton, that: 'The bouncers work swiftly, ruthlessly and non-stop, dealing with girls in fits and girls in faints.' Some extraordinary instinct was causing teenagers to behave in the wildest fashion at the Rolling Stones concerts. The mania seemed to grow and grow, to feed on reports of violence and spurt further outbreaks elsewhere. By the time the Stones went on tour again at the beginning of August life was becoming intolerable. On 3 August they played a concert at Longleat in Wiltshire, where two hundred girls fainted. By 9 August the insanity was such that the door was ripped off their car as they were making their getaway after appearing on the television programme, *Ready Steady Go*. A rare virus of contagious hysterical violence seems to have gripped the English-speaking world that summer, beginning with pitched battles between Mods and Rockers at English seaside resorts at Easter. It was the 'long hot summer' of violence in the United States, when riots broke out in New York, Philadelphia, Chicago and other American cities.

On 17 August the third EP, *Five by Five*, was released and hurtled up to the top of the charts, again dislodging the Beatles. Sales were so enormous that it even featured in the *New Musical Express* singles chart, where it reached number 13. On 7 August the Rolling Stones played at the National Jazz and Blues Festival in Richmond. Absurd ruses were now being invented to circumvent the mad fans, and this time they were driven into the athletic ground where the festival was being held in a newspaper van and then used a tent marked 'Lady Artistes Only' as a dressing-room.

During this extraordinary year the Stones were transformed from a relatively unknown group into a cult. Stonemania surrounded them and invaded every aspect of their lives. Mick and Chrissie would wake up, on the few nights he spent in London that year, to find that girls had managed to climb into the flat during the night

75

and were hiding somewhere. Outside the flat there would frequently be a gaggle of girls loitering with unspecified intent, except just the thrill of seeing Mick. For months on end he would see nothing of his family and they would hear nothing from him, although he had always been close to them. Shirley Arnold recalls a great many desolate telephone calls from a confused Eva Jagger, eager to have news of her firstborn that did not come through the newspapers. She was still uncertain how to view her son's career. Was it, as the press always suggested, something to be ashamed of, that was bringing disrepute upon the hitherto unsullied name of Jagger? Or should she be proud that he was obviously being successful? She had made no secret of her alarm when he had left university, although she had been somewhat mollified by the LSE's willingness to take him back whenever he wanted to come. Singing in a pop group certainly did not conform to her social aspirations. On the other hand it was gratifying, in a bizarre way, to have teenage girls turning up just to gawp at 24, The Close, Wilmington, the house where their revered idol had lived. It was a nuisance and it irritated the neighbours, but it was not entirely unpleasant to have one's family regarded as objects of pilgrimage. Neighbours, who had girls trampling through their gardens and sometimes even sleeping in them, found it galling that Mrs Jagger's vanity was obviously being fuelled by these pea-brained visitors. But the pleasure of being able bountifully to invite the fans in for tea before sending them home was one of the few consolations for being publicly reviled by her son. Mick would endlessly describe in interviews how he disliked old people and could not get on with them, and how much he despised the surburban life that his parents lived. Paul McCartney later described in an interview a conversation he had with Jagger in which they had been talking about their attitudes to the adult world, and Jagger had been insisting that he really could not get on with his parents. Paul had said that he did not hate 'old' people. 'I like my dad. He's an "old" person and I like him. I get along with older people.' Paul's mother had died when he was quite young, and his father had had to struggle to bring up two boys alone. But since no such unhappiness had ever encroached upon Mick's life, he could afford to be prodigal with the love and support of his family.

On 5 September the Stones began yet another tour. Night after night they broke box-office records, and were besieged by bellowing fans. They played Brussels and Paris, as ever accompanied by rioting. Despite the frenzied activity of the year the Jagger/Richards songwriting team was becoming very productive. Having seen Lennon and McCartney in action when they were finishing off 'I Wanna Be Your Man', Mick had suddenly realised that writing songs was not necessarily a difficult, time-consuming procedure. On that occasion John and Paul had only written the chorus when they first talked to the Stones about the number. But they then borrowed a couple of guitars, went next door and came back a few minutes later with the song finished. The advantages of writing their own material were immediately obvious. It would relieve them of the endless frustrating searches through the canon of recorded rhythm and blues songs, looking for things that were suitable and had not been over-exposed. It would bring in welcome royalties — each member of the group was by now earning over £200 a week, but a bit extra would be welcome. And most of all, it would add to their prestige. The Beatles seemed to be treated more seriously than other groups because they wrote so much of their own material. So Andrew Oldham strongly encouraged Mick and Keith to do the same. Their first efforts had not been suitable for the Stones themselves to use, but at the end of 1963 Oldham had managed to flog two of their songs to the late George Bean, 'It Should Be You' and 'Will You Be My Lover Tonight?' He had then sold 'That Girl Belongs to Yesterday' to Gene Pitney.

In the spring of 1964 Andrew Oldham had met a seventeen-year-old schoolgirl at a party and had immediately spotted her potential. She had an ethereal elfin beauty and a pretty, slightly husky voice. Andrew decided to turn her into a star. Her name would help: it was Marianne Faithfull. She was doing 'A' levels at a convent in Reading and was at the party with her boyfriend, a short Cambridge undergraduate called John Dunbar. Although she harboured an ambition to join him at Cambridge, Marianne was not a girl to turn down the chance of stardom, even if at first she persuaded herself that it was just an amusing sideline and that she was really going to go to university and become a serious actress. Her first record was one of Mick and Keith's songs, 'As Tears Go By', another of the gentle, winsome ballads that they found it easiest to write in those days. It was released on 24 August.

The songwriting collaboration between Mick and Keith upset Brian. It had been natural for Andrew to encourage Mick and Keith to write, since they were the two members of the band he had lived with in Mapesbury Road. And they had known each other for so long that they found it easy to work together. In the beginning they tried to work with Brian a few times, but it was never as satisfactory. He was simply not as attuned to them as they were to each other. However arrogant Mick might have seemed to some people at this time, he was humble about his songwriting abilities. He recognised that Keith's melodies were good, and that his own talent as a lyricist was more doubtful. But he was determined to work at it, and Keith was easy-going and willing to work with him. Slowly, by dint of application and perseverance, Mick was turning himself into a superstar. He had learnt to excite and control an audience. His PR was being brilliantly handled by Andrew. And now he was learning to write songs.

On 23 October the Rolling Stones flew to the United States for the second time. Word of their extraordinary successes during the summer had spread. American teenagers had heard of the Stonemania rampant in England and were eager to see and scream for themselves. The Stones Fan Club in America had 80,000 members by the time they arrived. This tour was a triumphal progress. The fans reacted hysterically, just as they had done in England. And the 'old people' also reacted hysterically. Ed Sullivan announced, after they had appeared on his show: 'I promise you they'll never be back on this show ... Frankly I didn't see the Rolling Stones until the day before the broadcast. They were recommended by my scouts in England. I was shocked when I saw them. Now the Dave Clark Five are nice fellows. They are gentlemen and they perform well. It took me seventeen years to build this show. I'm not going to have it destroyed in a matter of weeks.' The teenage ecstasy and the adult anger were all that they could have asked for. The Rolling Stones had conquered America. The crowning achievement of this tour was the concert they gave in the Academy of Music in New York, immortalised in Tom Wolfe's 'The Girl of the Year' article, first published in the *Herald Tribune*. It remains the definitive evocation of the speedy New York Pop Society of the early sixties, opening with a cascade of ghastly hairstyles and then recalling the incoherent enthusiasm of the eponymous model 'Baby Jane' Holzer, the undisputed 'Girl of the Year', and her friends for the modernity and youth of the Rolling Stones. The frantic, gushing excitement of Mrs Holzer and her friends continues as the Stones play:

> The girls have Their Experience. They stand up on their seats. They begin to ululate, even between songs. The look on their faces! Rapturous agony! There, right up there, under the sulphur lights, that is them. God, they're right there! Mick Jagger takes the microphone with his tabescent hands and puts his huge head against it, opens his giblet lips and begins to sing ...

After New York one thing was indisputable. The Rolling Stones were world-class fashionable.

By December 'Time is on My Side' had reached number 5 in the American charts. At home they had two number 1 hits and the most successful EP and LP of the year. And they had had twenty-two nights off during 1964.

79

Chapter Five

The Rolling Stones' frenzied activity continued in 1965. The year began with a tour of Ireland and they then left for a tour of Australia and New Zealand, stopping off on the way in Los Angeles for a recording session. On the way back to England they played in Singapore, and in March there was a two-week British tour. Then eleven days in Scandinavia, three days in Germany and two in France before they began their third American tour in April.

Their records were getting better and better. No one knew whether the same could be said of their playing on stage, since no one heard any of it above the inevitable screaming. Certainly Jagger's performance looked better than ever. The second LP was released in England in January, and *Rolling Stones Now*, the American album containing similar tracks, came out in February. The English album, like its predecessor, was released untitled with just a Bailey photograph of the group. But this time the cover also contained some of Andrew Oldham's eminently imitable, Anthony Burgess-inspired prose:

> It is the summer of the night. London's eyes be tight shut, all but twelve peepers and six hip malchicks who prance the street

... 'There's a femme in a frock.' 'Come on luv,' says Bill, 'Give us a kiss of Christmas.' 'For why I should,' says she, 'you bods ain't Mistahs with hair like that! ... Travel to Chicago and ask the malchek plebbies where is Howlin' Wolf? Be he be not the one with Cheyanie Bodie. Oh my groogie back to your window box ... Cast deep in your pockets for loot to buy this disc of groovies and fancy words. If you don't have bread, see that blind man – knock him on the head, steal his wallet and low and behold you have the loot if you put in the boot, good another one sold! ...'

The same notes were used on *Rolling Stones Now*, but they were censored on later editions of the album in Britain.

'The Last Time'/'Play with Fire', the Stones' next single, went on sale on 26 February. It was the first time that Mick and Keith had written an 'A' side, and within a week it was number 1. Keith has said since that 'The Last Time' was the first song that he and Mick had written that they really liked. And Mick, in an interview with *Rolling Stones Monthly*, agreed: 'I suppose we'd been writing for almost nine months to a year by then, just learning how to put songs together. And with "The Last Time" it became fun. After that we were confident that we were on our way, that we'd just got started.' 'Play with Fire' was the first of many Rolling Stones songs to chronicle contemporary young life through vicious and cynical eyes. By the beginning of March the Rolling Stones were at the top of the English singles chart (with 'The Last Time'), the EP chart (with *Five by Five*) and the LP chart (with their second album).

When they arrived in Australia they were greeted by about 3000 rioting fans who beat their way through a chain wire fence and then advanced into the quarantine area, ripping through a steel barrier in the customs hall. Once the group had disappeared into the terminal building the fans outside turned ugly. Twenty were injured in the ensuing battle, two of them seriously. The Australian tour was such a triumph that by the time they left four of their releases were in the Australian Top Ten singles chart: 'Under the Boardwalk' (number 1), 'The Last Time' (number 2), 'Walking the Dog' (number 3) and their EP, *Around and Around* (number 6). Everywhere there were riots, and stories of the group having to be smuggled into concert halls to protect them from their admirers. Before they returned home the Australian Fan Club presented them with a solid gold map of Australia.

Although he was by now used to being a superstar, life was changing for Mick in other ways. His circle of friends had widened in the last year or so. He was getting to know a group of young people that included models and hairdressers, suddenly wealthy pop stars and slowly impoverished aristocrats. Their lives tended to revolve around the Kings Road, where many of them lived or worked. The Chelsea Antique Market was a favourite place for breakfast, and some of them would usually be found in the Baghdad House in the Fulham Road in the evenings. Other haunts included the Chelsea Potter, the Pheasantry and the Kenco Coffee Bar opposite the barracks. In this social mixture the proportions were more equal than they would have been in previous generations. It was not just a few talented outsiders crashing a smart world, nor simply upper-class slumming. Each group gathered real glamour through its association with the other. To the smart young Londoners the vitality and drive of the working-class was an inspiring catalyst – the necessary spark to save them from isolation and smugness. And the boys on the make picked up their best revolutionary ideas from patrician iconoclasts. They shared feelings of frustration with the dreariness and illiberalism of the established order. The alliance was also based on beauty, talent and marijuana. 'We all met each other huddling in the loo smoking a joint,' according to one *arriviste* of the time. He estimates that 'on an average night in the Ad Lib nightclub there would be about 65 per cent upper-class, and the rest new-wave, glamorous rich.'

It was a world into which Mick Jagger slotted naturally. David Bailey, the former boyfriend of Chrissie Shrimpton's sister, Jean, was a major figure in it, and he was by now a close friend of Mick's. Bailey had a more advantageous background – he came from the East End of London and had the cachet of truly belonging to the working-class. Michael Fish, the pretty young tailor, was seen in this circle and so was Ossie Clark, the brilliant Mancunian fashion designer. There were other musicians around as well, including Georgie Fame and Paul McCartney. Many of the key figures in the explosion of talent that had created Mod London were now part of this inter-caste aristocracy. 'The point was that all these people really liked each other and liked being together, and there was a great exchange of ideas and aspirations and feelings. They were all young, friendly and growing up together,' a middle-aged businessman says, remembering the friends of his youth.

The group included Christopher Gibbs, an antique dealer, Robert Fraser, who ran an art gallery, and Mark Palmer, who ran a model agency called 'English Boy'. There was the brilliant young photographer, Michael Cooper, and Michael Rainey, who had enjoyed an enlightened education in a series of Mediterranean bars and now ran a clothes shop called 'Hung on You'. There was the Irish grandee Nicholas Gormanston, flitting in and out of London, and his compatriots Desmond Guinness (with his wife Mariga) and Tara Browne. There were Jane, Victoria and Alice Ormsby-Gore, the daughters of the former British Ambassador to Washington, and on the fringes of the group were the young painter Donald Cammell (who lived mostly in Paris) and John Dunbar, Marianne Faithfull's boyfriend. There was also the foreign exotica, including Prince Stanislaus Klossowski de Rola (known as 'Stash') and the American magus Kenneth Anger. But Christopher Gibbs and Robert Fraser, who were at Eton together, seem to have had the greatest effect on Mick.

When the memoirs of the sixties come to be written Christopher Gibbs will be in a lot of the indexes. He was one of the most universally liked figures of that sparkling generation. He pulled off at an early age the remarkable feat of being seen to have both ruthless discrimination and also unusual kindness and generosity. 'He was the wisest person I'd ever met. And his conversation was, and is, effortlessly informative and illuminating,' according to an old friend. Nicky Haslam, a contemporary at school, says: 'He was very good at educating people's eye, and he was able to inject a lot of his taste into Mick, who was very receptive and understood the point of it all.' Christopher Gibbs' influence was not restricted to Mick and his other friends. According to Donald Cammell: 'Christopher started a Moroccan fad in London and soon everybody had Moroccan drapes and cushions and all that.' Gibbs first went to North Africa in the late 1950s and began to bring back painted furniture and textiles long before anyone else in London was showing much interest in them. It is believed by many of the old proto-hippies that it was through his influence that the taste for such things began to spread. Just as Harold Acton began to wear wide trousers at Oxford and was imitated by an ever-widening circle of people, until all England knew what was meant by Oxford bags and thousands wore them, so it is possible to blame Christopher Gibbs for the bastardised Moroccan-Indian-'ethnic' look that came to characterise hippiedom. It is an allegation that he naturally refutes. He clings to the 'nothing can stop a style of interior decoration whose time has come' explanation and insists that, as always, other people around the world were doing exactly the same thing at the same time and the effect was cumulative. But whether or not he changed the face of civilisation, Christopher was a vigorous intellectual mentor to many of his contemporaries, and especially to Mick Jagger.

Robert Fraser was an art dealer of great vision with a flair for ferreting out talent. His gallery was so publicly fashionable that it was featured in the famous *Time* article on Swinging London published in April 1966. Fraser was consistently in the vanguard of modernity, showing ever more controversial painters and sculptors. In 1967 John Lennon's first exhibition of paintings was to be held in his gallery. He was continually attacked by the critics and continually imitated by other dealers. Robert Fraser's craving for the new was not restricted to art. An elegant voluptuary with a taste for low life, he had spent a long time investigating the colourful goings-on a few blocks to the east of his flat in Mount Street.

Christopher, Robert and the others were a revelation for Mick. The whole Mod world was oriented towards the pursuit of pleasure – the wildness, the extravagance and the frenetic rush were all symptoms of a determination to have fun. Self-indulgence was suddenly a Good. No one needed to save any more, and everyone was encouraged to spend – on clothes, records, whatever they wanted. Clothes as well as machines now had built-in obsolescence. No one wanted dresses made to last – no one wanted to wear them often enough to find out whether they would. (1966 saw the ultimate in throwaway couture – the paper dress, made possible by the development of non-rustle paper.) Old morality was discarded along with everything else in the headlong dash for fun. And the nobs seemed to be aware of more interesting and elegant ways of amusing themselves than anyone Mick had ever known before. They provided him with a real alternative to everything he had hated about Dartford. At the Grammar School education was oriented towards exams. Any area of human knowledge or experience that did not crop up on an 'O' or 'A' level syllabus was deemed irrelevant. And any awakening interest among the boys in such distractions would be severely discouraged. Although he had taken English 'A' level Mick seems to have been extraordinarily ill-read at this time, and to have had virtually no knowledge at all of music or painting. If you were not part of the rat-race you were a slob, in which case there were several recognised modes of slobbishness between which you could choose. There was the Games Slob, the Jazz Slob or the Pure Slob. But no dilettante could have survived. His new friends were indisputably better educated than he was and did not seem to view the acquisition of learning or experience merely as a step on the many-runged ladder to a good job. They seemed to have a negligent brilliance, an offhand learning, an impudent, over-familiar attitude to the arts. In an England governed by the dapper little Mr Wilson and the puritanical Dr Leavis they seemed to have come from another, more graceful world where all the men were beautiful and all the women clever.

The attraction was not all one-sided. The *gratin* took to Mick as strongly as he to them. He was becoming beautiful – an almost imperceptible slimming of his face was leaving it lean and electric. He had always been criticised until now for his narcissism. Although plenty of his contemporaries from school and from the LSE were vain, self-important or egotistical, they had no sensual appreciation of themselves as aesthetically pleasing objects. But most of Mick's new friends had grown up at schools where there was a widespread appreciation of ephebic beauty that was not necessarily homosexual. They were not appalled by his enlightened narcissism. Acquaintances from school and employees still found Mick 'full of himself', 'bumptious' and 'bullying'. But the new friends seemed to bring out a different personality, endearingly self-effacing for one of the greatest pop idols of the day. They discovered that he had an enquiring, if untutored, mind, and was interested in everything. If they mentioned a book that he had not read he would scuttle away, assiduously read it and then come back and discuss it.

Mick was bowled over by this world, and with all his suburban instincts for self-improvement he began thoroughly and unrelentingly to learn from them what he could. If she had seen him at all during this time his mother would have been delighted to see him carrying on her good work. He was quite straightforward, even camp, about what he was up to. A Boudin Ball was held at Christie's, and before it Christopher Gibbs gave a dinner-party at his flat in Cheyne Walk. Michael Fish recalls Jagger, during the party, sitting between him and Nicholas Gormanston and explaining, 'I'm here to learn how to be a gentleman.' He learnt fast. Just as he had spotted Andrew Oldham and Phil Spector as people who had a lot to teach him, so he befriended key social figures.

86

By the end of 1965 Mick was a fixture at smart gatherings, and he even hobnobbed with royalty. He was seen at nightclubs with Cecil Beaton and Princess Margaret. Mick and Chrissie Shrimpton went to the Ormsby-Gores' famous party in Ladbroke Grove, which Jane Holzer tried to gatecrash and was turned away from. 'It was the first party which included that kind of mix of royalty, aristocrats, very important Americans, the Rolling Stones, photographers and riff-raff,' according to Jane Ormsby-Gore (now Rainey). The surrounding streets were packed with people straining to catch a glimpse of the glamour of it all. 'Mick seemed to be entranced by the whole Ormsby-Gore family,' according to a friend. 'They probably provided his first glimpse of a family existence in which people of his age did not hate and despise their parents and frequently went to see them.'

Mick was a nifty social climber and had the intelligence not to dispense entirely with the punkish outlaw pose that had got him so far. He just modified it, and developed a Salon Rocker style, which did not quite compromise his independence. He was not the only sortable member of the Rolling Stones. Jane Rainey: 'At first Brian was much more sophisticated and was the easiest to talk to.' But although he had more polish than Mick in the beginning, he was also difficult, temperamental and unreliable.

In 1965 Anita Pallenberg, a German–Italian actress, entered the lives of the *jeunesse dopée*. She had been working with an avant-garde theatre group called Living Theatre in Rome, and then moved to Paris. There she met Donald Cammell who was living with his girlfriend, Deborah Dixon, in the rue de l'Ambre. While she was in Paris she encountered Brian Jones in Donald's flat, and also Jane Ormsby-Gore, who invited her to come and stay in London. Anita looked marvellous. She was slim and blonde, with the most magical, sparkling smile. A friend: 'There was nothing genteel about Anita. She had an almost masculine sense of humour, which could be very savage, and a completely unrestrained laugh. She was very wicked, very intelligent and very, very alluring.' She was much sought after, and people who were around at the time say that she could have had her pick of Mick, Brian or Keith. They all had girlfriends – Mick had Chrissie, Keith had a girlfriend called Linda Keith who was a model, and Brian was living with Linda Lawrence and their baby. Brian was the most smitten by Anita, and he soon ditched Linda and the infant and began to live with Anita. But she was to exert a strong influence over Mick and Keith as well. Donald Cammell: 'At the time she first started to hang out with those guys she opened up a whole world to them. She was the most attractive girl any of them had ever been around and she had a genuine feeling for books and poetry, and the guts to get involved with things.' Anita was constantly becoming involved with new interests – she would discover new painters or writers and decide that they were the greatest thing ever and would share her enthusiasm with Mick and Brian (Keith was less easily galvanised). She developed other obsessions, too, such as that Christopher Gibbs looked exactly like her dead grandmother. 'Look, look, it's a dead ringer,' she would say, pointing at photographs.

She was a descendant of the nineteenth century Romantic painter, Böcklin, best known for a picture entitled *The Island of the Dead*, in which a tall, shrouded figure stands on the prow of a little boat which is being rowed towards a rocky island. There are vaults carved into the rock, and a clump of cypresses growing among them. Most sinister of all in the painting is the coffin lying in the boat. It is unclear whether it is intended for the shrouded figure, who is perhaps already dead, or whether it already contains a stiff. If the latter, is the standing figure the murderer or the guardian of the body? It is a painting that seems appropriate to Anita – the mysterious, solitary luminous figure always game for any voyage into the unknown. And the landscape of the painting, imbued with a sense of the tantalising presence of evil, is one into which Anita would fit happily.

During their affair Anita and Brian began to look remarkably like each other. They were both blonde and they were about the

88

same height. They would dress alike, usually in near fancy dress, often in satin or leather. Anita was the first girl with whom anyone had ever seen Brian really involved. Linda Lawrence survived longer than most, but Brian made it clear to at least some of his friends that it was because she was prepared to accept the relationship on his terms. Brian and Anita became a powerful couple in London. They looked fabulous, Brian was part of the currently most successful group, and everyone was fascinated by Anita. 'The acquisition of Anita increased Brian's social desirability,' according to one observer, 'and certainly increased his confidence.'

The Rolling Stones' next single, 'Satisfaction', was one of their greatest ever. Written on the road during their third American tour in April 1965, it was to become one of the handful of characteristic sixties songs, a slogan for the decade during which young people all over the world declared themselves to be opposed to the values of their parents. Despite the phenomenal success that they were enjoying at the time, the Stones aligned themselves, in 'Satisfaction', with the universal teenage feelings of alienation and frustration: feelings which result from both the oppressively materialistic advertising pumped at them from the television and car radio, and also the difficulty of getting a 'girl with action', sexual satisfaction. Curiously, the Stones themselves were not happy with the song. It was not released until August 1965 in England, after its appeal had been verified by the American audience. It was released in May in the United States, and within four weeks was at the top of the charts, where it stayed for a month. Its success encouraged them to release it at home. It was a huge success in England, and was also number 1 in Argentina, Australia, Austria, Bermuda, Brazil, Bulgaria, Burma, Canada, Czechoslovakia, Denmark, Finland, France, Germany, Greece, Hong Kong, Hungary, Ireland, Israel, Italy, Japan, Lebanon, Luxembourg, Malaysia, Netherlands, New Zealand, Norway, the Philippines, Poland, Portugal, South Africa, Singapore, Spain, Sweden, Switzerland, Turkey and Yugoslavia. 'Satisfaction' was the first Stones song to involve the blend of rhythm and blues and soul that was to become the staple Stones sound. As David Dalton put it in *The Rolling Stones:* 'The synthesis combined the ecstatic momentum of Motown with the disdainful tone of the blues in a lethal brew that scathingly indicated the hypocrisy, corruption and folly of the society they lived in while at the same time celebrating their release from it . . . "Satisfaction" is the greatest of the Stones' inner-city hymns blues words with a soul sound in a rock song.' If 'Satisfaction' dealt with feelings general to most adolescents, the flip side, 'The Spider and The Fly', concerned the specific dilemma of a rock singer on the road, who is meant to be faithful to the girl at home, but is inevitably seduced by a 'rinsed-out blonde' who picks him up in the hotel bar. Since the Stones were spending months almost constantly touring, it is not surprising that Mick should have begun to feel a weariness about life on the road. Although Keith later told his biographer, Barbara Charone, how much Mick had enjoyed it all, especially in Los Angeles where the group frequently went to record: 'Mick loved it all. He loved the whole Hollywood bit. He loved renting a car and driving down Sunset Boulevard picking up groupies.' But however exciting it was at first to find scores of available girls wherever they went, it might have been beginning to pall by the later half of 1965.

And although they were now the second most successful recording group in the world, Mick was beginning to suspect that they were not earning as much money as they might have expected. Since they signed with Andrew and Eric they had earned about £100,000 – not an enormous amount considering the scale of their achievement. And Mick was aware that they could not expect to retain their world-wide appeal for much longer. Oldham and Easton were still their managers, but the Stones were beginning to feel increasingly alienated from the old pro Easton. Oldham's allegiance was by now far more to the group, especially Mick and Keith, than to his business partner. In August Andrew met Allen Klein, a figure famous in the music business. He was an accountant who had made a vast amount of money out of handling entertainers' financial affairs. He had grown up in an orphanage in New Jersey, and after learning accountancy at night-school had worked for a firm of accountants who specialised in show business clients. During the late fifties and early sixties he developed an efficient way of making money. It took a lot of work, but it was foolproof. Klein was experienced enough to know that almost anyone who had had dealings with a record company was likely to be owed a great deal of money, either through the negligence or the dishonesty of the company. So he set about becoming the Robin Hood of showbiz. By the time he met Andrew Oldham he had been wanting, for some time, to get his hands on the Beatles' financial affairs. But these were still being handled by Brian Epstein. The Rolling Stones were the nearest he could get to his ambition. But he was sufficiently well informed to know that the Stones and the Beatles were friends, and sufficiently shrewd to realise that if he could do a good job for the Stones it would be an ideal recommendation to the Beatles. Mick, Keith and Andrew were all seduced by Klein's slightly gangsterish image and his promises of untold wealth. Eric Easton was fired. Andrew Oldham became the Stones' sole manager, and Klein became business manager for the Stones and also for Oldham himself. The deal attracted quite a lot of attention in the press. Judith Simons wrote in the *Daily Express*: 'A year ago their (the Stones') fee was about £500 a show. Now they are paid £1000 for a shorter 25–30 minute appearance. There are lucrative sidelines too – like their spot in the American beat film, *The Tami Show*. They received £25,000 for that.' She estimated that in America alone they had each made £4000 from 'Satisfaction', £3000 each from 'The Last Time' and also from 'Little Red Rooster', and that Mick and Keith had each earned another £8000 in songwriting royalties. 'It isn't all profit, of course. Expenses are high. Each guitarist owns about eight instruments and the total cost of their present equipment was about £4000. When the Stones are on tour hotel bills are about £700 a week. Salaries for secretarial and other staff accounts for £200 a week.' But she had not taken into account the cost of studio time, and had probably underestimated other expenses. There had been no vast profits so far.

Shirley Arnold remembers the first time that Klein visited the Stones office. 'Mick had told us that Klein was coming, and we had to tidy the place up and make sure everything was okay, and that there were drinks in the place. But then he came in, drinking whisky from the bottle, and I didn't think he looked very impressive at all.' But Klein certainly did his stuff. The Stones' first contract with Decca had expired in February. Klein renegotiated it, and secured the group a £3,000,000 advance against royalties from record sales from Decca and London–American, the North American distributors. That sort of advance was unheard of at the time, but due to the extraordinary success of 'Satisfaction', their latest record, and the persistence of Allen Klein, Sir Edward Lewis, the head of Decca, decided that he should pay up, in order to keep the Stones for the company, and Klein quiet. By the time of their fourth American tour in the autumn of 1966 the Rolling Stones felt themselves to be rich for the first time. Suddenly they were staying in better hotels, being driven around in better cars. There was money to spend. And they all enjoyed the sensation of feeling rich.

The Stones' schedule at this time was completely insane. On 2 September they taped *Ready Steady Goes Live* in London. On 3 September they flew to Dublin for a concert, and went on to Belfast the next day. On 5 September they all flew to Los Angeles for a recording session, on 8 September they played the Palace Ballroom in Douglas, Isle of Man and from 11–17 September they toured Germany. And then on 24 September they began a British tour. When they had occasional time off they seemed unable to relax completely. If there was a free evening Mick, Keith, Brian and Andrew seemed always to gravitate towards London nightclubs where they would be recognised, so they did not unwind even when they had the opportunity. They were often at a loose end before they were scheduled to start touring again. It was not only the excitement of performance that was addictive. It was also the constant travel, the pleasure of moving from one world in which they did not belong to another. But the relationships within the band were undoubtedly strained by the close proximity in which they had to exist for so long. Mick and Keith wrote a great many of their songs while they were on the road. And the songwriting was causing increasing difficulties with Brian. After 'Satisfaction' Mick and Keith's confidence naturally mushroomed. Brian was becoming increasingly bitter that the Stones were using so many Jagger/ Richard compositions, and that they did not seem to want to use his material. But he was highly defensive about his own songs and never allowed any of the rest of the band to hear them. Having to go along to one recording session after another only to learn to play more and more songs that Mick and Keith had written was nearly intolerable for Brian. Not only did it mean that they were being seen to be the most important members of the band, but it also suggested the existence of an alliance between Mick and Keith that excluded him. He would still try to establish a particular rapport with one or other of them, by conjuring up some sort of hostility towards the third. 'He seemed unable to be friendly to everybody. There always had to be an enemy. And if he couldn't turn anyone else into an enemy, he assumed that everybody else was treating him as one,' according to a fellow musician. Bill Wyman also felt excluded by Mick and Keith, and peeved that it should be taken for granted that they were the only songwriters for the Stones. But he was able to keep his feelings of resentment under control. Brian was practically deranged by his. His affair with Anita did nothing to allay his sense of persecution. It became another area of anxiety – he was continually afraid that she would go off with someone else. Although she increased his social confidence, she could do nothing about his real problems. It was becoming obvious to everyone who worked with the Rolling Stones that there was something profoundly wrong with Brian. He was attractive, and many people found him endearing. Shirley Arnold: 'He radiated sunshine, but you could see that he had all the problems of the world on his shoulders. There was such an ugliness there as well as the beauty.' Fan mail was pouring into the Stones office daily, and Brian would always ask how many there were for him, and how many for Mick. 'Brian was just obsessed by the adulation.' Mick did not reveal any competitiveness with Brian, although he was the only member of the group who could be a real rival for the fans' devotion. But then, by now Mick's pre-eminence was becoming secure, cemented by the success of the songwriting partnership and by Brian's own insecurities.

Despite the enormous amount of work that he put into the Stones, Andrew Oldham was not neglecting his other clients. The career of Marianne Faithfull was flourishing, carefully tended by Oldham. She had a series of successful records, including 'This Little Bird' and 'Summer Nights'. In May 1965 she married John Dunbar, and in the autumn of that year her son, Nicholas, was born. There was, inevitably, some conflict between the demands of her career and her role as a wife and mother of an infant. It was not easy to be a rising pop singer. Nor was it easy to be married to one. John had left Cambridge and was now running the 'underground' Indica Gallery in Mason's Yard, off Duke Street, St James's. Before Nicholas was born Marianne spent some time in hospital, and was visited there by her husband's partner, Barry Miles, now known to everyone by his surname alone. The telephone rang while he was in her room. It was Andrew Oldham calling from New York. He told Marianne to go and look out of the window. She did, and waiting for her in the road outside was a black Mini with darkened windows – the absolute epitome of sixties flash. But however indebted she was to Andrew, and however lavish his presents, she did not have to like the other members of his stable. She had seen Mick and Keith quite often while she was recording 'As Tears Go By', and had hated them. After cutting the demo tape she complained to

94

Miles, 'God, those Rolling Stones are horrible. They're all greasy and spotty.'

But the fortunes of the Rolling Stones had changed dramatically since then. On 6 September the next LP was released, entitled *Out of Our Heads*. The American version, which contained different tracks, had been issued in July and had already sold phenomenally well. The English version contained four original tracks – 'Gotta Get Away', 'Heart of Stone', 'The Under Assistant West Coast Promotion Man' and 'I'm Free'. The American *Out of Our Heads* contained several tracks that had already been released as singles, 'The Last Time', 'Satisfaction', 'The Under Assistant West Coast Promotion Man' and 'Play with Fire'. Although so much of the material was already familiar, it was a more potent collection than the English version, which was commercially successful but did not seem to represent any real advance on their previous albums, nor to match the standard of 'The Last Time' or 'Satisfaction'. The last two singles had been of such a high standard that it seemed unlikely that the Stones would be able to find a suitable follow-up. But they succeeded admirably with 'Get Off of My Cloud'/'The Singer Not the Song'. It was released in England just two months after 'Satisfaction', and within a week it was number 1 in the hit parade. It was also at the top of the charts in America at the same time, giving the Rolling Stones their first simultaneous number 1 in Britain and the States.

The touring continued. The German tour, early in September, was the most violent yet. Thousands of rampaging teenagers were firehosed as they broke through the barrier when the plane carrying the Stones touched down. But that was only the beginning. Fifteen minutes later the local police called a press conference to say that they could not guarantee to protect the Stones. The hotel where they were to stay had already cancelled the reservation, through fear of what their admirers might do to the place. The frenzied hysteria that greeted the Stones throughout that tour was compared with that of the Hitler Youth Movement, although it seems unlikely that baby Nazis were allowed such freedom of expression. Not only did the fans stomp, scream and bellow along with the words during the concerts, they also ripped out fifty rows of seats in one theatre. Mick did not help matters by goose-stepping on stage during 'Satisfaction' at one concert, and giving a Nazi salute. The hall was too well-policed for the fans to do much damage, but afterwards they overturned 130 cars and pulverised every carriage on the trains leaving the city. The police had to help the group to escape safely, according to *Rolling Stones Monthly*: 'The police lead them through an old Nazi bunker – the Aryan inscriptions still on the walls – and up into some pinewoods a mile and a half from the theatre. But still they had to run.' They would have been lynched by their adoring fans if they had tried to get out through the main entrance.

An autumn tour of Britain was much less violent. In October they flew to New York to begin another American tour. The entire tour was sold out, and Klein was working his magic. Andrew Oldham said at the time: 'This is the boys' fourth American tour, but the first one that is going to pay dividends. During this six-week period of concerts and TV appearances we will gross an unprecedented $1,500,000.' Their next American LP, to be released in November, was advertised on an eighty-foot high Times Square billboard. *December's Children* was a collection of singles and tracks that had earlier been rejected from other LPs. Keith admitted that they would not have been able to release such an album in England. But the American market was enormous, and was happy to buy albums that were compilations of songs it knew already. Although the group were still being mobbed by little girls, they were also being treated more seriously in the United States. As Mick said to *Disc* magazine at the time: 'They (the press) don't like most of the groups anymore. They quite like us, but they have this ridiculous attitude towards us – a sort of intellectual approach towards the group.' The Rolling Stones were being treated as some sort of natural phenomenon and their pronouncements on morality, or music, or anything else were being seriously discussed by journalists and sociologists looking for symptoms of what was really going on among young people. 30 November was declared Rolling Stones Day in Denver, Colorado, by Governor John A. Love, as evidence that the adults of America were no longer anti-Rolling Stones.

On 6 December the Stones had another long recording session at the RCA studios in Los Angeles where they laid down nine tracks, including those that would be used on their next single – '19th Nervous Breakdown'/'Mother's Little Helper' (UK 'B' side) and 'Sad Day' (US 'B' side). '19th Nervous Breakdown' was phenomenally successful on both sides of the Atlantic. It was becoming clear that the Rolling Stones had reached a peak in their career and that they would have to change their tactics slightly in order to consolidate their position. It was also evident, by the beginning of 1966, that they would be unable to go on working at the same pace as they had during the preceding year. The whole group took a holiday for two months after the autumn 1965 American tour, and Andrew Oldham announced that they would not be touring Britain again for six months. They had had such extraordinary success during the last two years that it was obvious that they were going to have to become less accessible, in order to consolidate their superstar status. There was no point in being giants if everyone in the world could see them play and every journalist could interview them. They were running the risk of devaluing themselves by their availability. The Oldham-staged outrages were to diminish during the next year, they were to play fewer concerts and there would be fewer records. In 1966 they were to release only one album of new work – *Aftermath* – compared with two in 1965. But they were still to work extraordinarily hard by the standards of other groups, especially the Beatles. And the fuss did not suddenly disappear – in February a fifteen-year-old boy in Cleveland, Ohio, committed suicide when his guardian made him cut his hair. He was, according to neighbours, a 'quiet and studious type' and a 'fanatic follower of the Rolling Stones Rock and Roll group.' And the Stones' spring

97

tour of Australia and New Zealand was accompanied by the usual chaos – there was a riot in Wellington during which dozens of seats were slashed. The disturbances which seemed to occur wherever the Rolling Stones played had become a major nuisance. They were one of the reasons why the group could not continue to tour as often as they had been doing. They began a tour of North America at the end of June, and were refused accommodation by fourteen hotels in New York, for the usual reasons. *Aftermath* was the first Rolling Stones album to be released in stereo, and the first to be completely written by Mick and Keith. The *Daily Express* reported that the Beatles, who were themselves in a recording studio at the time, working on their next single (it was to be 'Paperback Writer'), were so keen to hear it that they sent Mal Evans, their road manager, out in the middle of the session to buy them a copy. It included a much wider variety of instruments than any of their earlier LPs, and was their most polished album so far. But the mood of many of the songs, of playfully smashing up women who had no dignity to lose anyway, could have been offensive to some. A pillar of Swinging London he might be, but Mick's lyrics suggested that his attitude to women was a brutal parody of that of some other, nastier generation. There was 'Under My Thumb':

Under my thumb's a squirming dog who's just had her day
Under my thumb's a girl who's just changed her ways
It's down to me, the way she does just what she's told
It's down to me, the change has come, she's under my thumb.

There was the unambiguous 'Doncha Bother Me', and 'High and Dry', in which the heroine has finally done a bunk:

Anything I wish for I only had to ask her
I think she found out it was money I was after . . .
Lucky that I didn't have any love towards her.

98

But those were as nothing compared with 'Stupid Girl', which must be one of the most venomous songs ever: it is just a vitriolic catalogue of the wretched creature's defects, with the dainty refrain, 'Look at that stupid girl':

> The way she talks about someone else
> That she don't know herself . . .
> It doesn't matter if she dyes her hair
> Or the colour of the shoes she wears . . .
> She's the sickest thing in the world . . .

There were also 'Out of Time', which included the memorable line, 'You're obsolete my baby', and 'Mother's Little Helper' about a slovenly modern housewife begging her doctor for pep-pills. Nestling uncomfortably among all these unblinkered images of contemporary life was the nostalgic ballad, 'Lady Jane'. But even here the message is that the narrator is ditching Lady Anne for Lady Jane, ruthlessly for all his gentle courtesy:

> This play is run, my love
> Your time has come my love
> I've pledged my troth to Lady Jane.

But dull would she be of soul who was more responsive to the nastiness of the words than to the hypnotic sensuality of the album as a whole. Most of the Stones' earlier LPs sound fragmented, as if they are an almost random jumble of tunes. *Aftermath* was the first to be recorded in two marathon sessions in Los Angeles, and as a result it works as a single entity in a way that was new for a Stones' album. Not only were there recurrent themes, but there is also a unity of sound that builds up a momentum of excitement. The American *Aftermath* was only slightly different from the English version – the most memorable tracks appear on both. It was released in the United States in June, and on both sides of the

Atlantic it sold hugely. It was beginning to seem as though anything the Rolling Stones put their names to would be a success.

Mick and Chrissie had come up in the world. They had by now moved to a much larger flat in Harley House in Marylebone Road. Shirley Arnold recalls being amazed that the rent of the flat was £50 per week. She was very impressed by the luxurious gadget-filled kitchen, although much of the flat seems to have stayed half-furnished for some time. But Mick's domestic life was still unpredictable. His relationship with Chrissie had never been tranquil. Maldwin Thomas, a friend and later an employee of Mick's, says that they used to have 'famous, plate-throwing, Hollywood-style rows'. Shirley Arnold recalls that whenever she saw them they were 'always, always arguing'. Mick was not easy to live with. He had always tended to niggle people and to enjoy bickering. Chrissie was not sufficiently placid to ignore, or to be impervious to, his tetchiness. It was a difficult time – he was constantly on the move and suddenly becoming rich, famous and very sought after. They seem to have had their ups, downs and even further downs during 1965 and 1966. The plans for their marriage were revived increasingly infrequently. Mick was beginning to tell people that he felt he should have a more glamorous girlfriend than Chrissie, to match his new status. It was a manifestation of the women-as-accessories attitude of which he was to be accused often in the future.

Marianne Faithfull had been seeing more of the Rolling Stones since 'As Tears Go By' was made, and she had drifted into bed with Brian, and Keith, and eventually Mick. In October 1966 she left John Dunbar, finally. In December of that year Chrissie Shrimpton, apparently despairing of any future in her affair with Mick, but unable to envisage coping without him, tried to kill herself by taking a drug overdose. She survived, and moved out. Marianne had been much courted since she began singing professionally. Gene Pitney had been struck by her, so had Bob Dylan and so had Michael Cooper, the Stones' photographer friend. But although she had several affairs none of them was very serious, until she took up with Mick. He had been smitten by her when they first met, and had made it obvious. But at that time she had not been impressed by him. Since then she had got to know him better, and he had become a more impressive figure. And he now seemed to adore her. She had an air of vulnerability and a gossamer, unworldly quality. And she had been rather well educated by her mother, the Baroness Erisso, and John Dunbar. She moved into the flat in Harley House, where Mick had lived with Chrissie, and she was at first easier to live with than her predecessor. Mick seemed to be happy with her. Shirley Arnold says that the difference immediately struck people in the office. 'When Marianne shouted, Mick jumped. It was a change after all the battles with Chrissie.'

It was inevitable that people should frequently compare Marianne with Anita. They were very beautiful blondes and they were connected with the two best-known Rolling Stones. And the contrast between the dynamic vitality of Anita and the slightly helpless frailty of Marianne was intriguing.

Chapter Six

1967 marked the zenith of the hippy dream. For the generation who were young then it remains a sort of mythological golden age, a 'season of everlasting spring'. There is a double nostalgia – for the period itself, and for its own dream of a lost pastoral life. The young seemed to create, briefly, a world that was a long way from reality. The idea of the countryside, neglected for a few futurist years, came back into fashion as romantics tried to reinhabit a pre-industrial paradise. Their clothes were gypsyesque, garbled medieval or quasi-eighteenth century – anything that was not twentieth century or urban. Mark Palmer carried the fantasy so far that he and a friend, Maldwin Thomas, actually became gypsies, and lived on the road in a horse-drawn caravan. And all good hippies asked for nothing more than to wander through fields of unmown hay, joint in hand, bell round neck, thinking beautiful thoughts. The songs of that year were memorable. The summer was heavenly. And the images supplied by the outside world were satisfactory – brave little Biafra declared its independence, there was a war in the Middle East which lasted less than a week and was won by the goodies, and the first human heart transplant was performed in

South Africa. All manner of marvellous madness flourished – alchemy and astrology, the belief that King Arthur was to rise again, or that devaluation of the pound could be avoided. There was a feeling that all things were possible. It was a different sensation from the optimism of the early sixties. Now, more crucial walls seemed to be breachable than those of material wealth. Drugs made many feel that they were capable of spiritual journeys more daring than any that their parents had taken. It was not yet apparent that some would never come back.

A generation that had grown up almost to adulthood without drugs had now begun to experience them together. A member of that generation describes a period of 'contagious joy – a kind of psychic infection. There is a process at work when a lot of people turn on together which means that the whole experience becomes more than the sum of the individual parts.' Greater visual awareness helped to create a new unified style. For a long time young people's clothes and songs had been loosely related – both reflected the spirit of the time in their different ways. But there had hitherto been no organic connection between music and design. Under the influence of LSD ('acid') and other hallucinogenic drugs, sounds and images seemed to interact, and unsympathetic surroundings, objects or images became physically painful. Sharp lines and primary colours, the essentials of the Mod look, could hurt. Hence the appeal of romanticised opium-den living – the floor cushions, textiles, rugs and so on. Over the next year or two the blurred, indolent, incense-burning, patchouli-laden style would be welcomed into a million newly hippified North Africanish rooms. Patterns that reflected drug experiences, mellow or vibrant 'psychedelic' designs rampaged over the world. The Flying Dragon, in the Kings Road, now became the favourite breakfast haunt of Mick and his Chelsea friends. Here it was possible to spend all day, lying on cushions on the floor, being served breakfast by beautiful young dope fiends. There was a hippy boom in the decorative arts. The poster became the crucial visual art form for the young, and big business. Two 'English Boy' models who traded under the name of 'Hapshash and the Coloured Coat' led the field in technicoloured, mind-expanding posters. The essential clothes designers were called collectively 'The Fool' and consisted of four young designers, three of them Dutch, who wafted around looking beautiful. They wore their own extravagant clothes, fairy-tale images shoplifted from all over the world and made in brocade, tapestry and velvet. 'The Fool' promoted their somewhat banal spiritual beliefs, along with their pretty clothes, with hefty backing from the Beatles.

The first signs of the souring of the sixties had already appeared. In 1966 people in high places had begun to worry about the balance of payments crisis, precipitated by a six-week national seamen's strike. And in December of that year people in high places and low had been saddened by the death of Tara Browne in a car accident. He was the first of the casualties among Mick's friends. But for the time being these seemed to be mere aberrations in a world of hope.

The Rolling Stones fitted somewhat awkwardly into the benevolence of the time. They had got where they were by projecting an image of nastiness and violence, and it was tricky for them to adapt. Although he was an idol to millions of hippies, quasi-hippies and neo-hippies, Mick never became closely identified with their ideals. 'I'm not involved in this "Love and Flowers" scene, but it is something to bring people together for the summer,' he was to say in an interview later in the year. The first Stones' single of the year, 'Let's Spend the Night Together', did not seem to owe much to the 'love movement'. It was outrageous in the best Rolling Stones tradition, and incurred predictable criticism, simply on the basis of its title, for corrupting youth. Nevertheless, the Stones were invited to perform it on *Sunday Night at the London Palladium*, a massively popular television variety show. At the end of the programme all the contributors were lined up, each week, on a revolving stage to wave goodbye to the by then tumultuously applauding audience. The ending of the programme was as firmly established in the national consciousness as the theme music of *Coronation Street*. But having done their turn, the Rolling Stones refused to take part in the ritual. The storm of protest that followed this particular act of iconoclasm was one of the worst the Stones had yet encountered. And Mick made it worse by telling journalists that 'it was a mediocre show and it made us the same. It was all terrible.' The album *Between the Buttons* was also released in January, but was considered to be a disappointment by most reviewers. It included some good songs, such as 'Yesterday's Papers' and 'Backstreet Girl', but it immediately felt familiar. Even the bitchy lyrics seemed to be talking about exactly the same girls who had been dealt with earlier. 'Let's Spend the Night Together' was more successful in America, where it topped the charts, than in England, where it only reached number 3.

It was during 1967 that most people in England heard for the first time the term 'Underground' to describe a hard core of several hundred painters, writers and apolitical activists, and their few thousand followers. The term was first used by themselves, around the end of 1965, but by 1967 they were beginning to repudiate its use. It had been used in America since the early 1960s to impart some sort of ideological significance to independently made, low-budget movies. The English Underground was committed, in so far as it was a unit that could be singly committed to anything, to changing society through bypassing most of its institutions, including the normal channels of protest. It rejected a world that it saw to be dreary, rigid and hypocritical. Despite commonly held instincts about the direction in which those changes should lie, and several imaginative Utopias, the Undergrounders insisted that they were not interested in politics. Even over Vietnam, according to one, 'We all felt moral outrage, but we were not politically involved.' A tenet that did matter, though, was that Underground capital, talent and initiative should be kept among themselves. No one was squeamish about making money, but they insisted that they should not be exploited by outside entrepreneurs. There were even plans to establish an Underground bank. It was all a dashing if befuddled attempt at Revolution, although it seems odd to use the word 'Underground' to describe something so public. The national press published endless articles about this new youth phenomenon, and its house newspaper, *International Times* (*IT*) and its magazine, *Oz*, could be bought on the streets of London by anyone who wanted them.

John Hopkins ('Hoppy'), a former Cambridge physicist who had worked at Harwell Atomic Research Station, was one of the seminal figures of the Underground. A great many of its activities were organised from his flat in Queensway. He was one of the founders of *IT* and of the UFO Club (pronounced Yoofo, held by some to stand for Unlimited Freak Out – an explanation hotly denied by others who claim that it had no meaning). The UFO Club, in Tottenham Court Road, was started to raise money to pay the *IT* staff, many of whom worked there in the evenings. Miles was another of the newspaper's founders, and was also the publisher. He distributed *IT* from the basement of the Indica bookshop, which, along with the Indica Gallery, was an important landmark on the Underground Map. Both Indica enterprises had been started on a total capital of £1600, which Miles and John Dunbar had borrowed from Peter Asher, the singer brother of Paul McCartney's girlfriend Jane. Jim Haynes was the third founder of *IT*, and he also ran the Arts Lab in Drury Lane, an experimental centre involving films, plays, exhibitions, food and, of course, happenings. Jim Haynes was an American, as were many of the people in the English Underground, including his partner in the Arts Lab, Jack Henry Moore (who was also at one time the editor of *IT*). Much inspiration had come from the United States, especially from the American Underground papers. Warhol was in England quite often at this time, and was known to most English Underground people, through Robert Fraser, who was his London dealer. More important American mentors included William Burroughs and Allen Ginsberg, who was in England during 1965 and 1967. The organisers of the UFO Club were delighted when an East End street gang, who called themselves The Firm, and came along to do the place over, ended up by becoming involved with it. They were just what was needed to refute the suggestion that the Underground was simply a bunch of art-infested middle-class university graduates: genuine working-class teenagers. Mick Jagger knew most of the people in the Underground, and was quite friendly with some of them. 'He was careful to know what was going on, and to keep a certain distance away from it,' according to a former pillar of the Underground. But Miles says that he was always keen to be interviewed by *IT*. Mick and Marianne were among those who went to the all-night party at the Roundhouse to launch *IT*. Mick said at the time that he had thought 'everyone would be freaking out and wearing weird clothes but they were all wandering around in dirty macs – it was the most boring thing I've ever seen.' Paul McCartney showed up dressed as an Arab and Marianne, dressed as a nun in a bottomless habit, won a prize for the shortest/barest costume.

For many middle-aged people, the emergence of a self-proclaimed Underground was the final straw. For the last few years the young seemed to have talked incessantly of 'revolt'. Those who had fought at least one war to safeguard freedom found themselves and their mores constantly attacked by a generation who had grown up in safety, with housing, education and medical care guaranteed by the Welfare State. And now, the young really seemed to be throwing down the gauntlet by annexing a term used by serious revolutionaries to describe their own peevish little quarrels with their elders. But there was life in the old guard yet, as the events of 1967 were to show. Robert Fraser had already incurred the wrath of the law for his 1966 exhibition, 'London Series', by the American painter Jim Dine, and was fined for causing a nuisance. As was to be the case again, the heavy hand of the law seemed to pick on a strange token victim. Dine's pretty watercolours of disembodied phalli hardly seemed likely to drive anyone into a satyriatic frenzy. The offices of *IT* were raided in February following the publication of issue number 7 in which the word 'motherfucker' was used in an interview with Dick Gregory. The police confiscated every scrap of paper in the office – past issues, manuscripts, even address books belonging to members of the staff. But far from viewing such excitement as a necessary part of life underground, those involved whined petulantly, as though they expected to be treated like sweet clever children, not proper grown-up freedom fighters. But it all ended happily – issue 8 was read aloud triumphantly at the UFO Club, since it could not be printed. And in the end the pigs returned everything they had confiscated, without prosecuting anyone for anything.

To the perceptive it was obvious that the real showdown was going to come in the area of drugs.

By 1967 drugs were becoming a considerable problem in England. The ignorance of everyone, young and old alike, about the effects and possible dangers of narcotics of all sorts was staggering. Bored housewives were still being prescribed amphetamines and other goodies to cheer them up and then some other sort of bonbon to calm them down enough to go to sleep. There were a great many people, even in the government, who genuinely did not know whether marijuana should be compared with 'hard' drugs, or whether it was harmless. Life was even made difficult for those who wanted to investigate the effects of drugs. Steve Abrams, an American PhD student at Oxford, was keen to carry out an investigation into the effects of cannabis. But any research that entailed administering cannabis to volunteers, or observing its effects, would have been illegal. It was not even possible to be granted a permit to carry out such research. Steve Abrams contacted the Home Office to discuss the possibility of getting money for his investigations, and to find out how far he would be allowed to go in them. The Home Office advised him to talk to the Chief Constable of Oxford, with whom he had a long and friendly talk. He also met the Head of the Drugs Squad, whom he describes as a 'good cop, very zealous'. The good cop described to him where he kept his stash of goodies, and the exact layout of his flat. There were, he said, two reasons why Steve had not been raided. The first was that the Chief Constable would not allow it, and the second was that the police knew that he had ten years of correspondence in his flat, and they couldn't face having to read through it all. But despite his good relations with the police, Steve was not given permission to carry out any experiments. The Drugs (Prevention of Misuse) Act 1964 forbade possession of cannabis, and a 1965 amendment made it an offence even to allow it to be smoked on premises you owned, even if you did not know that anyone had been doing so. There was a case in Oxford involving just that principle. A woman had let her flat, the tenants were found to have been smoking pot, and she was prosecuted. The injustice of the prosecution was flagrant, and Robert Graves came to her defence. By 1966 it was becoming urgent that something should be done about the problem. A survey had shown that there were 500 people at Oxford University who smoked pot regularly. The University authorities disputed the findings and insisted that there were only about twenty. But they then had to admit that they were wrong, that there were 500 regular smokers, but that they only caused as much trouble as the authorities would have expected from twenty. At Steve Abrams suggestion, the Vice-Chancellor of the University, Alan Bullock, wrote to the Home Office, suggesting that the government should investigate what was becoming a national problem. As a result of this, the enquiry that eventually resulted in the Wootton Report was initiated.

The newspapers were also becoming interested in the question of drugs by the beginning of 1967. The singer Donovan had been convicted of possessing marijuana in July 1966, and fined £250. Various people had been trying to sell stories concerning the Rolling Stones and drugs to the newspapers for some time. But until the Donovan case the newspapers had been holding back on celebrity drug stories. After that they were prepared to publish. At the beginning of 1967 the *News of the World* began a series, 'Pop Stars and Drugs', which had already been planned for *The People*, but had never been published. It was the work of Mike Gabbert, a journalist whose investigation into soccer corruption, which led to the imprisonment of seventeen people, had entailed the use of some resourceful, if unorthodox, tactics. The *News of the World* series revealed the 'shocking' 'inside story' of drug orgies, with lots of emphasis on bare-breasted girls. The series included all the typical ingredients for one of that newspaper's successes – sex, glamour and law-breaking. Most of the pop stars mentioned in the series had in fact admitted publicly to taking some sort of drugs, and the *News of the World*'s lawyers would have read it carefully for libel. On 5 February 1967 the second instalment was published. Most of it dealt with parties held by the Moody Blues, described as 'Roehampton Raves', held at the house in Roehampton where members of the group lived with their road manager, Phil Robertson. The article mentioned Denny Laine, Ray Thomas and Mike Pinder (of the Moody Blues) as LSD takers, along with 'Ginger' Baker of Cream and Pete Townsend of the Who. There was also a bit about Mick:

Another pop idol who admits he has sampled LSD and other drugs is Mick Jagger of the Rolling Stones.

He too was a visitor at the Roehampton home of the Moody Blues.

Investigators, who saw Mick Jagger at the Blaises Club in Kensington, London, reported:

He told us: 'I don't go on it (LSD) now the cats (fans) have taken it up. It'll just get a dirty name. I remember the first time I took it. It was on our first tour with Bo Diddley and Little Richard.

During the time we were at Blaises, Jagger took about six benzedrine tablets. 'I just wouldn't keep awake in a place like this if I didn't have them,' he said.

Jagger was at Roehampton when (a) popstar believed he was a historical character. He said of the incident: 'We thought he'd gone starkers. He was charging around the room.'

Later at Blaises, Jagger showed a companion and two girls a small piece of hash (solid marijuana) and invited them to his flat for a 'smoke'.

Mick was furious about the article. He had always been alert to the possible legal dangers of drugs, and he had been careful not to be seen taking anything, even an aspirin, publicly. And he didn't like bad publicity that he had not orchestrated. That evening he was to appear on the Eamonn Andrews show on television. It was inevitable that the subject should come up during the chat. 'What's this we've been reading about you, Mick?' the genial host asked him, on the air. 'Oh, I can't discuss that,' Jagger answered. 'It's all untrue, inaccurate and misleading. I am issuing a writ and suing the *News of the World*.'

That did it. He had made a very serious accusation, and one that if it were proved to be true could cost the *News of the World* a great deal of money. From that moment battle was joined, between the biggest newspaper in the world (with sixteen million readers) and the boy from Dartford. The *News of the World* was a seasoned, ruthless fighter and had staved off more libel cases than Mick had had speedballs. But the fight was not as unequal as it might seem. Mick was not little David, armed only with a sling. The Rolling Stones organisation was by now worth a great deal of money. And ready to line up behind Mick were all those forces that already felt themselves to be in opposition to the repressive adult world.

The next day, Monday, 6 February, the rest of the English press was full of the story, and by Tuesday it had hit every corner of the world where the Rolling Stones were big business. Although he had said on television that the whole story was untrue, Mick and his friends knew that things were not that simple. The *News of the World* would not have invented it. Mick, Keith and Brian all went to Blases (the name of the club had been mis-spelt in the article) and there was an unpleasant but plausible explanation. It seemed probable that the reporters had been talking to Brian, who, they were all afraid, would be capable of sitting in a nightclub gobbling pills, talking to strangers about drugs. It was possible that the reporters had mistaken him for Mick, or that they knew it was Brian, but had decided to write the story as if it were Mick, because he was more famous and made better copy. Each side rallied advisers and lawyers, preparing to wade through the slow processes of the law. Jagger's lawyer duly issued the writ, and the *News of the World* carried on its series, but without any further reference to Jagger.

The next weekend Mick and Marianne went to stay with Keith at Redlands, the thatched farmhouse in Sussex that Keith had recently bought. West Wittering is a small village near Chichester, quiet except in the height of summer when tourists from London and the Home Counties drive down to the wide, safe beach. Redlands was the perfect place to relax after a week that had been dominated by fuss over Mick's coming lawsuit. The gang were all there – Keith himself, Robert Fraser, Michael Cooper, Christopher Gibbs and Nicky Cramer, 'a sweet-natured, feckless Chelsea layabout, a sort of romantic hippy figure with masses of curly red hair.' Also in the house was a glamorous newcomer, who went by the name of David Schneidermann, or sometimes David Britton, or occasionally 'Acid King David'. He had emerged during the last few weeks in London, hanging around with musicians, as a purveyor of worldly wisdom and narcotics. He seemed to be a North American, possibly Canadian or Californian – no one was quite sure. 'He carried around an extraordinarily chic briefcase absolutely brimful of every possible kind of narcotic, mostly with initials that no one had ever heard of. All the girls fancied him, and he wouldn't have anything to do with them, and all the boys fancied him, and he wouldn't have anything to do with them either.' He was young, attractive and lively, rolled the longest, thinnest joints in London and had the added social advantage of his marvellous briefcase.

Most people at Redlands were woken up early on Sunday morning by Schneidermann, who brought them cups of tea and tablets of 'white lightning', a pleasant hallucinogenic drug with effects something like those of LSD, but less violent. Most of them went back to sleep and woke up later already tripping. During the afternoon Robert Fraser and Christopher Gibbs organised a 'mystery tour' to the house of Edward James (the millionaire collector and aesthete) at Monkton, just north of Chichester. 'We drove all the way up to Monkton through the woods with endless painted gates. At the time Edward had painted all the tree guards in beautiful stripes and patterns, which made it seem like a dreamland. When we got there, there was no Edward, and we were sent away again,' Christopher Gibbs recalls. Unperturbed, they went for a walk on the beach before returning to Redlands. Robert Fraser's Moroccan servant cooked a meal, and afterwards most of the house-party gathered in the drawing-room, where some of them were smoking a joint. Marianne had had a bath and, she was to explain later, since she did not want to put on her muddy jeans again, wrapped herself in a big fur rug. The television was on, with the sound turned down, incense was burning and they were listening to Bob Dylan and the Who records.

At about 8.30 they were interrupted by a hammering on the door. When Keith answered it he found a man in a white trenchcoat standing there, accompanied by a gang of uniformed policemen. Chief Inspector Dinely, their leader, asked Keith whether he was the owner of the premises, and then thrust a search warrant into his hand. Before any of those present had really taken in what was happening, Dinely and his men had entered the drawing-room. Someone put Dylan's 'Rainy Day Women' on the record player, so they were all searched to the abrasive strains of Dylan singing, 'Everybody must get stoned'. Marianne, still wrapped only in the rug, which slipped down once or twice, just enough to embarrass the constabulary, was marched upstairs to be searched by a tough policewoman. Despite the bewilderment they must have felt, the local cops began resolutely to do their job, putting joss sticks, cigarette butts and pipes into plastic bags. Robert Fraser was searched, and the police found that he had in his pockets two phials of tablets. He said that they were the medicines he needed for his diabetes. The policeman seemed to accept that but said that he would have to take a sample of them for analysis. Mick's jacket was found, lying around, with a plastic phial containing four tablets and a small piece of hashish in the pocket. To the amazement of the Redlands guests, the policeman who found it had obviously never seen hashish before. He showed no interest in it, and put it back, deliberately wiping his fingers on his handkerchief. He kept the tablets, however, and asked to whom they belonged. Mick said that they were his, and that his doctor had prescribed them. They were parcelled up and labelled, along with everything else that was being confiscated. Schneidermann was the last to be searched. They began with his famous briefcase, which they opened and found to be full of little foil-wrapped bundles. Surprisingly, they believed him when he said that he was a filmmaker, and the bundles were unprocessed film which would be ruined if exposed. But in Schneidermann's jacket they found a small tin of hashish and some grass. Everyone present was aware, as the police were about to leave, that things could have been worse. There was far more in the house that they could have found if they had tried. It almost seemed as though they were not interested in anyone but Mick – the others had been searched, but almost cursorily.

The coincidence of the bust was remarkable. Just when the whole newspaper-reading world was aware that Mick was suing the *News of the World* for libelling him by saying that he used drugs, he was involved in a police raid that almost anyone would feel substantiated the paper's accusation. It was especially odd since the police had tried, hitherto, to avoid arresting pop stars on drug charges. Steve Abrams remembers a significant conversation with Detective Inspector Lynch, from Scotland Yard Drugs Squad, in the presence of the head of the Home Office Drugs Branch. He said that his job, as a policeman, was to control the use of drugs, and to keep it within bounds as far as possible. 'Obviously my job is not going around busting people – that's incidental. I'm satisfied that if I went out and arrested Mick Jagger every kid in the country would go round wanting to smoke dope the next day. Therefore I refused to arrest him, just to help the *News of the World* out of their scrape.' And, so conveniently, Mick had been busted outside London.

The situation was worse than most people present at Redlands knew. Robert Fraser's 'medicine' was heroin, which he had been snorting increasingly often. If the week before had been energetic, this one, after the lethargy of Sunday, was frantic. For a while it seemed possible that there would be no prosecution. 'Spanish' Tony Sanchez, who later worked for Keith as a fixer and procurer, has said that Robert Fraser asked him to try to buy off the police. A conviction for heroin possession frequently resulted in a prison sentence, but it was generally believed that there were ways around drug prosecutions if you could find the cash. Steve Abrams pointed out to the Wootton Committee that one of the serious aspects of the drug laws was that they encouraged police corruption. A great many young, not very well paid, policemen were first tempted off the path of probity by being offered hefty bribes to overlook a drug offence or to falsify the evidence. It was the one area of the law that might entail serious penalties, but where the offences did not seem to most policemen to be morally outrageous. And it was also an area in which the offenders were likely to have plenty of cash available. There was already substantial evidence of police corruption by the beginning of 1967. One of those present at Redlands when it was raided is even said to have been buying drugs from a West End police station – the source, presumably, being substances that had been confiscated from other people. So Spanish Tony, he says, spoke to people who could fix the forensic laboratories to say that the heroin found on Robert Fraser really was insulin, as he had claimed. It was going to cost several thousand pounds, but for that none of those concerned would have to worry any more. Mick sent the money in a suitcase, and later the same day (the Tuesday after the raid) Spanish Tony handed it over in a Kilburn pub. There followed a spell of peace and quiet. No stories about the raid appeared in the papers, no police visited Mick, Keith or Robert. It seemed that the police had been satisfactorily corrupted. But Sundays were becoming increasingly unrestful for Mick, and on the following one the *News of the World* published the story of the raid under the headline 'Drugs Squad Raids Pop Stars Party'. The report was vague: 'Several stars, at least three of them nationally known names ... at a secluded country house near the South Coast.' But it was enough to blow it. Once any story of the bust hit the papers it was virtually impossible for the police to hush it up. The further coincidence struck everyone. It was remarkable that the very paper that Mick had announced he was going to sue should now have the exclusive story of the raid. Keith later suggested that he thought the bribe would not have worked, even without the *News of the World* story: 'In the States you know the cops are bent and if you want to get into it, okay, you can go to them and say, "How much do you want?" and they'll drop it. In England you can drop fifty grand and the next day they'll bust you and say, "Oh, it went into the wrong hands. I'm sorry. It didn't get to the right man." It's insane.'

But despite the *News of the World* story there was no summons. For nearly a month the phoney war continued. Mick and Keith were daily expecting to hear from the police, but nothing happened. The charm of Redlands was somewhat tarnished, so they planned a holiday in North Africa. They were desperate to get away from all the fuss, the constant fear of being watched and the dreary consultations with lawyers. Two separate parties made their way out to Tangier. Keith, Brian, Anita and Deborah Dixon (the American girlfriend of painter Donald Cammell) were to go out together in Brian's Bentley with his driver, Tom Keylock. They were to meet Mick, Marianne, Michael Cooper, Robert Fraser and Christopher Gibbs at the El Minzah Hotel.

On the way through France Brian was taken ill with a bad attack of asthma and had to be taken into hospital in Toulon. The rest of them carried on to Tangier, although Deborah turned back before they arrived. By the time they reached Tangier Anita and Keith had become entangled. Brian besieged the hotel with telegrams demanding to be fetched. Anita went back to France to collect him and they then returned together. For some time Keith had been living, while in London, with Brian and Anita at their flat in Courtfield Road, South Kensington. For the last few months Keith and Brian had been getting on well together, and neither Keith nor Anita, at first, seems to have taken the fling very seriously. Brian, forever suspecting betrayals, for once had grounds. But his at first unvoiced, yet apparent, suspicions probably gave the affair more significance than it would otherwise have had. Keith seems to have been very cool about it, waiting to see what would transpire, while Anita simply enjoyed the intrigue. The rest of the party assembled and they all moved on to Marrakesh, where they met Cecil Beaton. He recorded in his diary:

I didn't want to give the impression that I was only interested in Mick, but it happened that we sat together as he drank a Vodka Collins and smoked with pointed finger held high. His skin is chicken-breast white and of a fine quality. He has an inborn elegance. He is very gentle, and with perfect manners . . . He has much appreciation and his small, albino-fringed eyes notice everything. 'How different and more real this place is to Tangier – the women more rustic, heavy, lumpy, but their music very Spanish and their dancing too.' He has an analytical slant and compares everything he is seeing here with earlier impressions in other countries.

Most of the party had been taking quite a lot of LSD during the holiday, and Mick enthused about it to Cecil Beaton:

'Have you ever taken LSD? Oh, I should. It would mean so much to you; you'd never forget the colours. For a painter it is a great experience. One's brain works not on four cylinders but on four thousand. You see everything aglow. You see yourself beautiful and ugly, and other people as if for the first time. Oh yes, you should take it in the country, surrounded by all those flowers. You'd have no bad affects. It's only people who hate themselves who suffer.' He had great assurance. 'If you enjoyed the bhang in India this is a thousand times better: so much stronger – good stuff. Oh no, they can't stamp it out. It's like the atom bomb. Once it's been discovered, it can never be forgotten, and it's too easy to make.'

During the holiday Brian began bringing local women back to the hotel and expecting Anita to go to bed with him, with them. It seems to have been the individuals, not necessarily the idea in general, that upset Anita. But it caused trouble between her and Brian, and made it very easy for Keith to rescue her. Brian was taken by a friend to meet the Mejdoubi, local 'holy madmen', with whom he got totally stoned. The same afternoon Keith and Anita decamped, leaving Brian stranded. To make matters more insulting, they took Brian's driver with them. Brian was devastated by the defection of Anita, especially since it was with Keith, who had become his best friend in the group. He followed the others back to London, stopping off in Paris to see Donald Cammell.

As soon as he arrived home Mick discovered that he was to be prosecuted. On 18 March West Sussex police announced that they were charging him with the unauthorised possession of four tablets containing amphetamine sulphate, Keith with allowing his premises to be used for the smoking of cannabis resin, and Robert Fraser with the unauthorised possession of heroin and eight capsules of methyl amphetamine hydrochloride. Mick's doctor, Raymond Dixon-Firth, was prepared to testify that he had authorised the use of amphetamine sulphate tablets. Allen Klein flew back to London when the news broke, to coordinate the Rolling Stones' defence. The principal concern at the time was that if either Mick or Keith was convicted on a drugs charge, the immigration authorities might ban them from entering America, which would be financially dias- trous for the entire group. There was no need to worry about the fans' reaction – they would be loyal to their idols whatever they did. Mick was genuinely horrified, not only by the idea that he was going to be prosecuted, but by the feeling that there was a tide of resentment lying in wait for him, as the most vociferous repre- sentative of the new generation who were now able to enjoy all sorts of drugs and sex, and seemed unmotivated by the forces that had guided their parents' lives. Mick had always seemed, to himself as well as to other people, to be able to get away with everything. 'I don't think it had ever occurred to him that he would get into real trouble, but once he did he was simply ashamed of being arrested. He worried about what the folks back home would think. Mick was still very bourgeois, really.' Now that he realised that perhaps he was not immune, he began to worry about shadows. He became convinced that his telephone had been bugged. He refused to be convinced that it was highly unlikely – he had no evidence that the line had been tapped, and the procedure, even for the police them- selves, was too cumbersome to be worthwhile. Finally he managed to find someone who said that they could 'sweep' his flat and remove the bugging equipment. For Mick it was a bargain exorcism at £100, even if there was nothing there.

The European tour which began on 25 March can have done nothing for Mick's peace of mind. It was successful – the tickets sold well and as usual the fans got over-excited and things ended in tears and pitched battles. In Sweden the police had to use dogs to break up a riot and in Vienna 154 fans were arrested. In Warsaw 2000 youths tried to storm the city's Palace of Culture to see the Stones, and in Zurich Mick was hurled to the floor and stamped on by a youth who broke through a cordon of 300 policemen. But this sort of violence was not new. What was more upsetting was the hostility from the authorities in many of the countries that they visited. Swedish customs officers searched all the Stones completely, even going through their underwear looking for drugs and ransacking all of their luggage. The same thing happened almost everywhere they went. In Paris Mick complained to the *Daily Mail* that he was on the customs international 'red list': 'Of course there is a list. And of course they are after me. In the last two months there have been about four occasions when, on landing at London, I have been taken to a private room and searched – obviously for drugs . . . I feel as if I am being treated as a witch. And I have no broomstick handy.' A Customs and Excise spokesman, also quoted in the *Daily Mail*, said that he knew nothing about any such red list: 'Britain is a member of the Customs Cooperation Council. As far as I am aware there is no official list of suspects circulated around the member-countries. It is possible, however, that customs officials at various ports keep unofficial lists of their own.' Mick was becoming more and more frightened. But he was a pro, and was managing to convert some of his anxiety about police persecution into useful material for supporting his image. He could now portray himself as the victim of oppression by the authorities. If the police and the *News of the World* wanted war, Mick would cast himself as the youthful martyr. While he was in Paris he was interviewed by *Melody Maker*:

People talk about the riots that happen when we play. Of course there is a certain violent element, and, to a certain extent, the kids are conforming to what is expected of them. But there is more to it than that. . . . I've seen this wild behaviour in so many countries and the pattern is always the same. Because it is the same symptom. Frustration. And these kids are from all kinds of environments . . . you can't solve the problem by locking them up . . . that isn't the answer –

Narcissism.

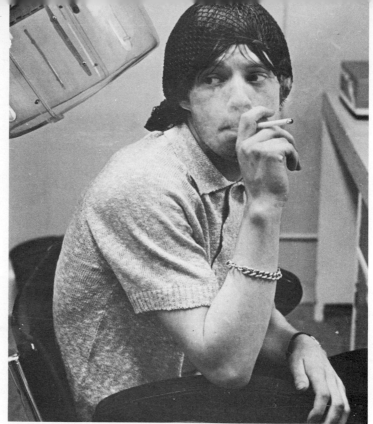

Mick (*standing, right*) in the school basketball team.

Longleat, 1964—the Glimmer Twins.

Portrait of
the superstar
as a young man.

Joe Jagger
at his son's
wedding reception.

The wedding: Ahmet Ertegun is on the left; Anita and Keith are behind the bride and groom; Nathalie Delon and Roger Vadim are Bianca's left.

The Misses Hunt.

Saloniers.

The price of fame: Mick and Jerry hounded by paparazzi.

A man
of wealth
and taste.

The Stones
photographed
by Mick's friend,
David Bailey.

Four Stones celebrating the release of *Let's Spend the Night Together*.

Mick and Woodie.

His Satanic Majesty in *The Rolling Stones' Rock 'n' Roll Circus.*

Jade.

On stage in Rotterdam, 1982.

The new sportif Mick.

you have to find out why it is that kids are discontented. They are not all morons just spoiling for a fight with the police.

Back in England he talked to the *Daily Mirror*. By now he was sounding increasingly messianic:

I see a great deal of danger in the air ... teenagers are not screaming over pop music any more, they're screaming for much deeper reasons. We are only serving as a means of giving them an outlet. Pop music is just the superficial issue to it all ... when I'm on stage, I sense that the teenagers are trying to communicate to me, like by telepathy, a message of some urgency. Not about me or about our music, but about the world and the way we live ... teenagers the world over are weary of being pushed around by half-witted politicians who attempt to dominate their way of thinking and set a code for their living. They want to be free and have the right of expression; of thinking and living aloud without any petty restrictions. This doesn't mean they want to become alcoholics or drug-takers or tread down on their parents. This is a protest against the system. I see a lot of trouble coming in the dawn.

The next bit of trouble for Mick was his appearance in the magistrates court, scheduled for 10 May. A crowd of several hundred fans and newspapermen waited outside the courtroom. While the court adjourned for lunch Mick and Keith went away and changed their clothes. 'After lunch Mr Jagger had changed his bright green jacket to one of charcoal grey and Mr Richard had changed out of a jacket with thick black and white stripes into green,' the *Evening Standard* reported. The committal proceedings were quite straightforward. Mick, Keith and Robert were all given £100 bail and sent for trial at West Sussex Quarter Sessions in June. But there was reason that day for Mick to feel that the police were out to 'get' the Stones. In the morning Brian Jones' flat was raided, in time to make the noon headlines. The announcement, 'Third Rolling Stone on Drug Charge', on every newspaper hoarding in the country was not going to help Mick and Keith. Once again, the timing seemed too perfect to be accidental. It was not surprising that Mick claimed that the Courtfield Road bust had been orchestrated to prejudice the Chichester court against him and Keith, since the police knew that their evidence was weak. But there was nothing at all that Mick could do about it, except whine. Brian, and Prince Stanislaus Klossowski de Rola ('Stash'), who was in the flat at the time of the raid, were charged with unlawful possession of cannabis.

The Beatles spent the spring of 1967 recording the songs that were to end up on the greatest rock album of them all, *Sergeant Pepper's Lonely Hearts Club Band*. They had given up touring and had already become more remote from their fans than the Rolling Stones have to this day. They were, in 1967, much the most famous people in the world and had been almost God-King figures for years. In their privileged unreality, their friendship with other massively successful musicians was a crucial line to life of a sort. And there was a part of John Lennon which resented the Epstein processing he had endured, which had turned him into the world's Nice Guy. Before he had been turned into a Beatle he had been rather more of a bad boy than Mick. But some people suggest that at the same time as being very friendly with the Beatles, Mick was also very jealous, especially of John Lennon. John Dunbar discovered that he only had to call Mick a 'ten cent Beatle' to annoy him. It would be more surprising if Mick had not felt some envy for the Beatles. They and the Stones were the two most successful English groups, they were roughly the same age and they had known each other since the beginning of their careers. Teenagers tended in England and America to be divided between 'Beatles fans' and 'Stones fans'. And yet, and yet. There was really no comparison. Even those who were most avidly devoted to the Rolling Stones knew that in some way the Beatles were the 'greatest'. The Stones might speak to one's personal condition in a way that the Beatles did not, but the Beatles were universal. Everyone, of any age at all, who owned a wireless, a television or just listened to what postmen were humming, knew at least some Beatles songs. And *Sergeant Pepper*, when it was released in June, was so obviously more advanced than anything that had been done before that it caused a crisis of confidence in a great many musicians. Brian Wilson of the Beach Boys is said to have burnt the tapes of an entire LP after hearing *Sergeant Pepper*. The Stones were devastated. Mick and Keith were upset by the feeling that suddenly everything they had been doing, and were still trying to do, was rendered obsolete by this one record. It was not just the dazzling quality of the songs themselves, with one really great number coming after another. Even the jacket, designed by Peter Blake, seemed quite different from, and far in advance of, anything seen before. It was a work of art in itself and seemed to herald the ultimate fusion of pop art and pop music. The mixture of the Victorian band and the acid imagery, on an album crammed with everything from a steam organ to a note so high that it could only be heard by dogs, was quite simply dazzling. Mick became convinced that *Sergeant Pepper* showed the way forward. The Stones would have to produce their own 'psychedelic' album to rival the Beatles'. Keith was prepared to go along with this idea, but Brian resisted it. He seems to have felt that Mick had undermined his confidence, and Keith had stolen his girl. Now that they were forcing him into playing music that was quite foreign to everything the Stones had been involved with, it seemed to him as though Mick and Keith between them had destroyed him. For much of the time that the band were working on the new album, Brian was unable to play at all. He seemed bent upon doing to himself what he was accusing Mick and Keith of wanting to do to him. He was taking vast quantities of acid, as well as anything else he could get hold of. He would walk into the studio and just collapse. Inevitably he was slowing down the whole

123

group. And since Mick and Keith had the drug case hanging over them, they were not inclined to be supportive to Brian, especially when his self-destructive sprees meant that Keith had to overdub his sections of the music. And as they worked on the album, none of the group seem to have been very happy with it. They intended to call it *Her Satanic Majesties Request . . .*, recalling the passage at the beginning of all English passports, 'Her Brittanic Majesty's Principal Secretary of State . . . requests and requires in the name of Her Majesty all those whom it may concern to allow the bearer to pass freely without let or hindrance.' It was to be a satire on the Establishment that not only offered no protection to such as the Stones, but actually attacked them. But none of the Stones felt comfortable with this sort of music, and working on the album only heightened the tension that surrounded Mick and Keith.

Consultations with lawyers continued to occupy a great deal of time, and it was impossible for either of them ever to forget the case that was hanging over them, although Keith seems to have been calmer about it than Mick. The notion that the whole thing had been set up gained credence when it was discovered that the bountiful Schneidermann had somehow slipped out of the country, as mysteriously as he had arrived. It was not unnatural that Mick and Keith became convinced that he had been an agent of the *News of the World*. Mick was alarmed still more by the imprisonment on 1 June of John Hopkins for possession of a miniscule quantity of cannabis. It was, according to a friend, 'the first time that one of us had been sent to prison'. It was widely felt that six months was an unduly harsh sentence, and that the judiciary had decided to crack down on the Underground. It boded badly for Mick, Keith and Robert.

On 27 June the proceedings at West Sussex Quarter Sessions began. The case was heard by Judge Block, a retired naval officer. Mick turned up dressed in a pale green double-breasted jacket, olive green trousers, a flowery shirt and a black and green striped tie. There were fewer teenagers than on their previous appearance, although the police had taken special precautions to deal with crowds. Robert Fraser pleaded guilty and was remanded in custody until the end of the hearing. The case against Mick was heard next. Malcolm Morris, QC, led for the prosecution. He called policemen who had been involved in the Redlands raid to give evidence. Sergeant John Challeñ described finding a phial of four tablets in a green jacket. Mick told him that both the jacket and the tablets belonged to him, he said, and that his doctor had prescribed them. Michael Havers, QC, for the defence, called Dr Dixon-Firth. He said that he had been Mick Jagger's doctor since July 1965, and that he recalled a conversation before February during which Mick told him that he had some Italian pep pills. He did not say what they were called, but Dr Dixon-Firth assumed that they were amphetamine-based. He had told Jagger that it was all right to use them in emergencies, but that he must not take them regularly.

Mr Havers: 'Having been told this and being told he could have them, was he properly in possession of them?'

Dr Dixon-Firth: 'Certainly.'

Judge Block: 'Had he had none, would you have prescribed something similar?'

Dr Dixon-Firth: 'Yes.'

The prosecution then had a go at him. Judge Block asked whether he had seen Jagger's pills and Dr Dixon-Firth admitted that he had not done so.

Mr Morris: 'A doctor must know what he is prescribing. You didn't know at all what you were prescribing.'

Dr Dixon-Firth: 'I knew they were pep pills. I did not know the precise formula.'

Mr Morris: 'Are you saying that if a patient came to you, as Mr Jagger did, and said, "I have some pep pills," you would say, "All right, you can take them if you need them, but not too many"?'

Dr Dixon-Firth: 'Yes, providing I was satisfied after discussion with him that they were appropriate for him.'

There was some dispute between the lawyers as to whether Dr

Dixon-Firth's sanctioning of the pep pills amounted to a prescription. The judge said that he had no hesitation in saying that it did not amount to the issue of a prescription by a duly authorised medical practitioner, 'and it therefore follows that the defence open to Mr Jagger is not available to him. I therefore direct you that there is no defence to this charge.' The jury returned after five minutes and delivered a verdict of guilty. Judge Block, granting Mick Jagger leave to appeal, said to Michael Havers, 'I wish you the best of luck.' Mick was then remanded in custody, along with Robert, until after Keith's trial. They were driven away from the courtroom in a grey van with other prisoners. Before the van left, about a dozen girls banged on the gates of the courtroom yard, screaming, 'We want Mick!'

Michael Cooper went with Marianne Faithful to visit Mick in the remand wing of Lewes jail that night. Mick was distraught and told them that he did not think he could stand being in prison. He was only cheered by Michael, who took a roll of photographs of him in the jail, which he knew would cause a sensation in the press. But sadly the film was confiscated by the warders as Michael and Marianne left. Keith had been allowed to return to Redlands for the night, presumably shaken by the day's events. The next day it was his turn.

For Keith's trial a new jury was sworn in. In his opening speech Mr Morris made much of the behaviour of Marianne, although she was not named during the trial. He told the jury that they were to hear evidence about the smell of cannabis, 'and of its effect of tranquillity and happiness, and how it tends to dispel inhibitions.' He went on to say that they might think that it had had exactly that effect upon one of Keith's guests: 'This was the young lady on the settee. All she was wearing was a light-coloured fur skin rug which from time to time she allowed to fall, disclosing her nude body. She was unperturbed and apparently enjoying the situation . . .' There followed some discussion about the exact smell of cannabis, and about the smell of joss sticks. Detective-Sergeant Cudmore gave evidence about the smells, but returned to the question of Marianne: 'On the sofa in the room were two males and one female wearing a light-coloured, fawn skin rug around her shoulders. From time to time one could see she was wearing nothing underneath. The lady went upstairs and returned. There were ten police officers in the room and she still had only the skin rug, nothing else.'

The trial seemed to be in danger of degenerating into a farce. The prosecution and the West Sussex constabulary seemed to be obsessed by the 'scantily clad young lady'. Eventually the crucial rug was even produced as evidence by Michael Havers. It was about eight feet long, and about five feet wide, orange on one side with a fur back. It was, as Keith said, big enough to cover three young women. In his opening speech for the defence, Havers lashed out at the *News of the World* and pointed out that the jury would have difficulty accepting that newspaper as a guardian of public morals. He explained the background to the case, beginning with Jagger's writ against the *News of the World*. 'And within a week this well-known national newspaper tips off the police to go to West Wittering – not just for anything, but for drugs. We know it was for drugs because the warrant was issued for drugs. If a newspaper publishes a story and it is found to be untrue, how many thousands of pounds would a jury like you award? ... In that party was a man not known to the Rolling Stones as a group, conveniently from across the seas and loaded to the gunwales with cannabis. Schneidermann was the only man on whom was found any cannabis. He has gone out of England.' Mr Havers reminded the jury that they had to be satisfied that Keith knew that someone was smoking cannabis in his house and permitted it. He said that if the house was full of cannabis, the guests might be expected to have rushed around trying to get rid of the traces of the drug when the police had arrived. But a policeman had been looking through the window, and there had been no such activity. And the behaviour of the girl did not prove that she had been smoking cannabis. He pointed out that much of the evidence was unfair to the girl in question, who remained technically anonymous. She was being described in court as a drug-taking nymphomaniac, and yet she had no chance to defend herself. He emphasised that he was not going to allow her into the witness-box, and 'tear that blanket of anonymity aside, and let the world laugh or scorn as they will.' Since Mick had been found guilty the day before, interest in the case had grown, and on the second evening there was a crowd of about 150 outside the courtroom. Keith was allowed to go home to West Wittering, but Robert and Mick, handcuffed together, were taken back to Lewes.

The next day the prosecution returned to the question of the *News of the World* plot, and highlighted the peculiarities in the story. Malcolm Morris pointed out that if Schneidermann had gone down to Redlands with the intention of planting incriminating drugs on Mick Jagger, it was curious that he had not done so, and that the only possible result of Schneidermann's action was that Keith himself was now in the dock, since no one suggested that Mick's pep pills had been planted by anyone, or even introduced into the house by Schneidermann. In his summing-up for the prosecution, Malcolm Morris suggested that the attack on the *News of the World* was introduced to distract the jury's attention from the real issues. The judge instructed the jury to put out of their minds any prejudice that they might feel about the way Richards dressed. He said that they should disregard the convictions of the two other members of the house-party, as well as the evidence concerning the state of undress of the girl in the rug. 'The issue you have to try is a comparatively simple one. You have to be satisfied that cannabis resin was being smoked in the house when the police went there, and you have to be satisfied that Richards knew of it.'

The jury was out for one hour and five minutes. When they came back they delivered a verdict of guilty. Mick and Robert were brought up from the cells for sentence. Michael Havers, in his final appeal, pointed out that over 150 million of the same type of tablets as Mick's pep pills were prescribed every year on the National Health Service, and they could not be classified as Dangerous Drugs. For Keith he said that there was no evidence that everyone at Redlands had been smoking cannabis. But Judge Block remained unmoved. He sentenced Keith to a year in prison, and ordered him to pay £500 towards the cost of the prosecution. Robert was sentenced to six months in jail, with £200 costs. And Mick was sentenced to three months and £100 costs. His shock was obvious, not only to his friends in court, but even to reporters: 'Jagger almost broke down and put his head in his hands as he was sentenced. He stumbled out of the dock almost in tears,' according to the *Daily Telegraph*. And the *Daily Mail* related, 'Jagger turned, put his fist to his forehead and started to cry. Girls in the gallery said, "Poor Mick".'

Steve Abrams had come down to Chichester for the third day of the hearing with Michael Cooper and another friend, Neil Winterbottom, to cover the trial for *IT*. As they arrived, Neil Winterbottom, who looked rather like Ray Davies of the Kinks, was mobbed by screaming girls. Steve's press pass was not considered valid, and he was not allowed into the courthouse. He waited outside, among the large crowd of fans who were waiting to see what would be done to their heroes. Suddenly, during the afternoon, a girl ran screaming out of the courthouse. 'He's been sent to prison. Mick's been sent to prison.' There was horror among the crowds. 'It was as if Society had now declared war on us,' according to Steve Abrams. Mick was driven to Brixton Prison, and Keith and Robert were taken to Wormwood Scrubs. Mick was visited by Marianne again that night. She said later that she had found him bitterly upset by the injustice of his sentence, and had had to tell him to pull himself together. On 30 June, the day after the trial ended, an advertisement appeared in the *Evening Standard*:

The Who consider Mick Jagger and Keith Richard have been treated as scapegoats for the drug problem and as a protest against the savage sentences imposed on them at Chichester yesterday, the Who are issuing today the first of a series of Jagger/Richard songs to keep their work before the public until they are again free to record themselves.

The tracks the Who had chosen to record were 'The Last Time' and 'Under My Thumb'. Less than twenty-four hours after they were sent to prison Mick and Keith were released on £7000 bail, pending their appeal. Robert Fraser was refused bail. The *Times* reported Mick's release:

> Mr Jagger smiled and waved from his chauffer-driven Bentley as he left Brixton Prison yesterday at 4.20 pm. As the car with darkened windows drove along Jebb Avenue, which leads from the gaol, into Brixton, Mr Jagger sat in the back seat by himself wearing a beige sports coat and a yellow shirt. He smiled at photographers and a small group of girls, most of them in school uniform, who were waiting to see him leave.
>
> The car then drove to West London to pick up Mr Richard at Wormwood Scrubs, in Shepherds Bush. When it arrived at 5.10, Mr Richard looked pale.
>
> After spending five minutes in the gaol the car came out again with Mr Jagger and Mr Richard in it. It stopped for half a minute as photographers thronged around. Mr Richard, wearing a dark blue Regency-style suit, gave photographers a grin. The car drove off towards London.

They went straight away to consult lawyers in Kings Bench Walk, and then went for a drink in a Fleet Street pub, where they talked to journalists. Mick told the *Times* that he did not bear a grudge against anyone for what had happened. And he told the *Daily Express* that he had written some poems in jail, had worked on an idea for a song and had missed having an ice-lolly.

The appeals were to be heard in October. This was an oddly

long wait, and the *Sunday Mirror* commented on it in an editorial headline 'Why are we waiting?'. When the UFO Club closed at 2 am on Saturday 1 July, most of the several hundred people who were there went down to protest in front of the *News of the World* office. City of London policemen moved in and sealed off Fleet Street. There had been a time when newspaper editors regularly had to be escorted to their carriages by the police, but it was fifty years since there had been a big demonstration outside a newspaper building. Michael X was, according to Steve Abrams, very helpful in organising this and the other, smaller demonstrations that took place so that they were kept peaceful. 'The police were holding back too, since they did not know quite what to make of it all. The tactics we used were quite different from those of the usual, highly organised left-wing politicians. There were very few arrests.' The protesters chanted, and someone threw a gauntlet into the *News of the World* building, with a message attached. It read: 'We take up your challenge.'

It was not only the Underground and the Rolling Stones' fans who felt that there was something wrong with the Rolling Stones' trials. Considerable support for them was coming from the press, although there were hostile voices. On the day after the trial ended Monica Furlong wrote in the *Daily Mail*, under the headline 'The Shallow Idols of Society and the Smell of Decadence', that: 'Some forms of protest, no doubt, are healthy and help to produce a useful tension against the rigid traditions of society. But in others, as I believe in this case, there is a smell of decadence, which is to say the absence of real ideas and real joy.' The *Evening Standard*, the same day, said that 'the swingeing prison sentences passed yesterday on Mick Jagger and Keith Richards of the Rolling Stones appear to be a fair reflection of the law as it stands today.' But it went on to question the law and to call for a Home Office investigation into the dangers of drugs. And it carried out its own mini-opinion poll by asking eleven people in the street what they thought of the Stones' sentences. Six approved of them, and five disapproved. But only one approver was under thirty, and none of the disapprovers was over thirty.

But it was the next day, 1 July, that things really hotted up. William Rees-Mogg, the editor of the *Times*, wrote an editorial for his paper entitled 'Who Breaks a Butterfly on a Wheel?' It began by saying that a sentence of three months imprisonment for possession of tablets which could be bought quite legally in Italy was sufficiently unusual to warrant discussion.

> If after his visit to the Pope, the Archbishop of Canterbury had bought proprietary airsickness pills at Rome airport, and imported the unused tablets into Britain on his return, he would have risked committing precisely the same offence. No one who has ever travelled and bought proprietary drugs abroad can be sure that he has not broken the law. Judge Block directed the jury that the approval of a doctor was not a defence in law to the charge of possessing drugs without a prescription, and the jury convicted. Mr Jagger was not charged with complicity in any other drug offence that occurred in the same house . . . We have, therefore, a conviction against Mr Jagger purely on the ground that he possessed four Italian pep pills, quite legally bought but not legally imported without a prescription. Four is not a large number. This is not the quantity which a pusher of drugs would have on him, nor even the quantity one would expect in an addict . . . One has to ask, therefore, how it is that this technical offence, divorced as it must be from the other people's offences, was thought to deserve the penalty of imprisonment. In the courts at large it is most uncommon for imprisonment to be imposed on first offenders where the drugs are not major drugs of addiction and there is no question of drug traffic. The normal penalty is probation, and the purpose of probation is to encourage the offender to develop his career and to avoid the drug risks in the future. It is surprising

therefore that Judge Block should have decided to sentence Mr Jagger to imprisonment and particularly surprising as Mr Jagger's is about as mild a drug case as can ever have been brought before the Courts. It would be wrong to speculate on the Judge's reasons, which we do not know. It is, however, possible to consider the public reaction. There are many people who take a primitive view of the matter, what one might call a pre-legal view of the matter. They consider that Mr Jagger has 'got what was coming to him' . . . One has to ask a different question: has Mr Jagger received the same treatment as he would have received if he had not been a famous figure, with all the criticism and resentment his celebrity has aroused? . . . If we are going to make any case a symbol of the conflict between the traditional values of Britain and the new hedonism, then we must be sure that the sound traditional values include those of tolerance and equity. It should be the particular quality of British justice to ensure that Mr Jagger is treated exactly the same as anyone else, no better and no worse. There must remain a suspicion in this case that Mr Jagger has received a more severe sentence than would have been thought proper for any purely anonymous young man.

It was unheard of for the country's leading paper to devote an entire leader to a matter that was *sub judice* and therefore ought not to have been commented on at all. Mr Rees-Mogg was risking imprisonment for contempt of court and the editorial was an indication of widely held feelings of unease about the sentence. Mick is said to have been overjoyed when Marianne showed him the article, and to have felt that it vindicated him more thoroughly than any court decision could have done. It was now clear to everyone that he had been the victim of great injustice. The next day the Sunday papers followed the *Times*' lead. The *Sunday Express* stated that 'the three months sentence imposed upon Mick Jagger is monstrously out of proportion to the offence he committed'.

Hugo Young in the *Sunday Times* went further – 'the trial proved to be a show trial in which the prurient press coverage played an essential and predictable part.' The *Observer* made the same point: 'To many hundreds of thousands of youngsters, those for whom the Rolling Stones are part of the pop Pantheon of heroes, it [the trial] was like a drum-head court-martial on the battlefield where the war of the generations is conducted.' Throughout the following week the newspapers continued to be absorbed in the story, from their leaders to their letter pages. The whole country seemed to be talking about Mick Jagger. The debate centred on the apparent injustice meted out in court, the handcuffing and overnight imprisonment of Mick and Robert during the trial and the broader question of the drug laws as they stood. But national opinion was not entirely in Mick's favour. On 14 July the *Daily Mail* reported the results of a National Opinion Poll, which revealed that 56 per cent of people aged 21–34 thought Jagger's sentence was not severe enough, 29 per cent thought that it was about right and only 12 per cent thought it too severe. Two MPs, the Conservative Paul Channon and the Socialist Tom Driberg, asked questions in Parliament about the handcuffing. Roy Jenkins, the Home Secretary, said rather limply in reply that it was a 'matter of discretion' for the prison governor concerned.

On 2 July the *News of the World*, under the dramatic front-page headline, 'A Monstrous Charge', denied the allegation made in court that it had planted Schneidermann in the Redlands party in an attempt to incriminate Mick Jagger. But it admitted that it had tipped the police off about the party, as a result of a telephone call from a reader, who said that he had had information about a party some of the Rolling Stones were holding in West Sussex. 'He rejected our suggestion that he should go to the police, saying: "I want to remain anonymous. But I think the police should know what is going on." The Editor of the *News of the World* was made aware of the information. He decided that since there was no doubt of the informant's sincerity, our duty was to pass this information to the police.' This sparked off a renewed wave of controversy, as to whether it was proper for the police to act on information passed on by a newspaper and whether it was responsible to pass on information that might be nothing more than a malicious rumour.

On 4 July it was announced that the date of the appeal hearing was to be brought forward to 31 July. As he waited for the appeal to be heard Mick was becoming, according to friends, almost divorced from reality. 'He had such a strong sense of injustice and of being persecuted that I think he knew that he was getting paranoid. He was sure that he had been set up, and had been given an over-harsh sentence, but he couldn't be sure whether it would all go away, or whether he really was going to prison. And he was more scared of going to prison than anyone would have believed . . . it really haunted him. And at this time he was having to deal with the fact that Brian was cracking up totally, and had to be taken into the Priory (a nursing home in Roehampton). It was only Keith who just kept on going, as if he didn't give a fuck what they did to him.' Marianne told friends that the tablets were hers, and that it was only because Mick gallantly refused to allow her to take the blame for her own drugs that he had been prosecuted at all. But whether or not that was true, it was now too late for Mick and Marianne to change their story. There was nothing they could do except hope that the appeal court overturned the Chichester verdict. And Allen Klein did his best to ensure that Mick and Keith did not while away the time consuming any illicit substances. He was aware of the risk that the police might bust them again, which would really sabotage their chances of getting their sentences reduced. And that would decimate their earnings.

The verdict against the Rolling Stones galvanised Steve Abrams into action. He had been considering for some time the idea of putting a full-page announcement in the *Times*, with signatories, to show that there was, as he put it, a 'body of respectable and informed opinion, much larger than anyone thought, in favour of a more enlightened attitude to pot.' He had been planning it for some time, but the imprisonment of John Hopkins, and then of Jagger and Richard, had outraged so many people that it was now easier than it would have been a few months earlier to persuade people to lend their names to it. A crucial problem was raising the cash to pay for the advertisement, but Miles solved it within forty-eight hours of the Chichester verdict by persuading Paul McCartney to put up the money. The money eventually came from the Beatles' advertising account which was, as Steve says, 'probably appropriate'. Steve had anticipated that it would be difficult to persuade the *Times* to accept the announcement, but the public furore over the Stones' sentences made it more likely that the paper would accept the advertisement, especially since the Rees-Mogg editorial.

The announcement, which appeared on 24 July, read:

> The signatories to this petition suggest to the Home Secretary that he implement a five-point programme of cannabis law reform:
>
> 1. The Government should permit and encourage research into all aspects of cannabis use, including its medical applications.
>
> 2. Allowing the smoking of cannabis on private premises should no longer constitute an offence.
>
> 3. Cannabis should be taken off the dangerous drugs list and controlled, rather than prohibited, by a new ad hoc instrument.
>
> 4. Possession of cannabis should either be legally permitted or at most considered a misdemeanour punishable by a fine of not more than £10 for a first offence and not more than £25 for any subsequent offence.
>
> 5. All persons now imprisoned for possession of cannabis or for allowing cannabis to be smoked on private premises should have their sentences commuted.

The advertisement also quoted Spinoza: 'All laws which can be violated without doing injury to anyone are laughed at . . .'

The sixty-four signatories to the advertisement included Jonathan Aitken MP, David Bailey, Anthony Blond (publisher), David Dimbleby, Tom Driberg MP, Brian Epstein and the Beatles, David Hockney, R. D. Laing, Tom Maschler (publisher), George Melly (jazz musician), Jonathan Miller (producer/director), John Piper and Patrick Procktor (both painters), and Kenneth Tynan (theatre critic).

In the middle of the drug debate that the Chichester verdicts had engendered Steve Abrams' advertisement added fuel to the fire. On 28 July, four days after it appeared in the *Times*, there was a debate in Parliament over the question of 'soft drugs'. It was inconsequential, but at least it aired the question officially and emphasised that responsible people held liberal attitudes towards such drugs.

The appeals were heard on 31 July. Teenagers had begun queueing before dawn for places in the public gallery. It seemed to everyone around Mick and Keith that, at least, their sentences would be reduced. But by now no one was certain – they had all realised the degree of animosity that existed, expecially towards Mick. Shirley Arnold recalls talking to Mick in the Stones' office, a few minutes before he left for the court of appeal. 'He tried not to show that he was nervous. I was due to get married on 13 August, and he said, "Well, if we go back to prison, have a nice wedding." I was quite frantic, and said, "If that happens we'll cancel the whole thing. I'll be too upset." And he said, "No, you just have a nice time." I remember looking at him and knowing he was really scared.' The Lord Chief Justice, Lord Parker, quashed Keith's conviction, on the grounds that Judge Block had erred in his summing-up, and that some of the evidence had been 'too tenuous'. Mick's conviction was upheld, but his sentence was reduced to a conditional discharge. After leaving the court Mick went to the Granada television studios for a press conference, and afterwards

137

he was flown by helicopter to the house of Sir John Ruggles-Brise, the Lord Lieutenant of Essex. There a discussion about drugs was taped for the television programme *World in Action*. William Rees-Mogg, Lord Stowhill (a former attorney-general), John Robinson, the Bishop of Woolwich (author of the famous *Honest to God*) and Father Corbishley (a well-known Jesuit) all took part. The debate was a farce – Mick had dosed himself heavily on valium, as he often did before interviews. But he overdid it, and seemed to have trouble even sitting up straight. He said practically nothing coherent and did little to persuade anyone that he was intelligent, reasonable or undrugged. But he remained the official front-man for the young in the generation war. The *Times*, the day after the appeal, carried a half-page interview with Jagger, conducted by Stephen Jessel. Everyone who covered the trial appeared to be fascinated by Mick's clothes, and Mr Jessel was no exception. He told his readers that Mick was 'dressed in purple trousers and a richly embroidered shirt' for the interview. He seems to have handled the interview better than the television debate.

> He is so unlike the cartoon stereotype as to be almost un-recognisable in reality. He is a slighter figure than you expect, and thin to the point of skinniness. He is quieter and has much more grace of manner than one would have expected. He is articulate, and the philosophy he outlines is obviously the product of sustained consideration. But the quality that impresses one most on first meeting him is his overwhelming self-possession . . . though Mr Jagger is the first to admit that he is not the stuff that martyrs are made of, he has the sort of certainty that he is right which is their special characteristic.

There followed Mick's own description of his beliefs: 'I believe in God but I'm not religious. One uses the term God when one gets to the end; to the "don't know" part. All right is just pointing in the same direction, right is a light on the path, the path to Nirvana if you like. The difficulty,' Mick admitted, 'is to articulate your experience.'

Despite the happy ending in the appeal court, there were elements of the whole affair that remained peculiar. Schneidermann was an entirely mysterious figure. The prosecution had ridiculed the suggestion that he was an agent of the *News of the World*, because he seemed not to have planted any cannabis on Mick, which was what he was alleged to be there for. But the police had, according to some witnesses, found some hashish in Mick's jacket, although they had failed to recognise it. It does not seem likely that Schneidermann would have been needed to introduce cannabis into Redlands, as the *News of the World* should have known. The timeliness of his disappearance is also difficult to dismiss. Then there was the question of the *News of the World*'s shadowy informant. Initially, Mick seems to have believed that he did not exist – that since the newspaper had orchestrated the bust, they had just invented their public-spirited 'reader'. But slowly he seems to have begun to consider that the *News of the World* story might be partly true. There was no definite proof, but circumstantial evidence and instinct began to weigh heavily against one hitherto trusted employee of the Stones. But it was difficult to reconcile Schneidermann as plant with the employee as Judas – if the *News of the World* had set them up, there was no need for a tip-off. Oddest of all was the fact that not even the prosecution questioned Mick's story that he had got his 'pep pills' quite legally in Italy. For five years those pills had been available there only on prescription, and Italian law was strict in the control of an even wider range of drugs than were dealt with by English legislation. The defence case could have been weakened considerably if it had been proved that Mick had obtained the drugs from an illicit source in the first place. Just as bizarre was a speech made by Judge Block later in the year, in which he showed a vindictive disregard for the principles of English law. Addressing the Horsham Plowing and Agricultural Society, he said: 'We did our best, your fellow countrymen, I, and my fellow magistrates, to cut those Stones down to size, but alas, it was not to be because the Court of Criminal Appeal let them roll free.'

The summer of 1967 became known as the 'summer of love'. Hippies from all over the United States and Europe made their way, hitching, walking, or flying to San Francisco. The city authorities became worried about the risk of disease in their over-crowded camp-sites, and were amazed by the upsurge in the number of reported cases of venereal disease. In England, too, 'flower power' attracted much attention. Even the butchest wore bells. The summer was long and warm, and everywhere *Sergeant Pepper* was playing. The Israelis had smashed the Egyptian, Jordanian and Syrian host, and occupied promising new land, all in six days at the beginning of June. Anglo-Saxon sympathy was with them – Europe's residual guilt over the holocaust, combined with their resounding military success, made them the heroes of the hour. There was a lull in the Generation War – it was not quite clear who had won the first round. Mick was not in prison, but he had been found guilty and he had failed to sue the *News of the World* for libel. The last episode in that adventure was a note in the paper which said: 'Mick Jagger of the Rolling Stones has dropped his libel action against the *News of the World* and agreed to pay all the costs incurred by this newspaper. Following an application to the High Court by his advisers, he was given leave to discontinue his action.' Jagger's lawyers had tried to persuade the *News of the World* that each party should pay its own costs and that no public announcement should be made about the settlement. The paper refused. Jagger's lawyers next suggested that he should pay the costs, but that there should be no announcement. That too was turned down. The *News of the World* held all the cards by now. But they too had been surprised by the ferocity of the first battle, and did not intend to skirmish again. The statement was as subdued as it could be, without the newspaper being seen to have lost face over the matter.

There were those going around London that summer who were bent not on love and peace but on revenge. One of the journalists who had worked on the original story about pop stars and drugs was offered money for information that might damage Mike Gabbert, who had masterminded the series. When he refused, his flat was broken into and a heroin needle sellotaped to the back of the drawer, in an attempt to incriminate him. He knew enough of the ways of the world to find the needle, and reported it to the police. A few days later Mike Gabbert's car was treated to the same attention – LSD was found planted in the boot. And the Stones employee who was under suspicion had the tyres of his car slashed and the windscreen smashed.

During August Mick, Marianne and Christopher Gibbs went to stay with Desmond Guinness at Leixlip. 'I remember we took an acid trip and spent the morning rearranging all the flowers at Castletown, because it had been opened, I think, for the first time. Then we went back to Leixlip and Desmond said that we were all going to see Lord Ormonde give Kilkenny Castle to the people of Ireland. So we went off there and it was a huge event and all the Butler family had gathered from all over the world to give it away. We were very doped up. We were all slithering about with all the pictures sliding off the walls. We were in a terrible state. There were people from all over the world with labels on, saying, "The Viscomte de Butler of France", and "Adam Van Butler III of Long Island", and they kept on coming up to us and saying, "What kind of Butler are you?" "Are you a Dunboyne Butler?" It was terribly funny. Mick made friends with a woman who came up to him and turned out to be William Rees-Mogg's secretary who was also a Butler. They weren't very pleased about us coming and spoiling their day.' Mick and Marianne seem to have been determined to outrage the Irish bourgeoisie during that holiday. They visited a Catholic brewing family in Kilkenny, who were friends of Mariga Guinness. While they were all having a drink Marianne picked up a photograph of one member of the family having an audience with the Pope. She sat down and began to roll a joint, using the photograph as a tray, while the entire family watched, speechless.

On returning to London airport Mick and Marianne found that every taxi-driver, except the very last one in the queue, refused to take them. Getting busted might have been good for publicity, but it was bad for the Stones' music. Their next single was intended to thank the fans who had supported them so loyally during their times of trouble. It was entitled 'We Love You' and Mick said that he had written it in prison. To promote it they made a four-minute film, based on the story of Oscar Wilde, in which Mick played Oscar Wilde, Keith the Marquess of Queensberry and Marianne Lord Alfred Douglas. It was a piece of bravado which did not amuse the BBC, who banned the film. And despite the love and loyalty of the fans, the single only reached number 8, even though it had the added attractions of slamming prison doors and the sound of footsteps on stone floors. On 25 August Mick and Marianne went with the Beatles and their womenfolk to see the commercially minded Indian guru, the Maharishi Mahesh Yogi. It was while they were there that the Beatles heard that Brian Epstein, who had been much more than a manager to them, had committed suicide. They were all billetted in a teachers' training college and had to listen with some show of piety to the Great Man's words. The Beatles seemed to be impressed by him, but Mick said afterwards that it all seemed 'more like a circus than the beginning of a religious event'.

Robert Fraser, languishing in Wormwood Scrubs, was not forgotten. Mick sent him books from the Indica Bookshop, including *Tantric Art* and *The Way of White Clouds*. And a group show was organised in his gallery which included paintings by Patrick Procktor, Peter Blake, Patrick Caulfield, Kitaj and Robyn Denny.

Chapter Seven

The relationship between the Stones and Andrew Oldham, which had been so mutually profitable, was beginning to sour. Andrew was convinced, just as Brian was, that the *Sergeant Pepper*-inspired psychedelic music of *Satanic Majesties* was a mistake for the Stones; they should not be trying to compete directly with the Beatles. It was hopeless to have a producer who hated the record he was working on. Andrew believed that Mick and Keith were no longer writing good songs, and they felt that their ideas were now far in advance of his. Mick and Keith were learning a great deal about the business of producing records, and they were well aware that Andrew had learnt everything he knew through working with them. They became surly and uncooperative with him in the studio and began to ignore every suggestion that he made. As they cut Andrew out of the operation they relied more and more on the expertise of Glyn Johns, the sound engineer who had been working with them since the middle of 1966. The Stones were irritated by, and un-receptive to, Andrew's criticisms of their work. They no longer felt the need for the sort of guidance that he had given them. The fact that Andrew seemed to be aligning himself with Brian, who was himself a problem to them, only exacerbated the situation. But Shirley Arnold insists that it was, in the end, Andrew who left the Stones – he was not fired by them. As a concession to Andrew, Mick and Keith agreed to record some of the blues-type songs that he preferred. But they played so badly that the whole session was a waste of time, and Andrew walked out in disgust.

At the end of September 1967 the Stones announced publicly that they had broken away from Andrew and in future would produce their own records. Allen Klein was to be their sole business manager and Tito Burns their European agent.

But Mick decided that they also needed someone to run the office. Shirley Arnold was still working for the Stones, but spent most of her time sorting out their travel and domestic arrangements – finding a nanny for Marianne's son, Nicholas Dunbar, looking for staff for Keith or Anita, or fixing seats for the Stones and their associates on flights that were already fully booked. Other people involved in the organisation felt strongly that Mick was being unfair to Shirley by not promoting her. 'But Mick likes the idea of hiring experts. If he has known people for a long time, since they were very young secretaries, he hates to accept them as something more. He'd rather bring in somebody new. It's to do with the fact that he's never really grateful to his employees, and doesn't consider how much they have done for him over the years,' according to a one-time employee. So the hunt was on for a 'business person' to run the office. Mick was keen to hire an American, Jo Bergman, who had experience of the musical world, and a reputation as a tough business woman. Shirley, without resentment, had to conduct the negotiations between Jo and Mick, by telex. She was a little surprised that Jo demanded £50 a week salary, and more surprised that Mick agreed to it.

One of the first tasks facing Jo when she arrived in London was to find a new office for the Stones. Now that they had split up from Andrew they had to move out of his office. But after all of the mixed publicity which surrounded the Redlands affair, it was not easy to find new premises. Many landlords were unaccountably deterred from letting offices to the Stones. Finally, in the autumn of 1967, the Stones moved into the building where Lily Langtry had once lived, in Maddox Street, between Regent Street and Bond Street. 'Mick loved the idea of having an office to go to like a businessman,' according to Shirley Arnold, 'and the Maddox Street place was lovely. Our office was upstairs – we had about four rooms, with sloping walls and original fireplaces. The lift had been installed specially by the King [Edward VII], so he didn't have to walk up all the stairs. And we had someone called David Jarvis whose job it was to go round the country buying antique furniture for the office. Mick kept a really tight control of the money. The reason he hired him was that he cost less than any of his antique dealer friends. There was a lovely atmosphere around that time – people were always coming in for a drink, it was very friendly. The Kinks' office was downstairs, in the boardroom there was a miniature stage, and we always had games and toys around for people to play with. It was all because of Mick. He loved it all, he wanted it to be a comfortable place where people could relax. He had this idea of having a huge, 3000-piece magnetised jigsaw on the wall, so that anyone who was waiting around could do a few pieces. But we found out what it was going to cost, and Mick said it was too much.'

Their Satanic Majesties Request ... was finally released in December. It was hailed by the critics, almost unanimously, as a wan imitation of *Sergeant Pepper*. Even the cover, with a three-dimensional photograph taken by Michael Cooper with a specially imported camera, was reminiscent of the Beatles' sleeve. It showed the Stones sitting in a mixed-up, Middle Eastern lurex fantasy land, with Mick wearing a witch's hat and black cloak. Among the psychedelic flora were four with Beatle-faces. But the album was not a total disaster. There were some good songs, including the first Bill Wyman song that the Stones recorded – 'In Another Land' is a charming, evocative drug ditty:

In another land where the breeze and the trees
And the flowers grow blue
I stop and hold your hand and the grass grew high
And the feathers floated by . . .

Certain songs dealt with familiar Stones themes: 'On with the Show' degraded adult pleasures and '2000 Man' chronicled a vision of total alienation. The orchestration was more sophisticated than on any of their records so far and there were technical advances, such as using different tempi within the same song. But the instrumental passages were unexciting and in songs such as 'Gomper' the imagery was hackneyed. '2000 Light Years from Home' totally lacked the excitement that usually characterised Jagger/Richard compositions, perhaps because the mood of the song was so incongruous for them – it was reflective, gentle, intentionally unearthly. 'She's a Rainbow' was even more unusual. 'She' was not, for once, horrible, nor was she someone who had been, or was about to be, beaten up: 'Have you seen a lady fairer?' The tone was one of sheer admiration, even if it was also hallucinatory. *Satanic Majesties* received more unpleasant criticism than any previous Stones LP.

With their next album they returned to their roots. It was recorded between March and June at the Olympic Studios in London. After 'We Love You' and *Satanic Majesties* the Stones could not afford another disaster. Mick and Keith's record-producing seemed not to have worked, and they now needed to hire someone first-rate. Jimmy Miller was approached by Mick at the beginning of the year. He was experienced, and liked the Stones' Music. Morale seemed to pick up almost as soon as Jimmy Miller arrived on the scene. And the quality of their output improved as rapidly. 'Mick and Keith both respond to other people's expertise. They try to put people down, but once they're impressed they really like to work with people who know more than they do,' according to someone who has worked with them.

146

Mick was fascinated by films, and was at this time considering all sorts of projects, either for himself or for the Stones as a whole. The first of these to get off the ground was shot while they were recording their next album with Jimmy Miller. Jean-Luc Godard's film involved his wife, Anne Wiazemsky, as Eve Democracy wandering through encounters with black militants, left-wing revolutionaries and the Rolling Stones. The film, which was to be called *One Plus One* but was eventually released as *Sympathy for the Devil*, included footage of the Stones rehearsing their song of the latter title. It reflected the chic radicalism that was emerging during 1968, to which Mick, alone of all the Stones, publicly aligned himself.

By the beginning of 1968 the first flush of hippy optimism was already waning. The Summer of Love had seen the worst race riots in America's history, with twenty-six dead and over 1000 injured in Newark alone. There was serious trouble in 127 cities. In October about 100,000 people had marched to the Pentagon to protest against the United States' involvement in Vietnam. And as the world began to look bleaker many young people found uncommitted, peaceful anarchy an insufficient response and took up their placards. Suddenly Revolution, or at least a desire for it, seemed to be in the air throughout the world. Vietnam provided a handy umbrella for protests in America – most people could find something to object to in the war, and more and more of them took to the streets to say so. In England, in May, thousands mobbed the American Embassy in Grosvenor Square to lend their support to the anti-war lobby. Newspapermen were delighted to find Mick in the front line of the demonstration, linking arms with ordinary people. Photographers battled to get photographs of Jagger in the vanguard of the Revolution and teenagers momentarily reverted to the bourgeois habit of begging autographs. Later, dozens of universities in Europe and America erupted as students protested. In France they were angry about admittedly bad conditions. In England they had fewer specific grounds for complain but they protested anyway. The militant craving for peace grew as the year progressed and the world seemed to be becoming more senselessly violent – Martin Luther King was assassinated in April, and Bobby Kennedy was shot dead in June in circumstances even more mysterious than those that had surrounded his brother's death. The year also saw one of the first real setbacks to the sixties belief that every day in every way life was getting easier. The papal encyclical, *Humanae Vitae*, outlawing artificial contraception, was greeted with stunned disbelief. Most Catholics and Protestants alike had come to assume that the Vatican was going to relax the ban. It came as a shock that the Pope was still telling people that there were things they couldn't do – especially when it meant attacking the most dearly held ideal of all – accessible, uncomplicated, inconsequential sex.

By this time Mick had moved into a large and pretty house in Cheyne Walk by the river in Chelsea. Christopher Gibbs had helped Marianne decorate the house and buy furniture. Marianne described later how she had bought a £6000 chandelier, and Mick had been both appalled at the cost of it and delighted to be able to possess such an object. 'Mick's own taste got completely confused. He lost sight of himself, and was torn between what people showed him, or told him to like, and what he liked himself. And I always thought that the effect of people like Christopher Gibbs made him slightly absurd, giving him ideas about country houses and such,' a very old friend says. A smart house in London was not enough. Mick also had to have a house in the country as well. He had wanted one for a long time – Christopher Gibbs had first been introduced to him as someone who might be able to help him in the search. 'We looked at a lot of very nice houses, including a wonderful William and Mary house in Shropshire with Chinese wallpaper. We didn't buy that one because Marianne thought Henley was on the way to Ludlow and insisted we stop on the way, for a picnic. So it took us nine hours to get there.' Mick needed to have somewhere that was within a reasonable distance of London.

Eventually John Michel, a friend of Christopher, suggested that Mick should look at a house that his family were selling. The party that went down to look at it consisted of Christopher, Mick, Marianne, Keith, Anita, Robert Fraser and the writer Terry Southern and Mason Hoffenburg, who was working with Terry Southern. 'I remember the nightmarishness of the journey down because both Mason and Terry insisted on stopping every three miles for drinks, and so we were two hours late arriving and it was dark and they weren't at all pleased to see us.' But despite the unpromising start the expedition was fruitful. Stargroves was a big, dilapidated Victorian house, just south of Newbury on the edge of the Berkshire downs. It had about forty acres of land, and stables and outbuildings, and was surrounded by marvellous woods. Mick got it for £22,000.

This was a period of great fertility for Mick. He was experimenting – with an aristocratic way of life, with ideas, with drugs, with sex, even with men. Allen Ginsberg, the American poet, told Miles on several occasions that he had spent a night in bed with both Mick Jagger and Tom Driberg. It was not the first suggestion of a homosexual encounter for Mick. Anita has said that Brian and Mick had a 'fling', and friends speculate about the exact nature of several of Mick's relationships. Driberg and Ginsberg certainly were both close friends of Jagger. Ginsberg was well known to the English Underground, to whom he was an older mentor. Tom Driberg had defended the Stones publicly over the Redlands bust – he had signed the *Times* advertisement, and had asked questions in Parliament about the prison governor ordering Mick and Robert Fraser to be handcuffed on the way to court. Driberg was a member of the National Executive Council of the Labour Party (later its chairman) and a self-advertised homosexual. He described in his autobiography, *Ruling Passions*, taking Marianne and Chris Jagger to a W. H. Auden poetry reading, and to dinner afterwards with the great man. 'Wystan's chair was next to Marianne's. As we sat down, he turned to her and said, in his curiously blurred, yet

149

attractive, American accent: "When you're smuggling drugs, d'you pack them up your arse?" '

Driberg said later that he had told Mick that he should stand for Parliament. Jagger was pleased by the idea, and often mentioned it to people. But he never seems to have tried to do anything about it. The notion that he had such an enormous influence over young people that he ought to be in Parliament was pleasing, but to implement it would have meant taking risks. Not everyone in the Labour Party might like the idea of Mick as an MP as much as Tom Driberg did. And it was always possible that he could stand and fail to be elected. After the Redlands affair he did not underestimate the hostility that existed towards him. He stuck, publicly, to an attitude of adolescent rebellion:

> Anarchy is the only slight glimmer of hope, [he told the *Sunday Mirror*]. Not the popular conception of it – men in black cloaks lurking around with hidden bombs – but a freedom of every man being personally responsible for himself. There should be no such thing as private property. Anybody should be able to go where he likes and do what he likes. Politics, like the legal system, is dominated by old men. Old men who are also bugged by religion. And the law – the law's outdated and doesn't cater enough for individual cases.

It was at this time too that Mick was most friendly with the American magus Kenneth Anger, whom he had met a couple of years earlier. Kenneth was then living in Notting Hill, and was friendly with Christopher Gibbs, Robert Fraser and Marianne. He alerted many young people to the intriguing possibilities of the occult – he was the first self-pronounced magician that most of them had ever met. He had been a disciple of Aleister Crowley, the 'Great Beast', the best known Satanist of the twentieth century. But many people insist that Anger was a salutary influence on his young London friends. 'There's a hard worldliness that enters people when they first get hold of substantial amounts of money, which they tend to think virtuous. Kenneth was disgusted by that and determined to show them that things are not always what they seem,' Christopher Gibbs says. 'He knows a lot about glamour, what it is and what it isn't. And he knows how masses of people can be influenced by one person's carrying on. He was an amusing, crazy creature with a very pronounced religious sense that just happened to be way off beam. He instilled a sense of mystery and adventure into our lives. He was a very puckish, "thorough bush, thorough briar" character.' He sent Robert Fraser a razor blade in an envelope, with a note saying, 'The final solution to your stuttering problems.' And on another occasion he hurled a copy of Blake, tied to a brick, through one of the windows of Jagger's house in Cheyene Walk. Anger was then working on his long-term project, a film to be called *Lucifer Rising*. His original Lucifer, a Californian called Bobby Beausoleil, had unfortunately been imprisoned for murder. Anger then decided that Mick should play Lucifer. Mick agreed to help with the film and wrote music for it. But he never committed himself any further, and eventually Chris Jagger and Marianne acted in *Lucifer Rising*, much of which was shot on location in Egypt. Anger's influence on the Stones was strong, particularly through Anita, who enjoyed all the spookery of demonism and, according to some people, spent a lot of time cooking up spells and muttering curses.

But although a whiff of Satanism was useful for pepping-up the Stones' image, Mick himself seems never to have had more than a dilettante's involvement with the powers of darkness. 'Look, Mick will never play with anything really dangerous. He's not going to mess with the Devil. It's just one of his games to pretend he is,' a friend from the time says. His account at the Indica Bookshop reflects the crash course that he was taking in the black arts, as well as the interest in poetry that was fostered by Marianne. In December 1967 he bought *Secret Tibet, Fairy Faith in Celtic, Masks of God*, Volume 2, *Vidyapati Love Songs*,

Mysterium Coniunctions, *Manuscripts of Witchcraft*, *Monkey*, *Nova Express*, *The Master and Margarita* and one or two other books. The whole lot came to £18/ 9/6d. *The Master and Margarita* provided direct inspiration for 'Sympathy for the Devil', which was to appear on the *Beggars Banquet* album. In April 1968 Jagger bought *Confucius to Cummings*, *Dylan Thomas*, *Penguin Modern Poets*, *W. B. Yeats Poems*, *Morte d'Arthur* and Jung, Volume 10.

'Jumping Jack Flash', released in Britain and America in May 1968, was the best Stones' single since 'Let's Spend the Night Together' (January 1967) or even earlier. It seemed to bridge the Stones' blues roots and their demonic phase and, like 'Satisfaction', to epitomise both an era and an aspect of Mick. This was the first Jimmy Miller production to be released, and it at once vindicated the decision to hire him. 'Jumping Jack Flash' was an enormous hit on both sides of the Atlantic. Suddenly the Stones were back on top again.

Mick was becoming more involved with the business side of the Stones organisation. He had always been fascinated by financial deals, and had kept himself closely informed of Allen Klein's movements. He was now becoming suspicious of him, and had hired a merchant banker, Prince Rupert Loewenstein, as his personal financial advisor. He had met the 'princely German dumpling', as *Tatler* described him, through Christopher Gibbs. Prince Rupert was to keep an eye on Klein's activities and to help Mick, in due course, set up his own company. In the meantime, Mick intervened whenever it seemed useful for him to do so in the business. He told several friends, including Ossie Clark, of one such incident. 'For some reason, none of the Stones' records seemed to be played on American juke-boxes. The Mafia controlled the syndicate, Mick discovered. So he set up a meeting with the Godfathers, to ask why they were vetoing the Stones and what their terms would be. The meeting worked out well for everyone. All the Godfathers asked for was Mick's autograph for their children. And the next day "Jumping Jack Flash" was blaring out of every juke-box in America.'

Mick's old friend, Donald Cammell, had begun to write movies in the last couple of years, as well as painting. He hatched the idea for a movie dealing with a confrontation between a retired rock star and a gangster. Warner Brothers agreed to fund the film once Mick had agreed to take part. They were expecting it to be a pop musical starring Jagger, who would, they supposed, have consider-able box-office appeal. Donald wanted to direct the film himself, but he was completely inexperienced, so he enlisted some help: 'Nick Roeg was a rather good cameraman who I rather liked and I asked him to co-direct it with me which turned out to be a great idea because we had a lot of fun, really. We made an agreement that Nick shouldn't talk to the actors if I wouldn't talk to the camera crew, because the camera crew were much more intelligent than the actors. I spent a lot of my time talking to the camera crew because I wanted to learn all about cinematography, all the things that Nick knew and I didn't, which was a hell of a lot at the time.' Donald's brother, David, was already involved with the movie business, and took a year off from his normal work making tele-vision commercials to produce the film, which was to be called *Performance*, with Sandy Lieberson. David Cammell already knew Mick. He had worked with Giorgio Gomelsky on his film about the blues in England at the very beginning of the sixties and had been interested in the Rolling Stones ever since. Donald's perennial girlfriend, Deborah Dixon, and Christopher Gibbs designed the sets and found most of the furniture and props that were needed.

It was part of David Cammell's job to find locations for the film. In the end three different houses were used – one in Hyde Park Gate, one in Lowndes Square and one in Powis Square, in Notting Hill Gate, for the exterior shots. It was not easy to find a big enough house that had not been turned into flats, but as he searched for one David remembered a game of poker in Lowndes Square when he had lost a lot of money. The house where it had

153

taken place was owned by the father of the man who had organised the game. The old man was called Lenny Plugge and claimed to have been a cabinet minister. 'He was only too pleased to get a pittance by renting it off. The whole place was festooned with paintings – the Plugge collection – and one condition of renting the house was that we should insure them for £2 million. I thought they were a bit dodgy and they were in rather battered condition. There was a Rembrandt, a Rubens and a Velasquez, but several were signed by Rembrandt as well as Rubens. Anyway, we removed the paintings, wrapped them in blankets and put them upstairs in the caretaker's flat. The caretaker was a strange sort of dogsbody who wandered around brandishing a luger. And there was another appalling creature who lived upstairs with him, a mongol whose bed we had to fumigate when we discovered that it was festering with lice. He took rather a shine to me and used to follow me around all day. Mr Plugge, who was about eighty-five, was also staggering about. He went to the opera every night, wearing an ermine coat, although he was completely broke, and was always being hunted by creditors. He was never seen without a pretty girl on either arm, and would totter up the stairs as we were filming, telling them he was going to get them into the movies.'

Donald initially envisaged an American gangster, and wanted to use Marlon Brando, who was a friend from Paris, for the part. 'But you know that a thing with Marlon takes forever,' he says. He then met James Fox. 'He was staggering-looking, and the charm of Jimmy is that he didn't understand how attractive he was. Mick was around at the time and they disappeared into the woodwork and there was a sort of romance . . . but they were both such closet queens . . . You'll have to ask somebody else whether he actually had an affair with Mick. I won't tell you, because I know that it would be misunderstood. But it was a joy to watch.'

Donald was inspired to cast James opposite Mick. He had seen him in Losey's *The Servant* and had realised then that there was a suggestion of sado-masochism underlying his clean, Anglo-Saxon

154

charm. Fox took some persuading that he could do the part, but Donald had no doubts. 'He was such a great, great actor that I knew he could do it. I knew that he could get totally into this character, which he did. He turned into this young hoodlum, East End character in front of my eyes. He went to live over a pub in the Commercial Road, down in the East End, and his best friends became two or three wide boys. The people I got for him were really frightening people. Jimmy Evans, whose real name was Mendosa, Jimmy Mendosa, was the most evil of the whole lot. And there was Johnny Bindon, who was very highly strung, a real psychopath of the greatest kind, a great actor, a great performer. Very excitable.' Bindon attracted publicity a few years later when he was involved in a spot of bother over a knife fight in a night-club. He was a massive man, frightening because of his sheer size. But Stanley Meadows, an actor who played one of the gangsters, says, 'Bindon a villain? No, no, he's a charming, cultured fellow.' He says that there always seemed to be a lot of beautiful girls around the set and that, oddly he thought, a lot of them seemed to find Bindon very attractive.

A key figure in the making of *Performance* was David Litvinoff, who was an old friend of Donald Cammell. 'I used to go around with David Litvinoff as a teenager. We hung around Soho together when I was still going to school. David was, apart from me, the most important person involved in the movie.' He shared Donald's enthusiasm for a louche underworld, their vision of which owed much to Jean Genet and Antonin Artaud. 'Really the only reason that anybody lived in Paris was to get a piece of that life, you know.'

'David was magnetised by the East End. He came from the poor end of a Jewish intellectual family that had got into the judge business. He had lived in the East End as a kid – he knew the real thing,' Donald Cammell says. According to David Cammell, he was 'very thick with the Kray brothers'. One of David Litvinoff's discoveries was a boxing promoter called Johnny Shannon. He ran the pub where James Fox went to stay, and telephoned David Cammell one day, in a state of some agitation. 'Look, I think you ought to know. You put Jimmy in my custody, and it's a bit of a worry. He seems to be over-identifying. He went out on a heist with some of the guys yesterday.' David shared his alarm – a lot of money would be lost if Fox were to get himself arrested for burglary.

It was not only James Fox who was encouraged by Donald to become the character he was playing. Mick also slipped into character. Turner, the retired superstar living a reclusive life with two women in his house in Notting Hill, was intended to be a over-dramatised, exaggerated version of some aspects of Jagger's character. Turner is never wholly involved with what is going on around him – he is an observer and a manipulator, sinister, playful and omnisexual. He inhabits a world of Baudelarian, seductive decadence, enlivened by his wanton viciousness. He luxuriates in psychological dangers that outstrip the perils of the underworld that Chas (James Fox) knows. It was an area that inevitably fascinated Mick, but that until this time he had not really explored. Originally Donald had wanted Mick and James Fox to move into the house into Lowndes Square, so that they would live out the movie. That plan did not work out, but Mick still seemed, during the filming, to be submerging beneath the weight of Turner. He did not even have the company of Marianne to give him a centre of reality. She was pregnant, and was living in a house in Ireland which Mick had rented from Molly Cusack-Smith, the Master of the Galway Blazers. Marianne's doctors had suggested that she should have a complete rest, and Irish friends had suggested that the west coast of Ireland would be an ideal place to go.

Anita Pallenberg appeared in the movie as one of the girls who lived with Turner. No one was as suitable as Anita for playing the sort of games that so fascinated Donald with Mick. She had always shared Cammell's impulse to plumb every psychological abyss and to explore the possibilities of excess of every kind. The other girl was played by Michel Breton, a young French discovery of Donald's. 'She was a peasant from the hills around St Tropez – her father was a *garagiste*. She was a great sexual catalyst in the film – very beautiful, very bright, no education at all. She was very good with Jimmy. She was about fourteen when Deborah and I met her and then we took her back to Paris and she was already destined for a bad end.'

The filming of *Performance* was anything but calm. Keith was just as disturbed by it all as Mick and James Fox, even though he had no real connection with the film. He knew that Anita had always been sexually interested in Mick, he knew that she and Mick made love in the film, and he supposed, accurately, that it would be for real. David Cammell remembers Keith sitting outside the house in Lowndes Square in his car. He was haunted by the idea of what might be going on, but could not bear to confront it directly.

One of the difficulties Donald faced was getting Mick and Keith to write the song that they had to produce for the film. 'Mick mishandled Keith badly over all that. They had been upstaging each other and it just turned into a kind of TV movie that was going on off the screen at the same time that my movie, which was the real movie, was going on. There was this unbelievable soap opera that had been scripted by Mick and Keith which they acted out for everybody's entertainment. It was quite serious, there was a lot of feeling on both sides. Anita was just having the time of her life with everybody. And my romance with Anita was on during all this time, too. Keith just wouldn't write the tune music. He was sabotaging the movie because of Anita. He was being beastly to Mick and putting down the whole project. Robert Fraser found it extremely entertaining and was sort of Keith's hatchetman. In the end I banned everybody from the set, especially Robert. Robert was much tighter with Keith than with anybody at that time, for pharmaceutical reasons.

'Mick was constantly trying to do James Fox in, because that's the only way Mick can operate, there's this sort of competitive thing that presumably is developed in the music business. But then he got over that, he's a quick learner, and then he actually got into the character. He would work with Jimmy up to a point and then he'd stop. And then he'd totally refuse to rehearse any more and Jimmy would be scrambling at the door of the dressing room: "Mick, Mick, just read the lines for me one more time." "Fuck off, Jimmy." It was all very good for the show. But Mick was very unkind to Jimmy, he's always been unkind to him, that was part of the relationship before that. He'd sort of not call him back. Jimmy would get very intense about people and he'd transfer a lot of that need for love from Mick to me and he rewarded me with this fantastic performance. He used to try and keep this character alive all the way through, and he did. But then there'd be a cut and Mick would tease him, and say, "Ah, but you know, it's not the real you, not the real you." In that sense he was a little destructive, Mick. It was just a conditioned reflex, the star thing, they're always getting at each other, stars. But Jimmy wasn't like that, he didn't know anything about this thing at all.

'It blew Jimmy's mind, and that was why he never worked again after *Performance* for so long. The story was about the Turner character, the Mick Jagger character, mocking him and that's why it was ultimately effective. It brought out the most contemptuous side of Mick, an almost arrogant side, prancing around, preening himself. When Mick performed he improvised some wonderful lines and of course Jimmy was going word for word by the script, just like inhabiting it. So you get two different kinds of performance there and it helps.'

The script was being adapted constantly, every day bits of it were rewritten, according to what had been happening on the set. Stanley Meadows translated quite a lot of his script out of standard English and into London underworld, an argot he picked up during some colourful holiday jobs in his youth. Stanley was virtually the only person in *Performance* who did not take all his clothes off. 'I had it written into my contract that I didn't have to display my genitals in front of the technicians.' Most of the other actors and the crew were unaware of the drama being played out between Mick, James Fox, Anita and Keith. They found Mick hardworking and self-effacing, which surprised those who had been expecting him to behave like a star and to think he knew everything about acting. He seemed eager to learn, and very cooperative. But David Litvinoff loathed him and, according to Donald Cammell, 'Mick treated him like shit.'

The complications which beset the production seemed endless. David Cammell, who was working so hard that he could only snatch a few hours sleep most nights, and would sleep fully clothed to save time, was woken up early one morning by the telephone ringing. 'The voice said that it was Inspector Whoever of Whatever Division, and he was calling about the missing Plugge collection. I thought that it was David Litvinoff or somebody having a joke, but it turned out to be true, the whole lot had disappeared. Then some of the film crew remembered that the caretaker had been looking rather flush and had bought himself a new motor-car recently. We discovered that he had whipped the whole lot. He was on the run for about two weeks, and was finally arrested at Paddington Station. He then rang up and asked me to stand bail for him. I told him that he had caused me more anxiety than anyone else on earth, and I hoped that he rotted. We found out that he had sold the paintings at auction – £3800 for the entire lot, which rather blew the lid off the fabulous Plugge collection. Then the next thing was that the woman who lived next door complained about what she called our ice-cream van. She called me in and said did I realise that there were more titled people living in Lowndes Square than anywhere else in London except Eaton Square. She said we were lowering the tone, and she put an injunction on us and stopped us filming. We had a lot of money at stake, so we had to get a vacation judge back to hear the case, which went on for two days in the High Court. It turned out that the house had been mortgaged twice over and old Plugge had no right to let it out at all. The Sun Life Insurance Company were delighted – it was a heaven-sent opportunity for them to get rid of him. In the end Plugge agreed to give up the remainder of his lease – there was only eighteen months left to run and it was a full repairing lease, so he was well out of it. And we were allowed to carry on so long as we behaved ourselves.'

But even that was not the end of the troubles. In one scene in the movie Anita climbed into bed with Mick and Michel. The scene was shot under the sheets but it was lit so that it was obvious that there was plenty of action. The rushes were seen each day by one of several different people at the lab where the film was processed. One of them was a woman, and David Cammell knew that she wouldn't like the bed scene, so he rang up and told the lab not to let her see the rushes – that she might be shocked. 'Inevitably she saw the rushes, and the managing director called me up and said, "Look, Mr Cammell, you know that we could be prosecuted for this. You've sent us questionable material, of a possibly pornographic nature." I tried to calm him down: "It's a complete misunderstanding." But he said he couldn't possibly release the print to me, and would have to destroy the negative. I went to fetch it myself and he produced a hammer and chisel, walked out onto the steps and chiselled the print they had made.' But David managed to get the negative which was then printed elsewhere. The filming was finished by December 1968, although Donald Cammell continued to work on it in 1969. It was not to be released for some time, because of Warner Brothers' horrified astonishment at the finished product. It was not at all what they had been expecting.

After the fun and games of *Performance* had ended everything more or less went back to normal. Anita and Keith went on living together, and Marianne, who had, apparently, a pretty good idea of what was going on while she was in Ireland, came home to Cheyne Walk. She had a miscarriage, which devastated both her and Mick. Mick seemed to recover more quickly, since he had a lot of work to do. But he had been looking forward to becoming a father and it was clear to friends that he had been upset by the loss.

Beggars Banquet was released on 5 December. To celebrate the event a party was held at the Queensgate Hotel. The record was sensational, and more than compensated for *Satanic Majesties*. It was the Stones at their best – exciting, vicious and seductive. Several numbers seemed to reflect the radicalism of the times – but this time it felt as though the Stones were leading the way, not emulating others. When Mick sang 'Street Fighting Man' his audience knew that he had been in Grosvenor Square, and they believed in him as Lucifer in 'Sympathy for the Devil'. The slatternly 'Factory Girl' and the felicitously faithless fiancée in 'Dear Doctor' are vintage Jagger, but without the unpleasant aftertaste of some earlier creations. Even 'Salt of the Earth', which comes precariously near to being maudlin, is confident, measured and moving. The album was intended to have been released in the summer, but a battle between Mick and Decca delayed its appearance. The record company objected to the sleeve design, which showed a photograph of a well-graffitied lavatory wall. But Mick refused to allow it to be changed. He said, 'I don't find it all offensive. Decca has put out a sleeve showing an atom bomb exploding [*Atomic Tom Jones*]. I find that more upsetting.' He then decided that as a compromise the record could be sold in brown paper bags marked 'Unfit for Children'. Decca held out. Finally Mick agreed that the album should be released with a plain white cover with just the words 'Rolling Stones Beggars Banquet' on it.

Relationships within the band were now colder than they had ever been. Brian was busted again in May, and charged with possessing cannabis. In September, when the case was finally heard, he was fined £50 and £105 costs. Mick was irritated by what he saw as Brian's incompetence in risking further legal trouble after his lucky escape in the autumn of 1967 when he had also got away with a fine. Brian was now consuming vast quantities of narcotics, especially DMT, one of the most seductive of all drugs. He was never without girlfriends, but he remained obsessed by Anita, and appalled that she had left him for Keith. He seemed to be becoming more and more unhinged, and to be bent upon destroying himself. He would consume insane combinations of drugs and alcohol, and would only stop when he finally passed out. Shirley Arnold remembers Brian telephoning the office, and begging her to come round and cook breakfast for him. He asked her to stop off at Selfridges Food Hall on the way, and buy some ham on the bone, eggs and instant mashed potato. When she arrived at Brian's flat she found that it was full of hangers-on who Brian had picked up the night before – he had no idea who most of them were. 'There was somebody passed out in the bath, and someone else shooting up in the lavatory. And Brian didn't even know what day it was. He watched as I cooked breakfast for him, and he kept saying, "How can you get it all together, how can you cook it all at the same time?" But he was in such a state that he'd passed out before I'd got it all ready.'

In November 1968 Brian bought Cotchford Farm in Sussex, the former home of A. A. Milne, the author of *Winnie-the-Pooh*, and he began to spend more and more time there.

Charlie Watts was as ever immersed in domesticity, except when the band was actually recording. His daughter, Serafina, was born in March 1968. For the first time there was a serious estrangement between Mick and Keith, as a result of *Performance*. But at the end of the year they all had to work together on the *Rolling Stones' Rock and Roll Circus*. This was to be a spectacular television show, a compensation to their audiences, who had not now seen them perform live for over two years. John Lennon and Yoko Ono came, as well as Eric Clapton, Jethro Tull, Mitch Mitchell, Roger Daltrey, Pete Townsend, and all sorts of circus acts – clowns, jugglers, tigers, a boxing kangaroo, a fire-eater and so on. It was planned to be broadcast all over the world, and was one of the most extraordinary gatherings of rock talent ever organised. There were also plans to release a record of the event. Recording took three days, at the

162

BBC studios in Shepherds Bush. The Stones themselves finally played at 5.30 am on the last day. Marianne was there, as well as a great many friends. The whole thing was directed by Michael Lindsay-Hogg, the director of the regular television show, *Ready Steady Go*. People who were at the studios when the *Circus* was filmed say that Brian was in worse fettle than they had ever seen him, quite incapable of doing anything other than strumming a few chords, and an embarrassment to the rest of the band. Most people present thought that the *Circus* was a triumph, but it has never been shown commercially. Mick decided that the Stones' performance was not up to scratch. It is also suggested that he spent a great deal of time haggling over the payment the Rolling Stones were to receive for their part. But if it did nothing else, the *Rock and Roll Circus* at least healed the *gêne* caused by *Performance*.

At the end of the year Mick, Marianne and Nicholas went with Keith and Anita to Brazil for a holiday. Keith told a reporter that they were going to Brazil because 'We've become very interested in magic and we're very serious about this trip. We're hoping to see this magician who practises both black and white magic. He has a very long and difficult name which we can't pronounce. We call him "Banana" for short.' They stayed first on a large cattle-ranch, then at a hotel in Rio and afterwards in a hut on the beach at Recife. Marianne said later that they found that a lot of Brazilians seemed to be fascinated by Mick, and slightly afraid of him at first. She said that Jagger decided that it must be because he looked very like the image of Christ on local crucifixes and statues and in paintings: he had become very sunburnt in South America, and had grown a small beard.

By the spring of 1969 the Rolling Stones were getting itchy feet. Mick and Keith were keen to organise another tour of America. But now that Brian had had two drug convictions he would most probably not be given an entry visa to America. And he was contributing little to the band in any other way. There had been several occasions already when he had been almost asked to leave. But the plan had been delayed, altered, put off. But now, finally, there was a pressing reason to act and a replacement lined up – Mick Taylor, a brilliant twenty-year-old guitarist who had played with John Mayall. Charlie Watts was recruited to go with Mick Jagger and Keith to see Brian in the country and announce the decision to him as unviolently as possible. But Brian seems to have made it easy for them. They agreed that it would be announced that Brian was leaving the group because of disagreements over music. On 9 June the Stones office issued a brief statement to the press. Several people were considered as replacements, but Mick Taylor was the one that Mick and Keith both wanted most. It was a decision that ultimately rested with Keith, since he would have to play with him. But it was equally clear that it would be impossible to have in the group anyone who Mick did not want. They were to play a free concert in Hyde Park on 5 July, which would be Mick Taylor's live debut with the Stones. As the date of the concert approached members of the Rolling Stones' staff tried to persuade Brian, on behalf of Mick, to come to the Hyde Park concert, and perhaps play a few numbers. It would show the world that there had been no ill-feeling over the breach, and reassure anyone who might think that Brian had been sacked, or dismissed against his will.

Although Brian was dismissed because his drug habit was making him incompetent as a musician and a liability when the group wanted to travel, it was at this time that Keith was acquiring tastes that were to land him in trouble later on. Anita already dabbled in most things, and Marianne first tasted heroin around this time. And Mick, who had been more careful than ever since the Redlands debacle, was busted again. Spanish Tony Sanchez said later that there had been an attempt to extort money from Mick. Marianne had been offered some heroin earlier in the day, and the police had found the white powder when they searched the house in Cheyne Walk. An intermediary then offered to bribe the forensic laboratories. But Marianne suspected that she had been sold talcum powder, and that the laboratory results would show that it was not heroin, even if they did not pay up. The policeman who organised the raid was generally considered to be one of the most corrupt in London, and Mick decided to call his bluff. He did not bribe him, and the forensic laboratories confirmed that the 'heroin' was talcum powder. But Mick still had to face the charge of cannabis possession. The case was not to be heard for several months, so Mick had to spend the summer with the prospect of it hanging over him.

Brian must have been expecting a final break from the Rolling Stones for some time. He had becoming increasingly separated from Mick and Keith who now were, to all intents and purposes, the Rolling Stones. Ossie Clark, the dress designer, who was a close friend of Mick and Brian, remembers Brian morosely saying to him, earlier in the year, ' "They're all in there, recording, and they've got someone else instead of me. I just don't have a place now". He was very unhappy about it. I got the impression that they were like deceitful children, rubbing it in.' But once the worse had happened, he seemed to be almost relieved. He began thinking about creating a new band, and he talked to Alexis Korner about his plans. He loved Cotchford Farm, and would delightedly show people who came to visit him the life-size statue of Christopher Robin in the garden, and the sundial with Pooh, Piglet and the other animals carved on it. He made friends with people in the local pub, the Haywagon, and invited friends from London down to stay with him. His parents came to visit him, and they found him happy, and physically better than he had been for some time. For the first time since he was a child they talked about Brian's sister, who had died when she was two years old and Brian was four. Now that he had finally left the group he seemed to be more optimistic than he had been for years. But there were also signs that his paranoia was getting worse than ever. He complained to friends that lights shone into his house all night, that he was being kept prisoner in his house, watched all the time and hardly allowed to go out. Sometimes he appeared to be blaming 'the office' for treating him as if he were mad, but at other times the enemy appeared to be the some of the nebulous crowd of hangers-on who were loitering around the house. There was a builder, Frank Thorogood, living in a flat over the garage with Janet Lawson, a nurse. Brian's latest girlfriend was also there, a Swedish girl called Anna Wohlin. Tom Keylock, who had been Brian's driver but had defected to Keith in Morocco, was now working for Brian again.

By now the Stones were working in the Olympic Studios, on songs that were to be used on the album *Let it Bleed*. As usual they were working well into the night. At about 3 am on 3 July they were telephoned by Tom Keylock's wife. She asked for Mick, and told him that Brian had been found dead.

Mystery surrounds Brian's death. Keylock claimed afterwards that he had not been at Cotchford that night. The story that emerged was that Brian and Anna had been watching television and drinking. At about 10 o'clock Brian went to the garage flat and suggested that Janet and Frank should join them. They then had several drinks together and Brian decided to go for a swim in the pool in his garden. Janet Lawson said afterwards that she had warned Brian that he was not in a fit condition to go swimming. Anna stayed in the house. Brian and Frank both went swimming. Janet returned to the house. Thorogood returned there as well, some minutes later, to fetch a towel, or a cigarette. Janet is then supposed to have returned to the pool, and discovered that Brian was lying at the bottom of the pool. She screamed for help, and Frank and Anna arrived. Anna had jumped into the pool, fully clothed, before Frank had taken his trousers off. They dragged him out of the pool, and pumped water out of him, massaged his heart and gave him the kiss of life. Brian is said to have feebly gripped Anna's hand, then moved no more.

The inquest, held at East Grinstead, ruled that Brian had died 'due to immersion in fresh water'. The coroner noted that he was swimming whilst 'under the influence of alcohol and drugs'. But the feeling persisted that there was something suspicious about the affair. Keith spoke about it some years later in a *Rolling Stone* interview. He was asked whether he thought Brian's death was an accident:

> Well, I don't want to say. Some very weird things happened that night . . . there were people there that suddenly disappeared . . . And someone called us up at midnight and said: 'Brian's dead.' Well, what the fuck's going on? We had these chauffeurs working for us and we tried to find out . . . some of them had a weird hold over Brian. There were a lot of chicks there and there was a whole thing going on, they were having a party. I don't know, man, I just don't know what happened to Brian that night. There was no one there that'd want to murder him. Someone just didn't take care of him . . . Maybe he did just go in for a swim and have an asthma attack . . . We were completely shocked. I got straight into it and wanted to know who was there and couldn't find out. The only cat I could ask was the one I think who got rid of everybody and did the whole disappearing trick so that when the cops arrived, it was just an accident. Maybe it was. Maybe the cat just wanted to get everybody out of the way so it wasn't all names involved, etc. Maybe he did the right thing, but I don't know. I don't even know who was there that night and finding out is impossible . . . it's the same feeling with who killed Kennedy. You can't get to the bottom of it.

At least a dozen people visited the house that night, although none of them gave evidence at the inquest. It is unclear whether Tom Keylock was in the house. At first it seemed that he had been, but afterwards he claimed that he had been at home in London all the time. And Les Perrin, the Stones' publicity man, had time to drive down from London before the police arrived on the scene. Yet it would have seemed that the most important thing was to call an ambulance, as quickly as possible. It has been suggested that Brian was murdered, possibly by people to whom he owed money for drugs: it is conceivable that someone went down to 'put the frighteners' on him, and he was killed by mistake. He had complained that things were being stolen from his house. Within a few days of his death almost everything that was left had been removed. And on the day of his funeral someone held a big bonfire in the garden. Someone also arranged for Anna Wohlin to go home to Sweden straight away, and there is a suggestion that she had little say in the matter.

On the morning of 3 July, after hearing about Brian's death, Shirley Arnold arrived in the office at 7 am. As the day went by more and more people gathered, stunned, in the office. They decided that rather than cancel the Hyde Park concert, it should be held as a memorial to Brian.

The day after Brian died the Stones' new single, 'Honky Tonk Women'/'You Can't Always Get What You Want', was released. The same day Prince Rupert Loewenstein was giving a big party for which everyone had been instructed to wear something white. Mick had been to Michael Fish's shop to buy something to wear. He found a short white tunic, based on a Greek soldier's uniform. Michael Fish says that he had designed it slightly too long, so that it did not look like a military tunic, but more like a dress. The photographer Patrick Lichfield had tried it on a few days earlier, for the same party, but had been told that he looked like a little girl in it. Michael remembers that he had been looking forward to the party, which everyone expected to be a very glamorous affair. But he suddenly had a marvellous offer of work in Toronto, which meant that he had to miss the party. He sent, in his stead, the most enormous bunch of white flowers that anyone had ever seen. The death of Brian inevitably cast a gloom over the party. Jane Rainey recalls that everyone there had obediently worn white, except Marianne Faithfull, who wore black, in mourning for Brian. Marianne seems to have been more upset by Brian's death than almost anyone else.

The next day, Saturday 5 July, was the day of the biggest pop concert that the world had yet seen. Half a million fans flooded Hyde Park, observed and described by hundreds of journalists, photographers and television cameramen. Hell's Angels, hippies, skinheads and schoolgirls gathered. Some told reporters that they had come from the continent specially to hear the Stones. Many had been encouraged to make the journey because of their sorrow at Brian's death, and had spent the night in the park. The police had been tolerant and allowed the fans to camp there, although they were flouting London by-laws. A series of bands played first – the Third Ear Band, King Crimson, Alexis Korner's new band New Church, Family and The Battered Ornaments. Ossie Clark went to the concert in the Stones' party: 'We all met at the Hyde Park Hotel. It was very exciting, there were quite a lot of people. Alan Dunn, Mick's driver and personal assistant, was in charge of organising us, and gave everyone their orders. As we got into the cars he said, "Right, now, usual procedure, lock all the doors," and we set off. Going into the park was like entering a great gaping mouth. The crowds were getting thicker and thicker. The Stones were quite blasé about it all, but I found it all incredibly thrilling. It was like one of those pictures of flocks of birds landing in a fertile bit of Africa, where there are birds everywhere, on the ground and in every tree. It was the same sort of thing, there was a person everywhere.'

As the Stones themselves took the stage the crowd roared their approval. Mick, again wearing Michael Fish's dress, made a half-hearted attempt to quieten them. 'No,' he shouted. But it was not going to be possible to calm them. He changed tack: 'Yeah. We're gonna have a good time, right?' Sam Cutler, the master of ceremonies, organised the day with schoolmistressy efficiency – relaying much practical advice, lists of lost children and thanks with the same bonhomie. He was assisted by a pack of Hell's Angels who had been hired as stewards. Intermittently he would ask them to move from one place to another, to control the pullulating mass.

Hundreds of girls fainted and were gently carried by Hell's Angels to first-aid posts. The Angels looked petrifying, in their full metal/leather battle-dress, but proved to be effective. Wild Child, their grandeval leader, exerted an unobtrusive authority over his pack. Fans and Angels danced. Many watched from boats on the Serpentine, or from the comfort of branches of trees. Others scaled the scaffolding surrounding the stage, until ordered down. The real police were there in force, but left the work of crowd control to the amateurs. The day got hotter. Coca Cola was being sold at 10/- a bottle. The camera crews had great difficulty filming as the crowds grew, and gabbled panicky instructions into radios. Suzy Creamcheese and Marsha Hunt clambered up to a platform that had been built for loudspeakers. Marianne and Nicholas sat by the side of the stage.

'Cool it for a minute,' Mick continued. 'I would really like to say something about Brian . . .' The crowd's noise murmured to a halt as he began to read two stanzas from Shelley's 'Adonais':

Peace, peace! he is not dead, he doth not sleep –
He hath awakened from the dream of life –
'Tis we, who, lost in stormy visions keep
With phantoms an unprofitable strife,
And in mad trance strike with our spirit's knife
Invulnerable nothings. – We decay
Like corpses in a charnel; fear and grief
Convulse us and consume us day by day,
And cold hopes swarm like worms within our living clay.

The One remains, the many change and pass;
Heaven's light forever shines, Earth's shadows fly;
Life, like a dome of many-coloured glass,
Stains the white radiance of Eternity,
Until Death tramples it to fragments. – Die,
If thou wouldst be with that which thou dost seek!

Follow where all is fled! – Rome's azure sky,
Flowers, ruins, statues, music, words are weak
The glory they transfuse with fitting words to speak.

The girls, boys and the camera crews went crazy, frenzied with excitement at witnessing this world historical moment. At a signal from Mick roadies opened brown cardboard boxes. A few torpid butterflies struggled painfully and then dropped to the ground. They had suffocated. They had been intended to flutter in a mass towards the heavens, somehow symbolising the release of Brian's tortured spirit. The Stones played indifferently. For pretty Mick Taylor, wide-eyed and innocent, it was a nerve-racking introduction to the Rolling Stones.

The next day Mick and Marianne flew to Australia to begin work on another feature film, *Ned Kelly*, about the life of the Australian folk hero. Mick had no real alternative but to go – the schedules for the film were already worked out, and he would have been sued by the film company if he had broken his contract. But some people suggest that Mick was glad to have an excuse not to go to Brian's funeral: 'He did feel awful about Brian's death, but it's the kind of thing he can't cope with. He wouldn't be able to go through seeing Brian's parents and saying how sad he was and all that. He would've cried. He cries very easily, Mick,' a close friend says.

The summer's adventures were not over. The next day Marianne took 150 sodium amytal tablets. She was also suffering from heroin withdrawl symptoms. She had been more severely affected by Brian's death than almost anyone else. She later told journalists that she had felt bound up with Brian's death, that both of them had been destroyed by Mick. She spent two days in a coma and was unable to act in *Ned Kelly*.

At Brian's funeral the vicar prayed for Marianne's recovery, and read the parable of the Prodigal Son.

Mick had no alternative but to carry on with the filming of *Ned*

Kelly. It quickly became clear that the film was not going to be as successful as *Performance* nor as much fun to work on. Not only was Mick inevitably under the weather because of his unhappiness at Brian's death and his concern for Marianne, but the script was uninspiring and the rest of the cast did nothing to improve it. And Tony Richardson, the director, was more difficult than Donald Cammell to work with, and less exciting. Marianne spent most of the two months that they were in Australia convalescing at Mount St Michael Hospital outside Sydney. The Australian police were interested to know whether Marianne had been legally in possession of the tablets with which she tried to do herself in. They were, finally, convinced after her doctor in London wrote to confirm that he had prescribed them for her. There was still more drama. Mick nearly lost a hand during the shooting of *Ned Kelly* – a gun backfired during one sequence, and the wound needed sixteen stitches.

The summer could hardly have been more eventful. Marlon, the son of Keith and Anita, was born on 10 August. On 18 July Senator Edward Kennedy drove his car off a bridge as he was returning home from a party, and four days later the first men walked on the moon. In June a gigantic free pop festival was held at Woodstock, in upstate New York, and in August half a million people gathered on the Isle of Wight for England's own little Woodstock. In the same month the Soviet Union invaded Czechoslovakia, to put an end to the liberalising reforms which seemed to be going on there.

Mick and Marianne returned home in September, and Mick was immediately plunged into work on the American tour, which began on 17 October. In September *Through the Past Darkly*, a collection of hits in memory of Brian, was released. The dedication read:

> When this you see, remember me
> And bear me in your mind
> Let all the world say what they may
> Speak of me as you find.

The American tour was their first since the European tour in early 1967 when they had been searched at every national frontier. Keith was delighted to be touring again, even though the baby was only two months old. Mick was still fairly preoccupied with trying to sort out Marianne. They had spent a quiet holiday in Indonesia on the way back from Australia, but she was still frail after the drug overdose. In October the band moved to Los Angeles, to begin the tour. The first date was on 7 November, in Fort Collins, Colorado. America had changed as much as England since the Stones had played there last. The change struck Keith, and he talked about it later in a *Rolling Stone* interview: 'Before, America was a real fantasy land. It was still Walt Disney and hamburger dates and when you came back in 1969 it wasn't anymore. Kids were really into what was going on in their country. I remember watching Goldwater-Johnson in '64 and it was a complete little sham. But by the time it came Nixon's turn in '68 people were concerned in a really different way.'

Reactions to the Stones varied during the tour. In many places it was like the old days – marauding maenads mobbing them and having to be beaten off the stage. But, as Mick said to a reporter during the tour, 'On the coast, and a lot of other places, there was a very large cross-section of people, all kinds of people, and they listened. A lot of them did. That was new in some ways.' As the tour progressed the Stones began appearing on stage later and later – at Inglewood Forum in Los Angeles they were four hours late. But their performance also improved – the first concert had been ragged, unpolished, almost a rehearsal. Mick admitted it: 'Compared to the way we sounded later along, we were terrible in San Francisco. Ragged. By the time we got to Detroit, I'd say, it was like one hundred per cent improvement.' Whatever the fans thought, the concert promoters were beginning to hate the Rolling Stones, and especially Mick. The Stones were outrageously greedy, demanding hefty guaranteed minimum payments for each concert as well as unusually high percentages of the gross takings. And the

173

promoters were appalled by the Stones playing hours late – it made the task of the administrators much more difficult.

As the tour progressed, and the Rolling Stones were given massive publicity wherever they went, Mick became increasingly determined to do his own gigantic free North American concert. He was peeved by the idea that Warner Brothers had filmed Woodstock, and were going to release it with a barrage of publicity. More people had come to the Hyde Park concert, but film of that had only been seen on television. He decided that if the Stones were to hold a free concert on the West Coast they could rush-release a film of it, and so scoop *Woodstock*. The concert would be held, he decided, around 6 December. Sam Cutler, the tour manager, tried to arrange for it to be held in San Francisco's Golden Gate Park, or failing that, in any of the city's other parks. News of the concert first broke the week before Thanksgiving. The tour promoters had been keen not to publicise it too soon in case it sabotaged the commercial concerts.

The tour was disrupted again, for Mick, when the band had reached Texas, by the story in the newspapers that Marianne had gone to Rome with Mario Schifano, a painter and film director whom she was describing as her 'prince charming'. Even though Mick was enjoying everything that was offered to him on tour, just as much as the next rock star, he was still outraged that Marianne should have publicly cuckolded him. But however angry he was, he had other things to deal with for the moment. As the tour progressed all America was talking about the planned free concert. If the reaction to the commercial concerts was anything to go by, the free one would be the biggest thing America had ever seen. In New York 6000 people were waiting outside the box office, two hours before it was due to open, on the first day the tickets for the Stones' Madison Square concerts went on sale. Within twelve hours the two shows were sold out – 30,936 seats. Mick's performance, once he had loosened up, was better than it had ever been on this tour. The *Beggars Banquet* material was ideal. He seemed far more

174

powerful than ever before: demonic, camp, androgynous, pumping energy relentlessly. Mick Taylor was fitting in nicely – he still seemed to be concentrating too hard on stage, but he had begun to wear make-up and snort cocaine during the tour. And now that he was not having to carry Brian, Keith had more freedom, and was enjoying himself.

Jo Bergman and Chip Monck, the lighting man turned stage-manager and production genius, spent weeks trying to find a suitable place for the free concert, and organising it. At such short notice even buying the wood to build the stage was going to be difficult. And Mick believed, until the last minute, that it was going to be possible to use the Golden Gate Park. He kept saying, and the Stones' satellites kept saying, that they always organised everything at the last minute and it always turned out fine. Mick had great faith in Jo and in Chip Monck and, in any case, since he was zapping around America, he was not involved in the minute-by-minute difficulties of setting up the concert. The tour was being phenomenally successful. Mick was on the cover of *Newsweek*. Everywhere there were riots for tickets. Every news bulletin, while the Stones were in the States, carried news of their progress. It was like the biggest royal tour anyone had ever seen. The Stones were seen arriving at airports, or being mobbed on stage, or answering with laconic scorn the eager questions of provincial newsmen.

Everything was going well. At the end of the Madison Square concerts thousands of pink rose petals showered from the ceiling onto Mick. There was plenty to celebrate. Allen Klein estimated that the tour had made $2 million, after twenty appearances. The Stones themselves ended up sharing about $1 million between them. *Let it Bleed* had been released to coincide with the tour and was also selling well. Herb Goldfarb, of London Records, said that it was the biggest selling record in the company's history. Before the tour began advance orders were almost one million. Once the tour started, that million quickly sold.

But still the struggle was going on to set up the free concert. By 2 December (four days before the concert was due to be held) the best site available seemed to be the Sears Point Raceway, a thousand-acre site about an hour's drive north of San Francisco, at the top of San Francisco Bay. It seemed that the troubles were over – it had suitable access roads, water and parking, and it would be possible to provide other services. But Sam Cutler is said to have objected to the site because it was 'aesthetically unpleasing'. Other advisers were aware that Governor Ronald Reagan or one of his political friends might enjoy making an example of this concert, and busting it. The San Francisco Parks Department had already temporarily prohibited rock concerts because of violence at previous events. But the Stones still hoped to be allowed to use the Golden Gate Park. Now there were hourly radio bulletins on the state of planning for the concert. Mick could hardly be blamed if he felt that the world was waiting with baited breath for the outcome. Thousands were ready to flock to wherever the Stones would play, the band was ready, the Maysles Brothers, the official film-makers, were ready. Other preparations could be made. All they had to do was settle the site. It seemed as though it would have to be Sears Point after all. The plans went ahead. Jerry Garcia, of Grateful Dead, suggested that they should use the San Francisco chapter of the Hell's Angels as stewards. They had done a good job at the Hyde Park concert, and they were good accessories for the current demonic image. They agreed to come and guard the stage in return for $500-worth of beer. But then there was another difficulty. Sharp employees of the company who had put on the Los Angeles concerts, Concert Associates, discovered that Filmways, their parent company, also owned the Sears Point racetrack. Within hours the Stones were told that they could no longer use the land without paying for it – it would cost them $125,000. But Filmways would accept, in payment, the right to distribute the Maysles Brothers film, so long as they were also indemnified against possible danger to the track. Concert Associates had been feeling disgruntled with the Stones because they had behaved badly when they had played Los Angeles.

Mick was outraged by this latest development, and refused to pay for the use of the racetrack. As radio stations continued to report this latest development, a local businessman by the name of Dick Carter offered the use of his stock-car raceway, Altamont, free. He hoped that the publicity would be good for business. Agreement was finally reached less than twenty-four hours before the show was due to start. There were people saying that it was not going to be possible to supply food, washing and first aid facilities, and lavatories for the expected crowds in the time left. But such people always warned of disaster. Woodstock had confounded all the prophets of unpleasantness by passing off almost peacefully. The fans began heading for Altamont as soon as the site was announced.

The Stones themselves were not even in San Francisco. They were recording at the Muscle Shoals Studios in Alabama. Bill Graham, the rock promoter, had been so appalled by Mick's behaviour during the tour that he had said, 'Mick Jagger may be great as a performer, but he's an egotistical creep as a person.' He now added his voice to those concerned about the concert. 'They can't do it, they should call it off or it'll explode in their faces.'

6 December was a Saturday. Chip Monck had worked the miracles that had been expected of him, and had managed to transport the technical equipment and everything necessary to build the stage at Altamont by Friday afternoon. By 9 pm it had been built. Floodlights fuelled by diesel-engines were hauled into place, and the technicians carried on working through the night. There were still wrecked cars lying around from the stock-car racing, and already the first fans were sleeping, or smoking, or getting in the way. Some played touch football under the floodlights. Among the first arrivals were a dozen portable lavatories and most of the West Coast's drug dealers. The track seemed vast that night, as the crew

slaved away and hippies huddled round campfires. Mick arrived at about 2 am, by helicopter, to see what was going on. He wandered around the site in a red velvet cape and cap, talking to a few reporters and fans. A girl gave him her scarf, another just kissed him then ran off, yelping with excitement.

The local press were as excited as anyone at the thought that they were going to have their own Woodstock. Having run the story of the preparations constantly for the last week or so, they were now determined to cover the event itself. At 3 am on Saturday radio KFRC told its listeners that the traffic was backed up twenty miles in each direction and that access to Altamont was completely closed off. In fact the roads were then clear – there were no traffic problems. But traffic jams had been a feature of Woodstock. So Altamont had to have bigger and better jams.

At about 7 am the Hell's Angels allowed the crowds who had been assembling at the top of the hills to go down into the valley where the stage had been built. They began to swarm in from every direction. Soon there really were traffic jams stretching six or seven miles away down the freeway. The occasional motorbike weaved through the cars, but no one else had much hope of driving to Altamont. Hundreds of people began ditching their cars on the road and getting out to walk. Some locals did very nicely out of charging $5 a head to fans who wanted to be guided to the site through the fields. It wasn't such a rip-off. Hundreds of those who didn't take them up on the offer never got there; they trudged away across the hills in the wrong direction. Helicopter charter companies made a lot of money out of Altamont and hot-dog sellers did even better. The day was warm and clear. But already it was evident that things might go wrong. Cheap wine, beer, every sort of pills and disorganisation combined to create an atmosphere that was already getting rough. The crowd was having to queue for everything – food, water, lavatories – except dope. The drug dealers seemed to be the only providers who had done their job properly. By noon 300,000 people were at Altamont, waiting for the Rolling

Stones. At about this time someone had the bright idea of giving tablets of acid, mostly laced with speed, to the Angels.

Santana played first. They were late, and there was already a feeling of violence in the air. Most of the acid at Altamont was probably of the ordinary street quality. But some of it was undoubtedly very bad. And the sense of violence engendered by the Hell's Angels seemed to combine with the contagious effect of the first few hellish trips to create a feeling of slaughterhouse terror. Most people hoped that it would evaporate once the music began. After Santana's first number a young man tried to get past a contingent of Angels, towards the stage. His face was kicked in and he lay for the next few hours where he had fallen. The Angels also started beating up a couple of people who had taken their clothes off during Santana's playing. They beat a photographer, who tried to record the event, about the head with pool cues, so that he needed thirteen stitches. Santana knew that the show had to go on, even though their next song was interrupted by a couple of Hell's Angels rushing across the stage to beat someone up.

Jefferson Airplane played next. Soon there seemed to be more Angels on stage than musicians. It was becoming increasingly difficult to tell why each bout of murderous violence had erupted, but each sent waves of helpless terror through those in the crowd who were tripping on LSD. The others were pretty scared too. As the group was beginning 'Somebody to Love' a young black man, shirtless, jumped onto the stage. Several of the Angels beat him about the head and back with pool cues and threw him down into the audience, where their comrades carried on the good work. Marty Balin leapt off the stage, into the audience, to try to prevent the security guards from murdering a member of the audience. The Hell's Angels then beat him unconscious. The rest of the group just carried on without him – no one could hear them anyway. Paul Kantner asked what the Angels thought they were doing, and why they had slugged a member of his band. Paul then nearly got the same treatment, but the Angel who most wanted to get him couldn't quite reach him. By now Marty Balin had come round and, since the stage was marginally safer than the audience, had staggered back on stage.

Already the few medics were having trouble coping. Medical facilities were one of the things that there had not really been time to organise. Richard Fine, the chairman of the Medical Committee for Human Rights, a volunteer group which provided medical aid at San Francisco events, complained that 'we as well as everyone else in the crowd were exploited by the promoters'. He said that they had been promised telephone communications and a helicopter, neither of which they received. 'We got shitty support from the people running the thing, who didn't realise what was crucial from a medical standpoint, and wouldn't give us the authority to do such things as set up a workable evacuation procedure. And we had no time to mobilise community people for help with bad trips. It was just piss-poor planning. A lot of the bad trips were violent because there was so much violence in the air.' It was now nearly 3 pm, and Mick Jagger, Mick Taylor and part of the entourage arrived in the first of the Rolling Stones' helicopters. A youth rushed up, as Angels tried to clear the way, and began screaming 'I hate you, I hate you' to Jagger, and punching him in the face. Jagger and Mick Taylor were quickly hustled into the trailer that was their dressing-room. The Flying Burrito Brothers played next and the turmoil seemed to quieten down. It is not clear how much news of the pandemonium outside filtered into the Stones' trailer. Mick later attacked the other musicians who had played at Altamont for not keeping him informed, but other reports suggest that they were constantly told of the afternoon's horrors. Mick ventured outside during the Flying Burrito Brothers set, but had retreated into the trailer again by the time Crosby, Stills, Nash and Young came on. Even if he was told of events, it is not surprising that the full impact did not strike Mick at once. Everywhere the Stones had ever played there had been riots and violence.

It was getting late. The last of the warm-up bands had played.

By the time Crosby, Stills, Nash and Young had finished bodies on stretches were being passed over the heads of the crowd. It was getting cold. Several fires had been lit, even though the only fuel was garbage – paper cups and plastic bags and cigarette packets and packing cases. (The fence of the race-track had gone for fire-wood the night before.) 'Flickering silhouettes of people trying to find warmth around the blazing trash reminded one of the medieval paintings of tortured souls in the Dance of Death,' a *Rolling Stone* correspondent wrote. 'It was in this setting that Mick sang his song about how groovy it is to be Satan. Never has it been sung in a more appropriate setting.'

At about 5 o'clock a dozen or so Angels drove their bikes up to the stage. Miraculously, they got there almost without incident. Sonny Barger, President of the Oakland Chapter of the Hell's Angels, described it later: 'We come down on our bikes, because we were told we were supposed to park in front of the stage, and so like when we started coming down through the crowd everybody was outa sight got up and moved and we come down in low gear and didn't try to run into anybody or do any of that kind of thing. Everybody got up really nice, some people offered us drinks on the way down and like . . . we must have come into approximate contact with at least a thousand people and outa them thousand we had trouble with one person . . . one broad jumped up and said some-thing that pertained to a four-letter word and then Angels and one of the Angels stopped his bike and he had his old lady on the back and he said, "Are you gonna let them talk about Angels like that?" and she jumped off the bike and slapped the other broad that said that that was in the crowd and got back on the bike and we pro-ceeded down with no problem.'

Still the Stones did not appear. One of the Angels assigned to guarding the Stones personally told a journalist: 'Jagger's so vain with the whole scene. We kept telling him, "Hey, you know what? You got a half million fuckin' people out there that made you what you are, and here you are, stalling!" The man says, "Well, my make-up looks better at night.'' Elsewhere, too, the Angels were getting restless. There was a spot of bother when some of the Angels' bikes got kicked, as Sonny Barger explained later: 'I don't wanna do it, man, but I'm a violent cat. I ain't no cop. I ain't never gonna police nothin'. I just went there to sit on the front of the stage and drink beer and have a good time, like we was told. But when they started kickin' our bikes, man, that started it. I ain't no peace creep, man.' So a few heads got mashed. There are things you just don't do to a Hell's Angel. As Barger put it: 'Ain't nobody gonna get my bike. Anybody tries that is gonna get got. And they got got.' It wasn't as though he pretended that the Angels were angels. 'Now I ain't saying nothing about no Angel hit anybody. I know some of them hit people.' The doctors were getting cross, too, because the organisers refused to turn the lights on so that they could patch up some of the wounded. To do so would diminish the drama of the Stones' entry.

Eventually the Stones came out to play. There wasn't much room for them, since there were about a hundred other people on the stage. Mick had to ask the Stones to step back a few paces so that he would have room to prance around the stage. It was not the most exciting 'Jumping Jack Flash' ever, but Mick's orange and black satin cape was impressively demonic. A fat, naked girl tried to climb onto the stage. Five Angels began to pummel her. Mick said: 'I'm sure it doesn't take all of you to take care of this.' The crowd tittered, and it was left to one of them to smash a pool cue single-handedly over her head. The rest smouldered angrily at Jagger. One began to dance alongside him on stage, mimicking his now nervous mincing. Another, only a few feet away, smiled at him homicidally.

In the middle of 'Sympathy for the Devil' yet another little battle broke out, this time about twenty feet from where Jagger was standing. The Angels were beating up a black man. He seems to have tried to approach the stage. But some witnesses insisted that the Angels just began beating him up because they did not like the look of him, and because he had a pretty white girlfriend with him. He tried to run away, was followed and stabbed in the back. He pulled a gun out of his jacket. The Angels wrenched the gun away from him and stabbed him again. He fell to his knees and one of the Angels held him steady by the shoulders and started kicking him in the face. He keeled over as another began kicking him in the ribs. According to some of the 300,000 people who were there, he went down muttering, 'I wasn't going to shoot you.' 'Why did you have a gun, then?' asked an Angel, picking up a dustbin and smashing it over his head. A few girls were screaming, and a few people seemed to be going mad, presumably having bad acid trips. Someone had the idea of helping the black man, but the Angels wouldn't let him get near enough. After a minute or two the Angels walked away. People nearby, drenched in blood, turned him over and noticed a 'big hole' in his back. Someone picked up his arms and someone else his feet. They tried to carry him to the stage, so that they could attract attention and get help for him, but the Angels guarding the stage wouldn't let him through. Wherever they turned the Angels blocked their path. About fifteen minutes later they got him to the Red Cross tent behind the stage. Mick appealed from the stage for a doctor. Some witnesses on stage later claimed to have seen the man, whose name was Meredith Hunter, point a gun at Mick Jagger. If they were telling the truth it seems likely that what they saw was the gun accidentally pointing towards the stage as it was grabbed from him. The music broke down. 'Brothers and sisters, come on now. That means everybody just cool it. We can cool out, everybody. Everybody be cool now. Come on.' The Angels on stage were mocking Mick now, laughing at him, menacingly. 'Everybody just cool down,' he went on. 'Is there anybody there who's been hurt? Okay, I think we're cool, we can groove. We always have something very funny happen when we start that number.' They began to play again, limply. The Angels hurled a body across the stage. Mick was babbling camply into the microphone. The crowd was not under his control. He began to whimper. The Angels jeered and growled. In front of the stage an Angel revved his Harley Davidson. Most of the crowd could not even see Jagger by this time – he was lost among the Angels. Those who could saw a sad, scared little figure with thin legs and a tatty cloak instead of the proud Prince of Darkness. Knives flashes and billiard cues flailed wildly in the crowd. Those who were not killing each other began shouting and booing.

Keith stepped forward and, pointing at some Angels beating a man's head in, ordered, 'Either those cats cool it, man, or we don't play.' The beating, smashing, pummelling carnage went on. 'Keep it cool! Hey, if you don't cool it, you ain't gonna hear no music!' An Angel wrenched the microphone away from him, and bellowed 'Fuck you' into it. Mick Taylor stood still, petrified. Bill and Charlie were hidden from most of the crowd among the hordes on stage. Only Keith seemed unterrified. The Stones pulled themselves together. 'Stray Cat Blues' went nearly peacefully. Then 'Under My Thumb'. Another body sailed across the stage. Sam Cutler, the supposed master of ceremonies, took control of the stage. 'First of all, everyone is going to get to the side of the stage who's on it now, aside from the Stones. Please, everyone. We need a doctor and an ambulance, right away. Just sit down and keep calm and relax. We can get it together.' The audience's heckling was unmistakable. But the Rolling Stones started up again and, amazingly, got better and better. Mick took a slug from a bottle of Jack Daniels, and waved the bottle at the crowd. 'One more drink to you all.' Keith had pulled them back together, was now pounding out megaton rock and roll. Mick was on top again. Suddenly it seemed as though the violence could be summoned and laid by him. During 'Satisfaction' the group were showered with roses. They thundered through 'Honky Tonk Women' into 'Street Fighting Man', an appropriate finale. 'We're gonna kiss you goodbye,' Mick yelled, blowing kisses to the crowd as he left the stage, before beating a hasty retreat back to the Huntington Hotel in San Francisco.

184

At about midnight a 1964 Plymouth Sedan drove straight into a ring of people sitting round a campfire. The car scrunched across the chests of two young men, killing them, and carried on. Two other people suffered head and internal injuries in the hit-and-run. There were no precise figures for the casualties since the medical facilities were so disorganised. A fourth person died, by drowning in an irrigation canal. The volunteers said that they had treated dozens of skull lacerations and fractures as well as other injuries. Dr Richard Baldwin, who coordinated the medical treatment, estimated that 'with all our units we probably treated about 700 freak-outs, plus all those we never saw that were handled by friends in the crowd'.

Astonishingly, the newspapers did not seem to have noticed what had happened. The next day's *San Francisco Examiner* headlined, '300,000 say it with music'. The story mentioned the four deaths and yet said that, 'But for the stabbing, all appeared peaceful at the concert.' For nearly a week the concert continued to be described as if it had been another Woodstock, where there just happened to have been a death. All reports insisted that there had been four births during the concert as well, as if that somehow evened up the score. However, none of the volunteer medical staff saw any new-born babies, and none showed up at any of San Francisco's hospitals claiming to have been born at Altamont. Ron Naso of KFRC News described Altamont: 'We think it was beautiful. Things went smoothly and people were happy. When you have a big amount of people together a couple of things happen, unfortunately; it's nothing anybody can do anything about. After all, look what happens in Vietnam every day.' There were others who clung to a blithely optimistic attitude. Sam Cutler appealed on the wireless, the day after the concert, for 'the beautiful people of San Francisco' to come and clear away the tons of garbage they had left behind. It was the *San Francisco Chronicle* which first wrote accurately about Altamont, unsparingly describing the chaos and violence. The truth was picked up by other papers as witnesses and photographs began to appear. Everyone had their say about the debacle. 'Leo H of Los Angeles' wrote to *Rolling Stone*:

Sirs,
 To those who know, it's been obvious that the Stones, or at least some of them, have been involved in the practice of Magick ever since the *Satanic Majesties Request* album. But there at least the color was more white than black. Since then the hue has gone steadily darker and darker.
 At Altamont he appeared in his full Majesty with his full consort of demons, the Hell's Angels. It was just a few days before the Winter Solstice when the forces of darkness are at their most powerful. The moon was in Scorpio, which is the time of the month when the Universal vibration is at its most unstable. It was held in a place dedicated to destruction through motion. Then Mick comes on only after it is dark enough for the red lights to work their magick.
 I don't know if they were truly aware of what they were doing or not. I feel that they are sadder and wiser from the experience. But an agonising price was paid for the lesson. And we were all guilty because we have all eaten of the cake the Stones baked.

Not everyone felt that the blame should be distributed. Bill Graham, for example: 'I'll ask you what right you had, Mr Jagger, to walk out on stage every night with your Uncle Sam hat, throw it down with complete disdain, and leave this country with $1.2 million? And what right did you have in going through with this free festival? And you couldn't tell me you didn't know the way it would have come off. What right did you have to leave the way you did, thanking everybody for a wonderful time and the Angels for helping out? He's now in his home country somewhere – what did he leave behind throughout the country? Every gig he was late. Every fucking gig he made the promoter and the people bleed.

What right does this god have to descend on this country this way?
... But you know what is the greatest tragedy to me? That cunt is a great entertainer.'

Meanwhile, back in Cheyne Walk, Mick was bracing himself for another court appearance.

Chapter Eight

Mick and Marianne had to appear in Marylebone Magistrates' Court on 19 December. Unlike most people who were approached by bent policemen suggesting that they should buy their way out of drug trouble, Mick publicly accused the man in question of corruption, in court. The policeman concerned said that he was going to sue Mick for libel, but then dropped the case. Mick's allegations were investigated by Scotland Yard, and were dismissed. But the policeman was subsequently moved out of the drugs squad. He had exercised something like a reign of terror in London during the previous few years. But Mick had done himself no good by trying to call attention to his corruption; he was fined £200 with £52/10/- costs. Marianne was acquitted.

After Christmas Marianne and Mick were reconciled. The fling with Mario Schifano was over. But it was obvious to everyone that she was in a bad way. According to friends, 'She was always falling about, drunk and doped, having to be carried into and out of restaurants, and falling into the soup plate sixteen times.' 'Marianne was strung out on smack constantly, and always trying to hide it from Mick. But it must have been obvious to him.' Mick seems to have been very patient with her. Christopher Gibbs: 'Mick has always been good with the afflicted. He's very gentle and takes a lot of trouble with them. I've seen him looking after Keith and Brian whenever they were in a mess, which was quite often.' Even so Mick and Marianne now had violent rows in public. She complained that Mick neglected her, that he was always out either recording or attending to the Stones' business affairs, and she was left alone with nothing to do. When he was made to feel guilty about it he would just shower her with presents. But she also admitted that it was her own fault that she was a junkie. Mick now allowed himself some relief from looking after Marianne. For some time he had been having an affair with Marsha Hunt, an American actress. Marsha had been seen at the free Hyde Park Concert, wearing white buckskin, and she had been backstage at the Stones' Christmas Concert at the Lyceum on 14 December. Her flat in St John's Wood provided a haven from the tempestuousness of Cheyne Walk and at Christmas, when Marianne had been away, Marsha had joined Jagger there. She gave him a basset hound puppy, which he called Grits. The unfortunate animal was eventually moved from Cheyne Walk to Stargroves, where Maldwin Thomas looked after him. He was, according to Maldwin, 'a wonderful dog, but Mick never appreciated him.'

Mick needed peace. Altamont and its aftermath had been shattering for him. Months later he continued to be reviled in the English and American press for allowing it to have happened. Just as Woodstock was regarded as a triumph for the alternative, non-capitalistic way of life, so Altamont became a symbol of the chaos and terror bred by anarchy. It was unfair. Good luck had contributed to the success of Woodstock, just as bad luck had dogged Altamont. The Stones' organisation had been appallingly irresponsible in allowing the concert to take place without proper preparation. And in this case, as in so many others, the 'Stones' organisation' meant people who had been carrying out the personal whims of Mick Jagger. It was Mick who was determined at any cost to have the San Francisco concert and rush the film of it out before *Woodstock*. But he had not been around while it was being organised – he had been recording in Florida. There were others who should have realised that the necessary preparations could not be made. Now, more than he had ever been before, Mick was the world's bad boy. The demonic image that he had been revelling in during 1969 made it all much worse. Throughout the tour newspapers had talked about the Satanism, the decadence, the drug-taking and the sadistic overtones of the Rolling Stones. The great songs that Mick had written in the last couple of years were taken to be autobiographical by outraged parents and captivated children alike. The Mick Jagger everyone knew was 'Jumping Jack Flash', a 'Street Fighting Man' with the Satanic leanings of 'Sympathy for the Devil'. But it was all partly accidental – the whole point was that Mick knew that there was nothing a poor boy could do 'except to sing for a rock 'n' roll band'.

Everything seemed to conspire against him. The recent conviction confirmed him in the public eye as a dope-fiend. And even accidents worked against him. Ossie Clark designed an orange and black shirt that was, he says, not intended to look devilish. But it was one of the many outfits that Mick wore during the tour that observers interpreted as intentional Satan costumes. And the problems that resulted from Altamont were not just adverse criticism. Landowners in the Altamont area filed a suit against the Stones claiming damages for the destruction of their land. There was talk of Meredith Hunter's mother suing for damages as well (she eventually filed her suit in October). The Stones themselves announced that they were to sue Sears Point International Raceway for $10 million, for breach of contract and fraud, which had meant that the Stones had needed to change the site of the concert at the last minute.

Work was still in progress at Stargroves, the country house that Mick had bought some time before. Christopher Gibbs was supervising it with Nicky Johnson, an architect friend, and the inevitable teams of quantity surveyors, contractors and so on. 'But then I had to try and feed back to Mick these terribly interesting decisions we had made about the plumbing or whatever it was. And he wasn't desperately interested in it always.' Mark Palmer and his co-fake-gypsy, Maldwin Thomas, had spent the winter before at Stargroves, still living in their horse-drawn caravan. The place had been briefly cheered up by their presence. Before they arrived, and after they left, it was abandoned, except for the builders. Mick never moved into the house. He would go down for the occasional day or two, but would then appear to forget about the house again for weeks. Christopher Gibbs: 'And then Marianne had brilliant ideas about what to do with the garden which never actually happened. She was always saying, "I want a very complicated herb garden here," and then some poor boy would be made to draw up some very difficult parterre in some particular place. There was a gardener called Mr White. He had been there before, he was almost taken over as fixture and fitting, and nobody ever told him what to do. So he just pottered on, sort of vainly patching up the greenhouse.' By the beginning of 1970 Mark Palmer had decided to give up his vagrant life. Several winters on the road had made him ill, and he was persuaded by Christopher Gibbs that life in a fixed abode might be preferable to none. Maldwin, who had been a hairdresser before he became a vagabond, went to work at Todd's, a London hairdressers, where Mick had his hair cut. Maldwin was already friendly with Mick. As the caravan idled around England, following the lay lines and occasionally pulling into a friend's house, Mick, Keith and Brian had occasionally turned up in their big cars for a picnic. They had been impressed by the caravan as an experiment, but put off by its discomfort. Mick asked Maldwin whether he knew anyone who could be persuaded to live at Stargroves and look after it. Since Maldwin hated living in London he offered to go himself. So the house at least had a caretaker. Maldwin lived in a converted stable, and helped to organise the builders and run the house. His life was made much more difficult by Mick's reluctance to pay bills. Shirley Arnold recalls frantic telephone calls to the office whenever Maldwin was having an especially hard time talking the workmen into carrying on even though they had not been paid. 'It often took three months to get Mick to cough up the money to pay the men,' Maldwin says. So naturally the turnover of builders was brisk.

Joe and Eva Jagger occasionally visited Mick at Stargroves. On several memorable occasions they stayed in the house while Mick was away, and they eventually moved in for long periods at a time. They seem to have taken to heart the role of the landowner's parents, and treated everyone who was working about the place with seigneurial disdain. Poor Mr White was kept standing outside when he went to the house to talk to them. He had been able to cope with the peculiar visitors and the parterres, but this was too much: he took umbrage and quit. Other people working at Stargroves also found Mick's parents tiresome. Maldwin Thomas finally left because of them. Chris Jagger also came to stay. He was over four years younger than Mick, so in 1963, when the Rolling Stones' success began, he had been fifteen. His adolescence had been dominated by his brother's success. All his life he had been acknowledged by people who knew them to be less intelligent than Mick. He had attended the same primary school, but had failed the 11+. The Jaggers had sent him to a local private school where he had enjoyed a certain cachet as the younger brother of a pop star. Later he made friends with many of the people Mick knew. He took part in a demonstration at World's End in Chelsea after Brian Jones' first drug conviction, during which he was arrested, along with about a dozen other people. Steve Abrams, who also took part in the demonstration, says: 'The Chelsea police were very excited by having him in tow. But they couldn't figure out whether or not it was Mick. One after another they came up and asked me whether it was Mick, and I kept saying, "No, it's his brother, Chris." But they weren't sure whether to believe me and they all kept coming up to have another look at him. They were probably relieved in the end that it wasn't Mick because there was nothing really to charge him with, and it would have meant fuss in the newspapers.' Mick was generous to his brother. Chris at one stage followed the hippy trail to India, and would repeatedly telex to the Rolling Stones office, asking for subsidies. And, according to Shirley Arnold, Mick always authorised them to transfer £50 out to the nearest bank, for Chris to collect. And eventually Chris and Vivienne, the wife he brought back from India, moved into Stargroves.

Stargroves fulfilled one useful function for Mick. It was a handy place to take his on-the-side girlfriends. Maldwin was woken up late one night by Mick hammering on the window. 'Maldwin! Maldwin! Come on! I've got a chick out here. It's Caroline Coon. George Harrison gave her £5000 for Release last week, so she thinks I'm going to do the same. She'll find out otherwise soon enough.'

In May 1970 Prince Rupert Loewenstein and Mick decided that the Rolling Stones were going to have to go into tax exile. Their financial affairs were in chaos. Despite all the money they had earned, they were in danger of being declared bankrupt because of the fortune they owed the Inland Revenue. A great deal of money seemed to have evaporated during the last seven years. On 30 July the Stones told Allen Klein officially, through their lawyers, that neither he nor Abkco (his company) nor anyone acting on their behalf had any right to negotiate contracts on behalf of the group. They issued a press release, making the same announcement. On 31 July their contract with Decca expired, and Prince Rupert Loewenstein speeded up his negotiations with other companies. They were to form their own recording company, but they needed one of the industry's giants to distribute the records. Prince Rupert was looking, on their behalf, for a contract that guaranteed at least $5 million. In the meantime, the five Stones could no longer afford to live in England. They had to be out of the country by the beginning of the next tax year, in April. They all decided to settle in France, at least for the time being. So the Rolling Stones office began to look for houses for them all to rent.

The move provided Marianne with an excuse to leave Mick permanently. 'She'd been turned into a junkie wreck by Mick. She had to get away from him. He had terrible, destructive power over her,' a friend says. Marianne said later in an interview with the *Sunday Times* that she had to leave because of her growing predilection for heroin, although she was not yet addicted: 'I truly didn't want to damage Mick any more than I had. People always assume I became a junkie while I was still with him, but I didn't. It was still an experiment I was making with my eyes wide open. I started on heroin knowing exactly what I was doing. I did love Mick very much, and he loved me. But I felt that an era was over and nothing could ever be the same again.' Once she had decided not to move to France Marianne left Cheyne Walk with Nicholas and went to live with her mother, in the cottage in Berkshire that Mick had bought for her. Both Mick and Marianne knew that the separation was inevitable.

Mick was not without company. There was Marsha Hunt, who was having Mick's baby. She has always insisted that both she and Mick intended to have the child, even though they never lived together. Since *Hair* Marsha had been a star herself, in a small way, and she liked living alone. There were also the one or two or three nighters, for most of whom their one or two or three nights were an important experience, even if Mick himself couldn't even tell them apart. According to Christopher Gibbs, 'It was like other people with Chinese waiters. They would come up to him in restaurants and he wouldn't think he'd ever seen them before. They used to get terribly upset about it.' A longer affair was with Suki Poitier, who had been Brian Jones's last girlfriend but one before he died. There was a pretty Californian – a Catherine James. Mick seemed to like American girls. But for a while there seemed to be no real Marianne substitute.

Mick had serious problems. In the summer *Ned Kelly* was

released. After seeing it Mick was so horrified he burst into tears. He was in Donald Cammell's house in Old Church Street, just round the corner from Cheyne Walk. He had apparently known that *Ned Kelly* was bad during filming. But the finished film exceeded his worst fears. *Performance* had still not been released, because of wrangles with Warner Brothers, so that was the first time that anyone had seen Mick acting. In the film Ned Kelly, released after serving an unjust prison sentence, returned to the run-down family homestead to find his brother in prison, his sister unhappily married and his mother hooked up with a horse rustler. After a series of confrontations with the local bigwig Ned decided to go crooked. He organised a gang of friends and relatives and set to work. His mother was arrested on a charge of attempted murder, and Ned offered to give himself up in exchange for her freedom. The deal was turned down – the authorities were determined to get Ned anyway. The gang shot three policemen. There was a shootout at Glenrowan where most of the gang were killed, but Ned was taken alive and hanged. The plot, which came more or less directly from life, was all right. But most critics found the script trite, and blamed Tony Richardson, the director, for failing to give the film direction. They also mauled Mick. 'Jagger delivers his lines with an almost catatonic lack of expression, battling with an Irish accent in which he would seem to have been coached word for word without yet graduating to sentences.' 'When he puts on the home-made armour he looks rather like a cut-price sardine . . . he's just about as lethal as last week's lettuce.' The cattlemen of Glenrowan, in Victoria, were asked what they thought of Jagger as the national hero. 'He's too bloody scrawny. Ned was a real good fighter and was nearly six foot . . . This bloke Jagger has shoulders like a Coke bottle. He looks too cissy . . .' Mick was as frank about the film as the cattlemen were about him: '*Ned Kelly*! That was a load of shit. I only made it because I had nothing else to do. I knew Tony Richardson was a reasonable director and I thought he'd make a reasonable film. The thing is you never know until you do it whether a film will turn out to be a load of shit and if it does all you can say is, "Well, that was a load of shit," and try to make sure you don't do anything like it again.'

It was fortunate that Warner Brothers had now decided that *Performance* could be released. The censors filleted it, and Warners themselves were even sterner. Donald Cammell and Mick were so angry when they first saw the cut version that they sent a telegram to the president of Warner Brothers:

Re Performance: This film is about the perverted love affair between Homo Sapiens and Lady Violence. In common with its subject, it is necessarily horrifying, paradoxical and absurd. To make such a film means accepting that the subject is loaded with every taboo in the book.

You seem to want to emasculate (i) the most savage and (ii) the most affectionate scenes in our movie. If 'Performance' does not upset audiences it is nothing. If this fact upsets you, the alternative is to sell it fast and no bullshit. Your misguided censorship will ultimately diminish said audiences both in quality and quantity.

In an interview with the *Guardian* Donald said, 'There are a number of people who hate the film and all it represents. They would love it to be a failure.' A public battle raged for the next few months. Warner Brothers seemed not to be distributing the film properly, although it did well wherever it was shown. But twelve years later Donald's attitude to the cutting of the film seems to have mellowed – 'it doesn't matter, what's left is fine.' *Performance* shocked people, but it was clear that it was a great film. *Time Out* interviewed Mick about his role in *Performance*:

It isn't me really. You just get into the part – that's acting, isn't it? You just get into the feelings of that person and I got into feeling like that. You know you don't want to make any

196

decisions and there's certain things you know you've got to do and there's certain things in your fate that you know. Some people like to sit down and get really involved in the things that they know and some people just want to take what they are and just carry on. Turner was just a person who'd stopped all that and become very tuned into it. After a while you really get into thinking like that and driving everyone crazy. I drove everyone crazy, I think, during that time.

Performance had provided Mick with a persona that he had inhabited throughout 1969. Donald Cammell: 'When Mick understood the sort of picture I was painting of him as an imaginary character called Turner he acted the part, he started to think, it made him more and more conscious of that side of himself, and I think it was very, very good for his work because he got a lot of mileage out of playing the demonic character, the bisexual – he started that long before David Bowie.' But Altamont had been a chastening experience, and afterwards the demonic decadence seemed to be toned down a bit. The people who know and love Mick the best have always recognised that he is constantly playing a part. 'It's not insincerity, it's a lot to do with self-protection. If he presents a well-worked out, slightly overstated image, no one is going to get at the real Mick, who he wants to protect. I think he's actually rather shy, although people wouldn't think so,' an old friend says. Donald Cammell's description of that aspect of Mick is slightly different: 'Because first of all Mick is a great, great artist he can be very sort of blank as a human being, like a lot of good artists are, like the best actors. It's a sort of emptiness, being not quite centred. It's got something to do with narcissism. It's thinking always in a mirror, living in too many worlds.'

For a few months Mick seemed a little lost. Suddenly there was a gap in his life. Having pared down the decadence, he needed something else to replace it. And it was not yet clear what that could be. The lack of a steady girlfriend made it worse, since there

197

was no one to reinforce his identity. 'He could be a different person with each of them. And since he didn't have much respect for any of them he wasn't picking up from them,' a friend who saw a lot of Mick in 1970 says. In the early summer the Stones recorded songs for their next album at Stargroves. But even then Mick did not really move into the house. He would just camp there occasionally. Maldwin Thomas says that 'they used Stargroves as a studio, but not really as a house. I was rather sad about that.' The Stones toured Europe in September, for the first time since 1967. Despite everything that had happened in America, the madness this time was the good old-fashioned sort. Fans ran wild in Helsinki, riot squads were needed in Hamburg, fifty people were arrested in Berlin, and sixty-three were arrested in Milan. On 23 September they played the Olympia Theatre in Paris, where policemen were injured in battle fighting off the fans. There was a party afterwards at the Georges V Hotel, attended by musicians, aides, friends and camp followers. Donald Cammell was among those present. He had been badgered for some time by one of his legion of girlfriends to provide an introduction to Mick Jagger. Donald had had reservations about doing so since he knew the girl in question would go off with Jagger if he did. 'She was an old style courtesan, the sort who was always basically saying to herself, "Well, who's going to be paying the rent five years from now?" But she had set her cap at him, and was determined, so I engineered a meeting. I procured Mick for Bianca.' He took her to the concert, and then to the party afterwards. 'As I introduced them, I said, "You two are going to have a great romance, you were made for each other." ' Mick, Donald, Bianca and another of Donald's girlfriends, an Ethiopian called Myriam, all went back after the show to Donald's flat. They drank a bottle of champagne, and Mick and Bianca spent the night in the downstairs spare bedroom, after rejecting a more companionable suggestion. The next morning they had disappeared before Donald got up. As Donald had foreseen, Mick was stunned by Bianca. For the rest of the tour she travelled with him. The world's press soon noticed Mick Jagger's new girlfriend, and photographers besieged them wherever they went. In Rome Mick punched a photographer who tried to snatch a picture of them, and was fined for assault. In Frankfurt a bodyguard dealt with a photographer while the young lovers made their get away. When they arrived at Heathrow after the tour Mick told the massed reporters that they were 'just good friends'. Bianca's method of evading them was more dramatic: 'I have no name. I do not speak English,' she said.

But Bianca was not a mysterious figure. She had already spent some time in London. Thea Porter, who had been a friend of Mick and Brian Jones for years, knew her of old. She had first met her when she had been staying at the Dorchester with Michael Caine. Bianca and Michael had come into Thea's shop, and 'Bianca went out wearing an enormous Elizabethan jacket with slashed sleeves and a great big doublet in black and silver. After that she came in often and I made her a lot of things. But then when she was with Eddie Barclay I made some things for her, including some harem pants, and took them over to Paris to deliver them. But she never paid me for them, in spite of endless reminders.' There were other people who had known her in Paris, where she had been one of the many rootless foreign girls without means or jobs who were seen in nightclubs, fantastically well dressed. They poured scorn on the idea that she was the daughter of a diplomat or a rich plantation owner, as she variously claimed. And since she had been around for at least seven years, they were amused when she told journalists that she was twenty-one.

Mick decided that he wanted her to be photographed by his old friend David Bailey. She turned up at Bailey's house in Gloucester Avenue. 'She was already being very difficult, she had already become the Jagger lady,' according to an old enemy. Bailey said something that irritated her. She screamed at him, and then added a remark, almost an aside, in a Latin American patois. Caesar, Bailey's enormous black Brazilian housekeeper, overheard, and said something to her, and suddenly the two of them disappeared downstairs to the kitchen. It was an hour and a half before they re-emerged, during which time she kept saying, 'I'm busy, I'm busy,' to anyone who interrupted them. When they came back upstairs Caesar was very excited and kept saying, 'My God, she's wonderful, she's wonderful.' Afterwards Bailey asked him what was so great about her. Caesar said that they had been talking in a rarefied patois that most people would not know. 'The only women who speak like that are tarts.' He said that she came from a very poor background but had somehow managed to get together enough money for the fare to Paris. And since then she had been living on her wits. Mick was aware of the scandal and even made jokes about it. Some years later he had dinner with Maldwin Thomas and Ronnie Lane, also a musician. Ronnie was complaining about the trouble a girl had been giving him. Mick said, 'Come on, Ronnie, I know a great whorehouse in Paris, I'll take you there.' 'I don't want some old scrubber,' Ronnie told him. 'Watch what you're saying,' joked Mick, 'that's where I got my wife from.'

It was inevitable that Bianca made enemies. She looked wonderful and it was obvious that Mick was entranced by her. Keith was appalled by her. The high chic, the lust for Society and the cost of her clothes were anathema to Keith, the eternal, uncompromising rocker. Anita was not mad about her either. Some people suggest that Anita still had an open mind about the possibility of moving in on Mick now that Marianne had gone. To Anita, and to Keith, as well as to friends, it seemed that Bianca would cause a rift between Mick and Keith – and might therefore destroy the band. Mick had always enjoyed smart restuarants and grand houses, and Keith had always been much less interested in that sort of life. But Bianca was exaggerating that part of Mick. She seemed to be leading him into a new mode – they were becoming nearly full-time *saloniers*, seen everywhere, constantly photographed looking immaculate.

In November 1970, not long after Bianca's arrival in London, Marsha Hunt gave birth to a daughter. Mick was reportedly pleased, and collected them both from St Mary's Hospital, Paddington. Marsha spoke to reporters and was photographed with the baby, whom she called Karis. But she refused to say who the father was. Although Mick continued to see Marsha occasionally, Bianca now absorbed most of his energy. He was also planning the Stones' farewell tour of Britain, finishing off the next album and preparing for exile. The London premiere of *Performance* was on 4 January, and it was to be in aid of Release, the charity set up to help people convicted of drug offences. Although the film had been seen in America it had not yet been released in England. Mick had promised to attend the premiere, and on the basis that he was coming Caroline Coon, the organiser of Release, had managed to lure a great many journalists along. By the time the film was scheduled to begin Mick had not shown up, but he sent a message that he would come along afterwards. The night went on, and the journalists grew more restless and Caroline more irritated as messages continued to promise the imminent arrival of Mick. He never did show up, although Caroline wasted a lot of time and money keeping the press happy in a nightclub while they waited for him.

The Stones' first tour of England for five years, in March, was successful, and coincided with the public announcement that the Stones were leaving the country, so many fans felt that it might be the last time they would see them. Marshall Chess, the son of the founder of Chess Records, travelled with them. The Stones were to form their own record label, Rolling Stones Records, and Marshall was to run it. The records were to be distributed by Atlantic and the company logo was a mouth – Mick's – with thick lips and outstretched tongue. Marshall had his first snort of cocaine on the tour, and according to Tony Sanchez he lost $12,000 to Bianca at gin rummy. A couple of weeks after the end of the tour the Stones held a party at Skindles Hotel at Maidenhead to mark the beginning of their exile. At about 4 o'clock in the morning the management began throwing people out, and said that they now had to close the place. Mick, who had spent good money on the party, was livid. Ossie Clark remembers him hurling a chair through a plate-glass window, in his rage, and John Lennon trying to calm him down, saying, 'Oh, come on Mick, it doesn't matter.' It was an unusually uncontrolled gesture for Mick, who did not often violently lose his temper.

Both Mick and Keith were delighted to be rid of Klein, and they both seemed pleased with their new business arrangements. Keith was pleased that the Stones' records were to be distributed by Atlantic, which had originally released the records of many of his heroes, including Ray Charles, and that their company was to be organised by the son of the founder of the great Chicago company, Chess Records. Mick probably also enjoyed these historical associations, but for him the real significance of the formation of Rolling Stones Records was that it forged alliances that would be crucial if the Stones were to survive. Mick was going to be twenty-eight in the summer of 1971. It must have dawned on him that he was no longer a teenager, and that he could not be a fake teenager for much longer. The band might have only a few years credible existence left. Or it might be that their ascendancy could be prolonged if they had the best advice in the world. Either way the financial insight of Prince Rupert Loewenstein and the professional guidance of Ahmet Ertegun were needed. Ahmet Ertegun was the president of Atlantic Records, and one of the most powerful and charismatic figures in the world of rock and roll. His family had served the Ottoman Empire, but his father had switched his allegiance to Mustafa Kemal and in 1934 he was named Ambassador to Washington. So Ahmet Ertegun, at the age of eleven, arrived in the United States. He developed an infatuation for the culture and artefacts of America that has never abated. George W. S. Trow wrote of him in the *New Yorker*:

What is most striking, of course, is that Ahmet mastered the American art of vogue-making (hit-making in the music business), which has reduced so many privileged foreigners, however infatuated, to confusion or impotence or mere greed and invitation-hustling . . . in taking the measure of Ahmet's sustained eminence in American popular music (and his more recent prominence in American social life), one should remember the long line of Chicos and Pepes and Alexandros at American prep schools and elsewhere who . . . have failed to achieve any kind of American cool. Ahmet, at some moments, has presided over American cool.

The deal was finally signed in Cannes at the beginning of April. The same month the Stones released a new single and an album. 'Brown Sugar' was a playful erotic fantasy that many of Mick's friends assumed had been inspired by Marsha Hunt. Other people, with no more reason to know the truth, insisted that it was dedicated to the black soul singer, Claudia Lennear. It was widely considered to be racist, sexist and a sensational rocker. *Sticky Fingers* presented the Stones as outlaws still, but hygienised. The dangerous debauchery of *Beggars Banquet* had been replaced by wallowing in the chicer drugs. Practically every song on the album seems to be packed with drug references – 'cocaine eyes', 'speed freak jive', 'I'm feeling so stoned', 'a needle and a spoon', 'a head full of snow'. And there is the harrowing 'Sister Morphine'. But in fact the content seems to be secondary. *Sticky Fingers* is essentially just a series of sensational songs revealing the Stones' mastery of a variety of styles. But several of the songs had been recorded during the Muscle Shoals session, days before Altamont. The Stones had not been as productive as usual since then. They planned to organise recording sessions in France as soon as they had settled down there.

Jo Bergman went 'into exile' with the Stones. Shirley Arnold remained in London to run the English end of the operation. In

May she was telephoned by Mick who told her that he was going to marry Bianca in two days time. Her job was to contact 150 people, tell them that they were invited to the wedding, and somehow get them out to St Tropez. The wedding had been planned for several weeks but Mick was desperately keen that the event should not be turned into a circus by newspapermen. So he decided that everyone, even his parents, should be told at the last possible moment. Most people accepted the invitation, although it was inevitable that some could not come at such short notice. Kenneth Anger says that he sent Mick a telegram saying that he would wait for the divorce party instead.

But a great many people wondered why Mick was marrying Bianca. It was quite normal for people in Mick's world to live together without getting married – he had already lived with Chrissie and with Marianne. Some observers accused Jagger of wanting to marry his own mirror-image, of needing to acquire Bianca because she looked so much like him. Just as he had once felt that the Baroness's blonde daughter would be a nice accessory, they said, now he wanted the girl who looked like him. Bianca herself was to say later that was why he had married her. None of Mick's friends seems to have guessed that she was pregnant at the time of the wedding. But that need not in itself have impelled them to marry. Mick had already decided twice to have children out of wedlock (by Marianne and Marsha). The real reason seems to have been that Mick actually liked the idea of marriage, whatever he said publicly to the contrary. He had tried continually to persuade Marianne to marry him, and had been angered by her refusal.

Like any good Catholic girl Bianca wanted to be married in church. She and Mick found a pretty little fishermen's chapel overlooking the harbour of St Tropez. But Mick was nominally Anglican and had to be taught the rudiments of the Catholic faith before he could be married in church. So he had been undergoing instruction for about four weeks from Abbé Lucien Baud. And Bianca needed to have clothes made for the wedding. They had turned up together late one day at Thea Porter's shop in Greek Street, Soho. 'I looked out of my office at the back of the shop and saw Mick, standing in the doorway, posing. Bianca was doing her usual impenetrable mask, and he said, "We've came to see whether you can make Bianca a wedding dress." I was feeling tired and jaded, so I just said, "Not until she's paid me for the last one." Mick absolutely shrieked with laughter and said, "I'll do anything for Bianca's honour," got out his cheque book and paid me. They looked at various things, but Bianca got more and more bad-tempered. Perhaps she didn't like being reminded of her debt.' On 8 May Mick collected two wedding rings that he had commissioned from a Paris jeweller. Shirley Arnold worked through the night and managed to contact almost everyone on Mick's list, and she arranged a plane to take them from London to Nice.

The wedding was nearly called off because of a last-minute hitch. Under French law a couple could elect to keep their property separate, or to own it all in common. Mick was keen, naturally, to keep it separate, and Bianca, equally understandably, felt that what was Mick's should be hers. He won. But the battle made them late for the Council Chamber where they had to go through the first, civil part of the contract. By now crowds of reporters and fans and interested locals were massing outside the building. The mayor, Marius Estezan, appeared to be enjoying his moment of stardom as he awaited the happy couple. When Mick heard that the Council Chamber was already besieged he ordered the long-suffering Les Perrin, the Stones' press officer, to get rid of the crowds – or else there would be no wedding. But there was not much that poor Mr Perrin could do. The mayor refused to clear the Chamber – it was, he said, a public place and everyone had a right to be there. The Chief of Police was by now having trouble keeping the crowds calm. And the mayor was becoming bad-tempered as well. He issued a counter ultimatum – that if Bianca and Mick did not show up within ten minutes there would be no wedding. Everyone gave in. The mayor waited for them, and Mick and Bianca decided to come along after all. The procedure took only few minutes. Roger Vadim and Nathalie Delon witnessed the couple's signatures.

Next, on to the church. The students protesting against the extravagance of the wedding and the local hooligans swearing at them and kicking the car did not cause much more confusion than Keith working over a photographer he didn't like the look of and smashing his camera. Good Mr Perrin was doing his best to prevent the real wedding ceremony being turned into a scrum by photographers and sightseers. He locked the heavy wooden doors of the church to keep them out. It was a pity that he hadn't made sure that Mick and Bianca were inside first, though. However, Mick finally managed to make himself heard, and his suit had not been badly damaged by the fans mauling him as he stood there. No one seems to have asked why the Queen's cousin, Lord Lichfield, gave the bride away. Like the rest of the congregation Fr Baud could hardly have failed to notice that the bride was inadequately dressed – her white suit was more than perilously low-cut. But he said nothing, and carried on with the ceremony with professional insouciance. He had obviously taken to Mick. In his sermon he said, 'You have told me you believe that youth seeks happiness and a certain ideal and faith. I think you are seeking it too, and I hope it arrives today with your marriage. But when you are a personality like Mick Jagger it is too much to hope for privacy in your marriage.' Much of the music for the wedding, chosen by the bride, came from the film *Love Story*.

The reception went on all night. Bianca had changed into a transparent black waistcoat. A local band played, followed by an English reggae group. The Stones themselves could not play as Keith had unfortunately passed out on the floor. Joe and Eva wandered around rather helplessly, looking for a opportunity to give Mick and Bianca their wedding present. Ossie Clark says that he 'quite enjoyed' the wedding. Christopher Gibbs, however, says that it was 'not the most jolly thing I remember doing. I didn't quite understand what it was all about.'

The wedding certificate recorded the marriage of Bianca Rosa Perez-Mora, twenty-six. Unabashed, the new Mrs Jagger, who had always described herself as Bianca Perez Moreno de Macias to Mick and his friends, continued to insist that she was twenty-one.

Mick and Bianca spent their honeymoon in the Mediterranean, in Venice and in Ireland. Later in the summer the Stones began recording the tracks for their next album in the basement of the house Keith had rented. Work was delayed because Mick was spending quite a lot of time with Bianca in Paris, where Jade was born on 21 October, in the Belvedere Nursing Home. Mick was ecstatic about the birth of his daughter, and telephoned Keith to tell him that he would not be back in the South of France for another three weeks. And Keith, despite his infatuation with his own infant, Marlon, seems to have blamed Bianca for this interference with the work of the band.

Chapter Nine

By 1972 it was clear that the seventies were going to be very different from the sixties. The creativity and the optimistic revolutionary energy of the previous decade were being replaced with disillusionment and exhaustion. In Britain the Heath administration was wrestling with the dreary problems that were in turn to dominate the decade – inflation and unemployment. In 1968 there had been widespread surprise at the discovery that a group of British subjects were deprived of the *sine qua non* of democracy – the vote. The Civil Rights movement in Northern Ireland had begun in a mood of hopeful conviction. It had seemed then that it was part of an inexorable world-wide tide of liberation that was to change the lives of the oppressed everywhere. By August 1971, however, the unhappy Ulster minority found themselves in an even more anomalous position compared with other Britons – they could be interned without even a show trial. 342 of them were snatched from their beds in dawn raids on the morning of 9 August. On 30 January 1972 the 1st Parachute Regiment killed thirteen Catholics during a civil rights march. The ancient grievances of the province, far from being buried peaceably, had been strengthened. The *New*

York Times, by publishing the Pentagon Papers in 1971, had revealed that the American public had been consistently lied to over Vietnam. And Nixon's bungling Plumbers had been at work for six months by the beginning of 1972, although few Americans yet knew of their activities. The United States were about to be plunged into their deepest crisis of self-respect ever. The 1960s land of dreams had already been revealed as having neither joy, nor love, nor light, nor certitude, nor peace, nor help for pain.

The chief Rolling Stones, as ever symptomatic of the times, reacted in different ways. Keith, living in his rented villa in the South of France with Anita and tribes of musicians, junkies and dealers, clung to a debauched sixties rock star's existence. Mick was immersing himself more than ever in the alternative world that Prince Rupert Loewenstein and Ahmet Ertegun represented. He had always been interested in the Stones' business affairs. Now more than ever he was fascinated by the process. One of his greatest abilities had always been to see what various people had to teach him, and to absorb the lessons. He was an assiduous student. From his new mentors he was learning about the workings of a world that had so far eluded him. It was an adult world of power and money that offered a more solid security than any to which Allen Klein, or most people in the rock world, had access. He was now establishing an unmistakable distance between himself and his audience. Mick had always enjoyed the company of rich people. And yet he had continued to seem accessible to fans, a god maybe, but one who shared their emotions and experiences, and seemed to inhabit a more lurid version of their own world. Now he was invariably described by newspapers as part of some 'jet-set'. He and Bianca seemed to swan around the world, everywhere tailed by paparazzi, looking exquisite. Bianca modelled occasionally, especially at charity functions. She was seen modelling wigs at Grosvenor House at an Oxfam function and later modelled clothes for Zandra Rhodes and St Laurent, among others. In New York she became a familiar Factory satellite, one of the people who hovered around

Andy Warhol. The Jaggers now seemed to be always on their way to or from a holiday when they were photographed – on their way to Ireland, or to North Africa, to Scotland, or to the West Indies. They went to stay with Gore Vidal in Italy, along with Andy Warhol and others of his entourage. Jagger now looked bored wherever he was seen, and the old insolence was overlaid with fastidiousness.

'In the early days Mick defended himself with bad manners – later on he used a kind of detachment. He found a way of looking at the camera which made it clear that he was keeping his distance. And Mick being the canny bugger he is, everyone found it the biggest turn-on yet,' an old acquaintance says. Richard Neville, the editor of *Oz*, was not seduced and wrote bitterly at the time of the Jagger wedding: 'The wedding was stark confirmation that Mick Jagger has firmly repudiated the possibilities of a counterculture of which his music is a part.' And David Dalton in *The Rolling Stones*: 'To many the Stones had become the very people they had once warned us against. Their image as jaded socialites parading an entourage of jet-set hangers-on seemed to trivialise them.'

The Rolling Stones' 1972 tour of America confirmed such accusations. Throughout 1971 the band had met intermittently to record the tapes for the next album, *Exile on Main Street*, which was released in May 1972 on both sides of the Atlantic. Despite the chaotic conditions in which it had been produced – much of it recorded in Keith's basement, whenever Mick could find the time to be there – it was a polished, unified collection. For some people it is the greatest Stones album of all, and it undeniably provided an authoritative sound track to adolescence in the seventies, although it lacked the dynamism and the feeling of direction of albums such as *Beggars Banquet*. But for Mary Whitehouse at least the Stones had lost none of their old pungency. She complained to the BBC about obscenities on two tracks. Lord Hill replied in an open letter that she was 'zealous is discovering obscenities', and perhaps heard what she wished to hear.

The tour was significant for the Rolling Stones. They had not played in America since Altamont. Chastened by the lessons of that night, they now had to reaffirm their appeal while keeping at bay the violent overtones of the '69 tour. Everyone close to the Stones noticed Mick's obsession with safety and security, especially his own, as the plans for the tour went ahead. He suggested that they should only play in small theatres where there was no risk of him losing control. But the cost of taking the Stones' entourage around the United States made that impossible. They had to perform in vast arenas to make the tour pay. But this time everything was minutely planned. Peter Rudge was the tour manager; Chip Monck was once again in charge of lighting and stage production. Marshall Chess, Jo Bergman and Alan Dunn, Mick's driver, travelled with the tour. Robert Frank was to make a film of the tour and Robert Greenfield was to write the book of it. By the time of the first concert *Exile on Main Street* was number 1 and tickets for Stones' concerts could only be had for a lot of drugs or $75 cash on the black market.

The first concert was at the Pacific Coliseum in Vancouver, where 2000 people who had been unable to get tickets for the show fought police in their attempt to crash the stadium. Thirty policemen were injured, but the show was a great success. The lifestyle of the Stones during the tour greatly impressed all observers. Reports described the tequila sunrises, the poppers, the cocaine and the groupies. Marshall Chess was quoted saying, 'When thirty-five chicks come to seduce the Stones, and there are only five Stones, that leaves thirty, so anyone close to the tour gets one. It's part of the ritual.' Keith was absorbing a lot of heroin by now, and was being characteristically generous with it. Marshall Chess is said to have fixed for the first time on 4 July in Washington. Mick often had a hefty snort of cocaine before going on stage, but seems to have disapproved of the 'smack' consumption on the tour. Robert Frank managed to capture some marvellous scenes of rock debauchery, especially aboard 'The Lapping Tongue', as the band's plane came to be known, because of the Stones' logo on the fuselage. Orgies involving young groupies and the road crew fascinated both Robert Frank and Greenfield. Other commentators were more interested in the glamorous camp followers that the tour attracted – Truman Capote travelled with the Stones for a few days and Princess Lee Radziwill came along for the ride. But Mick complained later about the coverage given to that aspect of the tour: 'That whole business was very exaggerated. After all, there were only two people on the tour and they were only there for a couple of days. I mean, really.' But the final concert of the tour, which coincided with Mick's birthday, encouraged still more the idea of the Stones as surrounded by celebrities. The concert was held in Madison Square Garden, and people who had been following the tour said that it was the most sensational yet. At the end Stevie Wonder sang 'Happy Birthday' to Mick, and there was a custard pie fight on stage. Afterwards Ahmet Ertegun gave a party at the St Regis Hotel, where the security was so efficient that crashing was almost impossible, although many tried. Among those with whom the gate-crashers wanted to rub shoulders were Andy Warhol, Zsa Zsa Gabor, Woody Allen, Carly Simon, Lord Hesketh, Dick Cavett, Tennessee Williams and Bob Dylan. And Warhol and Princess Lee Radziwill took Polaroid photographs. Muddy Waters and Count Basie entertained.

It is impossible to pinpoint precisely the moment when Mick stopped deferring the date of his birth. By the time of his marriage in 1971 most newspapers, but not all, got it right. In 1967 there had been a widespread belief that he had been born in 1944. But by 1972 he seems to have come clean, and so his twenty-ninth birthday could be celebrated freely.

Mick and Bianca returned to England for a while. They were seen, among other events, at the Test Match at the Oval. They spent some time in Ireland, but were back in England in September for Shirley Arnold's leaving party at the Stones' latest office, which was in New Oxford Street. Having worked for them for nine years,

Shirley had had enough of sorting out the minutiae of their lives. She had wrestled with hiring and firing their domestic staff, and with trying to protect everyone's *amour propre*. There had been the painful time when Mick wanted, at the very last minute, to go to the Olympics, and asked Shirley to arrange everything for him. The name of Jagger opened most doors, and Shirley managed to fix seats, hotel rooms and flights – all of which were generally impossible to obtain by then. 'But the next thing was that Bill Wyman wanted to go to, and of course no one had never heard of him. He gave me a very hard time because I couldn't arrange all the same things for him, and I had to try and protect him. I couldn't say why it was.'

Mick's relationship with Bianca also depressed Shirley and other members of the Stones staff. 'It used to get us down at the office, the way they were always arguing, right from the beginning. They just seemed to want to hurt each other, and there was never a time when they seemed happy. Mick didn't ever seem to us to love her, not the way he had loved Marianne. And she was very difficult.' The lack of communication between Mick and Bianca was evident. Mick turned up at Shirley's leaving party with a topaz cross from Phillips in Bond Street, which was, he said, from himself and Bianca. Soon afterwards Bianca arrived, and gave Shirley an enormous bottle of scent, 'from both of us', and there was then a memorable fracas as they argued about which of them had misunderstood the agreement over who was to buy Shirley's present.

Donald Cammell also recalls some dramatic rows between them. Mick and Bianca invited themselves to stay with a friend of Donald's in Spain: 'It just rained all the time. We were holed up in this huge old house, an incredibly beautiful Spanish ruin with a friend of mine who hated [Mick's] guts. Bianca and he were just at the torrid part of that romance. He never went out of the house and Bianca was roaming around the hills in one of these Mini Cooper jeeps with my girlfriend Myriam, who was a completely barbaric Ethiopian girl. They got into fights all the time and threw mud at each other. Most of the time Mick just sheltered in his room. He was like a little monk, living away in his cell, playing the guitar.' But although Bianca's rages were becoming famous – newspapers found out that she had shredded all his shirts during one – it seems that Mick sometimes gave her cause. There was the dinner-party in Los Angeles given by Nicky Haslam which included Mick and Bianca, a second-rate actress, an ageing *chanteuse*, a well-known New York socialite and several other people, during which Mick and the socialite went off with the actress and a couple of other girls to a hotel. They all returned before the end of the dinner-party, and Nicky says that Bianca did not reveal any irritation at the time. It is of course possible that she beat him up afterwards.

Bianca's brother, Carlos, had also come to Europe, although they do not appear to have spent much time together. He lived with Marion McEvoy, who worked for *Women's Wear Daily*, in the avenue Parmentier in Paris. He was, according to friends, 'a very bad painter and a very good man'. He was thought very good-looking when he first arrived in Paris, but his instinct for self-destruction matched Bianca's for self-protection. 'He was always high on something, or drunk. I remember a party in Paris when he tried to seduce absolutely everyone, without result. I think he finally went off with the dog. He frequently used to become belligerent when drunk, and would hit people, and break up dinner parties.' And yet many of Mick's friends who knew them both preferred Carlos, who was at least 'generous and vulnerable, whereas she was just like a cold idol, she never spoke.' But there were those who liked Bianca – who found her a refreshing change after the English and American girls that Mick had been surrounded by before. But even the people who considered themselves her friends found Bianca 'in a way graceless, because she was not at peace with herself. She was lovely, and funny, but never comfortable.'

After a couple of months recording in Jamaica Mick and the

missus returned to Cheyne Walk to spend a quiet Christmas with Jade before beginning a tour of the Far East and Australasia at the end of January. But a catastrophic earthquake devastated Bianca's hometown of Managua on Christmas Eve. 6000 people were reported to have been killed, but all communications had been cut off, so it was impossible to know what was really going on. Bianca was now frantically worried about her mother. Mick suggested that they should go to Nicaragua and find out whether she was alive, and whether anything could be done to help her. It was not possible to fly there directly. On 26 December Mick and Bianca left Heathrow for Kingston, Jamaica, and on the 28th they chartered a plane to take them on to Managua. They took with them 2000 doses of anti-typhoid serum (all that could be bought in the available time) and other medical supplies. They found that Bianca's mother was safe, but that most of the city had been reduced to rubble. Mick was shocked by what he saw. Thousands of people were homeless and in need of medical care that had not yet been organised in the chaos following the earthquake. Rebuilding the city and caring for its inhabitants was going to cost a fortune. After they had left Nicaragua Mick announced that the Rolling Stones would give a concert in aid of the Nicaraguan earthquake victims in Los Angeles. The concert, in the Forum on 18 January, raised over $500,000.

During one week at the beginning of January 1973 Mick was nominated one of the world's best-dressed men of 1972 (Bianca was on the list of the best-dressed women) and banned from entering Japan because of his drug convictions. On 4 January it was announced that Australia, too, was going to ban one (unspecified) Rolling Stone. Six concerts were already completely sold out. Astonishingly, it was six years since the Stones had played Australia. Mick had visited the country several times – he had stopped over in Sydney in April 1972 with Bianca and Jade on the way to Bali, and he had spent time there making *Ned Kelly*. But the Australian audience had not had a chance to see the Stones live since February 1966. On 9 January Al Grasby (known familiarly to his countrymen

215

as Grass-snake) of the Australian Immigration Ministry announced that he had lifted the ban on the unnamed Rolling Stone. The tour began with two concerts in Honolulu. The Stones then flew to Sydney for a press conference. The first Australasian concert, at the Western Springs Stadium in Auckland, New Zealand, attracted 30,000 people. The tour was a great success. Everywhere crowds gathered to see the Stones, and in Adelaide 5000 fans fought policemen in their attempt to get near the Stones. Even the authorities seemed to be won over. Mr Grasby said that the Stones were an example to Australian youth. 'I told them I was putting my faith in them and hoped they would do the right thing. I have no regrets that I let them in – yes, I went out on a limb to give them visas – to give a man a bad name and hang him is immoral and un-Australian.' In Auckland Mick donated sheets and pillow-cases that had been used by the Stones to an auction in aid of a local boys recreation centre. Altogether the Stones' dirty sheets raised about $NZ1100. After the tour Mick and Keith returned to Jamaica to carry on working on the next album, and by the end of March most of the tracks were complete.

In June 1973 Marsha Hunt filed an affiliation at Marylebone Court, claiming that Mick was the father of Karis. A great many people had known about the baby ever since she had been born, and Mick had never suggested to anyone that she was not his child. Marsha had always supported Karis alone. Now, according to friends, the little girl injured herself and Marsha, faced with medical bills, decided that Mick should help her out. But he was not prepared to pay up unless he had to. The day after the affiliation was filed, a statement from the Stones office said, 'None of the allegations are admitted. There are discussions between the parties about the merits of these allegations. Until these discussions have taken place no comment can be made by Mr Jagger or any of his representatives.' The discussions resulted in Mick's demand that he and Karis should have blood tests, to determine whether he could possibly be her father. The case was finally settled out of court, and Mick agreed to pay maintenance. It seemed to everyone who had known him during his affair with Marsha that Mick had behaved unusually unpleasantly over the matter.

The Stones were to tour Europe in the autumn, and in August a single, 'Angie', and the album, which was now called *Goats Head Soup*, were released. Most of the tracks on *Goats Head* were gentle and slow compared with old-style raunchy Stones. The exceptions were 'Dancing with Mr D', 'Silver Train' and 'Starfucker', which was hastily renamed 'Star, Star' at Ahmet's insistence before the album was released. 'Star, Star' by itself generated sufficient controversy to compensate for such apparent aberrations as the sentimental 'Angie'. The lyrics were more straightforward than any that Mick had yet produced. 'I suppose we ask for it if we record things like that,' Mick said of the row, 'Christ, I don't do these things intentionally. I just wrote it.' Mick displayed a new musical versatility on the album – he played piano and rhythm guitar. Even so, it was the second album in succession that seemed to be more the work of Keith than of Mick. *Exile on Main Street*, recorded in the South of France, was the first album that had not been a genuine collaboration. A great many early songs had been written while the band were on the road, or at least while Mick and Keith had been spending most of their time together. But with Mick away in Paris it was left to Keith to control the direction of *Exile*. The songs on *Goats Head Soup* were also, in general, written when Mick and Keith were apart. One or other of them would bring along a song that they had been working on, and together they would modify it. But in the old days ideas had been shared from the moment of their conception. Since *Between the Buttons* Mick had been writing some of the tunes as well as the lyrics. And Keith contributed words, but as Mick himself said in a *Rolling Stone* interview, 'People don't know who does what. And it's very difficult for me to remember who wrote what particular verse or song. Rock reviewers say: "That's a typical Keith Richards song." But they don't know. They often get it wrong, and it makes me laugh.'

By 1974 the Stones had been rolling for eleven years. And although four out of the original five were still together there had been a lot of casualties in their circle. Brian was dead, and so was Tara Browne. Michael Cooper, the Stones' brilliant photographer friend, with a fatal predilection for dope of any kind, finally OD'd, and so did his wife. Talitha Getty, Mick and Keith's neighbour in Cheyne Walk, died in 1971, according to her death certificate, from 'barbiturates mixed with alcohol'. And few of the people who worked with them had been able to take the pace for so long. 'Stu' was still around, and so was Mick's lieutenant, Alan Dunn. But Andy, the engineer brother of Glyn Johns, and Jimmy Miller, their producer, had both left the Stones by the end of *Goats Head Soup*. Jimmy was not replaced. After *Goats Head Soup* Mick and Keith produced the band's records, describing themselves in their function as producers as 'The Glimmer Twins'. At the time of *Satanic Majesties* they had lacked the experience to produce records, but they had learnt a great deal from Miller, and this time the experiment worked. Bobby Keyes, who had played horns on Stones' albums since *Let it Bleed*, had moved on. And Jo Bergman also left the organisation.

People who have worked for the Rolling Stones seem to find it an exhausting, and not infrequently destructive, experience. 'The trouble is that people always try to compete with the Stones, and it's impossible. No one can be as excessive as Keith, or compete with Mick in terms of a business brain,' Maldwin Thomas says. The most dramatic defection was that of Mick Taylor. On 12 December 1974 the Rolling Stones office issued a press release, on behalf of Mick Jagger: 'After five and a half years Mick Taylor wishes a change of scene – wants the chance to try out new ventures, new endeavours. While we are all sorry that he is going we wish him great success and much happiness.' Mick Taylor seems to have felt that he was inhibited musically by playing with the Stones. But he also seems to have been liberated in other ways. Tony Sanchez said that he needed to have a plastic replacement for the membrane that divides the nostrils, because his own had been destroyed by over-indulgence.

The Rolling Stones' sound depended on the interaction of two guitars – a replacement for Mick Taylor had to be found. There were various possibilities. Wayne Perkins, Harvey Mandel, Jeff Beck, Rory Gallagher and Robert Johnson were all auditioned in Amsterdam. But Mick and Keith were unable to agree on any of them. Shirley Arnold says that Mick Jagger first met Ron Wood at her leaving party – she went to work for the Faces when she left the Stones. Both Mick and Keith admired 'Woodie', but they did not want to break up the Faces by luring him away from them. But Rod Stewart told them that the Faces were in any case about to split up, so there was no impediment to his joining the Stones. There had been an earlier attempt to recruit Woodie – Ian Stewart had talked to Ronnie Lane (also of the Faces) about the possibility. Ronnie Lane did not pass the message on, because he knew enough of life with the Rolling Stones to know that it might be very bad for Woodie. Keith and Mick got their man anyway.

Woodie joined the Stones on the road for the first time for their 1975 tour of the United States. During this tour the Stones' stage was a massive, five-pointed, star-shaped construction, complete with built-in lights. At the beginning of each show the petals were folded up, but they would unfurl like those of some gigantic plant to reveal the band. In Los Angeles Keith was seen to kick down the petals, to make them open faster. Rumour had it that the petals were bullet-proof, and that at the first sign of trouble they would automatically fold up. Another essential prop was the forty-foot inflatable phallus that Mick rode during each performance. Once again the American tour attracted its share of celebrities. Raquel Welch, Liza Minelli and Olivia Newton-John visited the boys in Los Angeles. In New York Bob Dylan showed up, and Jack Ford, son of the President, arrived in Washington with Andy Warhol. At the concert in Madison Square Garden Mick sang 'Sympathy for the Devil' for the first time, publicly, since Altamont. A loud bang froze, momentarily, the audience and the band. It was only a fire-cracker, and everyone relaxed again after the instant of fear.

The routine was now well worked out. After the tour of North America there would follow one of Europe, the following year. Unusually, this time there was no major album to coincide with the American tour. *Made in the Shade*, released in June, was a compilation of the Stones' seventies hits so far. But by the time the European tour began in April 1976 *Black and Blue* was on sale. As the title suggests, the album attempted to reaffirm the Stones' roots, and explore various traditions of black music. It sold well, but it was not one of the Stones' most exciting productions. But the tour, on the other hand, confirmed that the band was still able to deliver the goods. Ron Wood seemed to project new energy into Keith. As Keith said during the tour, in an interview with Barbara Charone: 'Mick Taylor took eighteen months to knock into shape. Woody is there. As far as I'm concerned he's a lot more there than Mick Taylor ever was.' It was true, Woodie even looked like a Rolling Stone – scrawny, raddled but dynamic.

The Rolling Stones were by now very rich indeed. But the cost of staging their concerts was also enormous. The American tour cost about $10 million to stage, and it took, altogether, about $13 million. So there was $3 million profit. The stage for the European tour cost £150,000, lighting £125,000 and the sound system £44,000. The incidental expenses were enormous too. Mick's clothes cost £25,000. Transporting equipment from America and taking it around Europe cost £105,000. Not that the tour organisation, under the guidance of Peter Rudge, was profligate. In an attempt to cut costs Rudge even arranged to buy liquor wholesale.

But despite the scale of the operation it was becoming difficult to see how the Stones could survive much longer. *Black and Blue* had forcefully reminded audiences that the Stones had hijacked successive idioms, and that although they had produced wonderful songs they had never led the way. And during the seventies younger, raunchier iconoclasts were coming along. Glitter-rock, glam-rock, punk and other ripples of the New Wave invaded the charts with assaults on established mores more outrageous than any that the Stones had dared. Most of it was undeniably tawdry, but it threatened the Stones' territory. There were new and more credible outlaws now – it seemed that a world which had seen the Sex Pistols would find it difficult to believe in the menace of the Rolling Stones. Critics suggested, during the 1975–6 touring season, that Jagger in performance was now a parody of his old self. And yet, whenever they took to the road, the Stones justified again their self-assumed title of 'the greatest rock 'n' roll band in the world'. Whatever comparisons might be made with their earlier selves, there was still, quite simply, no one with whom to compare them.

But although with each tour the Stones defied the predictions of their demise, on the home front the late 1970s appear to have been unsettled for Mick Jagger.

Chapter Ten

Mick's marriage survived, legally, until 1977. But it had been obviously unhappy for several years before that. Mick was frequently seen with other women, and Bianca was photographed with other men. People who knew them at the time were convinced that the reason the marriage kept going so long was that Bianca was never subjugated by Mick. 'Marianne became a doormat and so he walked all over her. If she had been stronger and had fought back that affair would have lasted longer,' Ossie Clark says. Mick's affection for Marianne had survived his marriage to Bianca. They continued to have occasional assignations, and were seen by another member of the band leaving the Montcalm Hotel in London one afternoon. His wife was never under his thumb: she continued to challenge him. Bianca asserted her independence, publicly as well as privately. 'I've never been Mrs Jagger. Never. Always Bianca Jagger. There's a lot of difference. We are two very strong-willed people. Maybe each of us should have married somebody different, somebody quiet and easy-going . . . I should tell you Mick is very critical of me. He is always watching me, saying if he thinks I look wrong or something.' And on another occasion: 'He sleeps with many women but rarely has affairs with them. They are all trying to use him – they are all nobodies trying to become somebodies,' Bianca told the *Sunday Times* in 1974. She had a point. But Mick was said to be irritated with her for saying such things publicly. He tried for a long time to maintain a more decorous front with the press. Even by September 1977 he was telling the *Daily Express*: 'We are still living together and in love with each other. I haven't got the seven-year itch. In fact I didn't know we had been married for seven years until I read it in the newspapers . . . we spend six months of the year together. We take it just as it comes. I have to go and work in studios or on the road. Bianca doesn't like going on the road because there is nothing to do.' The domestic disturbance seems to have upset Mick, although he put a brave face on it publicly.

He went to stay at Leixlip, Desmond Guinness's Irish house, without Bianca. The Guinnesses were away, and Mick and Maldwin Thomas were the only people staying there. Mick seemed to be gloomy, and 'to be going through an emotional upheaval', although characteristically he did not discuss it. He lived a quiet and solitary life for about six weeks – an unusually long time for him. Occasionally he and Maldwin saw Irish friends. They went to a big party at the film-maker Kevin McClory's house. Sean Connery and his wife were there, and so was Garech Browne (Tara's brother), and Julian and Victoria (Ormsby-Gore) Lloyd. Maldwin recalls that Shirley Maclaine was at the party and continually pestered Mick about working on a rock opera dealing with oil slicks and pollution. Mick and Maldwin also visited Eric Clapton at Barberstown Castle, where Mick amazed the locals with a 'surprisingly good' 'Danny Boy'.

Ever since he had married Bianca Mick had been living a nomadic life. He never seemed to stay in one place for more than a few weeks, but Bianca spent most of her time in Cheyne Walk. The domestic arrangements there were chaotic. Staff were needed, but had a tendency to leave. One year the cook walked out a few days before Christmas. Mick, desperate, asked his greengrocer in

Chelsea whether he could recommend a cook. Bridget Matthey, a girl whose family lived nearby in Chelsea Park Gardens, was recommended, and was given the job. But although she was experienced, she had never made stuffing before. She called upon her parents for assistance. Her father, the chairman of Johnson Matthey, went round to Mick's house on Christmas Eve, and helped her out. He was delighted afterwards to be able to tell people that he thought he was probably the only chairman of a public company to have stuffed Mick Jagger's bird. For his daughter the job was enlivened by the persistent unwillingness of Mick to pay her, despite constant reminders.

Although they both seemed to be unhappy, the marriage dragged on. Friends of Mick believed that he hated the idea of divorce and was prepared to tolerate unhappiness and discomfort to avoid it. Above all, he doted on Jade and was determined to provide her with as happy and secure a background as possible.

Bianca's interest in Jade was more variable than Mick's. A friend recalls: 'Bianca has no glimmer about looking after Jade. It is all very Mommy Dearest, the whole carry on. Suddenly Jade's got to be dressed up in some wonderful new dress and brought down and shown to me or Manolo [Manolo Blahnik, the shoemaker] or whoever it is who has come to tea. It's awful, she's completely ignored for days, and then Bianca starts trying to impose her ridiculous ideas about food and stuff.'

Jade's teachers formed the same impression. She attended Garden House School in Sloane Square, where she was found to be obstreperous and uncontrollable. She would break up lessons and make a nuisance of herself, but afterwards she would climb affectionately on to a teacher's knee and curl up. 'She seemed like a classic case of a neglected child.' Bianca insisted that the school should provide special, non-fattening meals for Jade, and never allow her to eat any puddings or sweets. But her teachers say that Jade was frequently to be found trying to scrounge food from the cooks or from teachers after her meagre salad lunches. It seemed that no one took care of her. Because she was naughty her nannies tended to leave quite often, and Jade was frequently not collected from school until after 6 o'clock. Teachers or cleaners would be unable to leave the premises until someone had been to fetch her, and there would be frantic telephone calls to Cheyne Walk, trying to persuade someone in the house to come for her. But her teachers noticed her adoration of her father. She would tell them, with tremendous excitement, when she was going somewhere to see him. He showed more interest in the child's education than his wife, and when he was in London he would collect her from school and talk to the teachers about her work and her behaviour. Jade's music teacher once complained that she sang flat. 'Mick roared with laughter and said that she must get that from her mother.'

When her parents were away Jade would stay, fairly frequently, with her English grandparents. Joe and the Avon lady moved to a house in Westgate, Kent, that Mick had bought for them. Other frequent visitors were Chris and his wife and son Dmitri. The wife was later traded in for a Barbie doll look-alike, with an odd habit of gyrating mindlessly and adopting studied poses for no apparent reason. She and Chris had five children between them. He earned a living in a variety of ways – as a singer (briefly), waiter and decorator, and by selling Christmas trees.

Later Jade and Bianca moved to New York, where Jade would spend a great deal of time with Mick and Jerry Hall. She was still reported to be troublesome at school, and to have a somewhat disorganised life. But she had picked up quite a lot of worldly wisdom. According to an adult friend of Jade's in New York, she fell in love with a boy who was called Bobby Leibowitz, or something similar. But as she said, 'The thing is, I'd really like to marry him. But would you change a name like Jagger for Leibowitz?'

Bianca made sure that she was seen with men, and would intimate to reporters that her life was not lonely. But it appears to have been Bianca's ambitions to become a film star that lead to most trouble. Everyone found that she became intolerable during her movie star phase. Ossie Clark, who had always been fond of her, says that she became 'too big for her boots'. She involved him in making clothes for one of her films, but then refused to make up her mind about what she wanted. And finally it transpired that she had in any case made a pact with Valentino only to wear his clothes in the film. Her acting career never really took off. She appeared in a few films, including *The Ringer* and *Flesh Color*, but other projects had to be cancelled, not always because of Bianca. A close friend of Mick blames him for the change in Bianca: 'He certainly brought out the worst in Bianca. She got incredibly pretentious and silly.' And even her old friend Donald Cammell admits that 'her girlish charm soon wore off'.

Despite their mutual bad behaviour, Bianca's friends say that she was very upset when the marriage broke up. She had not thought that Mick would ever really leave her, even though they both had other affairs. When Bianca first filed for divorce she claimed half of Mick's fortune. She wanted the case to be heard in California, where she might expect a more generous settlement than in England. But the Appeal Court in London finally ruled in October 1979 that her case 'could not be weaker', and that the hearing should go ahead in London. It was November 1980 before the final financial settlement was reached. Although the amount was not revealed, it was generally believed to be about £1 million: less than Bianca had demanded, but more than Mick wanted to give her.

Mick was now estimated to be worth £10 million, although it was difficult to assess his wealth, since it had been obfuscated by complicated tax schemes. A constant accusation by friends and employees has been that Mick is financially mean. David Litchfield, David Bailey's *Ritz* magazine partner, was entertained that when he interviewed Mick in a wine bar Jagger not only seemed anxious that Litchfield should pay the bill, he even remembered, after a couple of hours, exactly how much he had drunk. But there are friends who have been lent money by Mick who emphasise how generous he is. His interest in the finances of the Stones' organisation, and his concern that the overheads should be as low as possible, and the profit as high, can be interpreted as a sign of business acumen rather than just stinginess. The Stones have never employed the enormous web of people that eventually bogged down the Beatles. Other rock bands, too, have found themselves supporting crowds of people, most of whose function was not quite clear. Although the Rolling Stones had offices in London, New York and Los Angeles by the beginning of the 1980s, their organisation was still taut, and employed no more people than were necessary.

It was in 1977 that the press first noticed a girlfriend who was a possible replacement for Bianca: the model Jerry Hall. Jerry was the daughter of a Texan truck driver who had risen to fame and riches on much the same circuit in Paris as Bianca. According to one informed observer, 'Jerry was the nearest thing to a real grand horizontal ever to hit town. If she was English she wouldn't even have been a starter. She's hopeless socially, she hasn't any idea how to get on with people. But because it's done in Texan it's cute.' Soon after she arrived in Paris she was taken up by the fashion illustrator Antonio, whose book, *Antonio's Girls*, provides a record of the glamorous models in that world. At one time Jerry and Grace Jones regularly performed a double cabaret act, that some people found erotic, at parties. She became the girlfriend of Bryan Ferry, whom she ditched for Mick. Ferry was understandably miffed and, while complaining to his friends about her defection, recalled that before she met him she had intermittently been flown out to Iran, at the Shah's expense, to see him. Some of Mick's friends liked her no more than Bianca: 'Very fashion crazy, this new one, Miss Hall. She's terribly pretty. She's got her ruthless streak – she obviously started off without too many advantages and glimpsed at the possibilities. Her sister's made a brilliant marriage and is terribly rich and very pleased about it. So Jerry wants to get on in the world, and she is frightfully keen on money and almost seems to equate it directly with sanctity and sex and worse. Every-

227

thing that's wonderful has got dollar signs in front of it.' And again, 'Jerry hasn't the faintest idea about how to do anything properly except how to look after her own interests and career. There's no reason why she should know how to look after a big house and so forth, and she certainly doesn't. Jerry's great failing [is] she's a great sort of bullshitter, she pretends she is doing things and knows how they should be done when nobody would mind if she just came off it and was a nice dumb model girl from Texas. But the swank that Mick seems to bring out in people is ridiculous.'

But Jerry has her admirers. Donald Cammell's wife China says: 'I think she's very, very talented. I think she could be a wonderful artist, Jerry, but people don't give her a chance. There's another much more sort of intellectual side that she doesn't let out very often, only when she's very, very relaxed – all of a sudden she'll start reciting poetry and doing things like that. She'll do sonnets and she's really very talented. I don't think people want to accept that side of her because she looks beautiful and blonde and she's Texan. If movie people could only see how talented she is. Because usually she just gets these parts where they always cast her in bedroom scenes and the two movies she was in, she was always in bed. She calls herself the Bedroom Girl.' Ossie Clark is another fan of Jerry's, and says that she absolutely dotes on Mick, even though he is rather cruel to her, and makes fun of her and imitates her accent. Other people think Jerry can cope with Mick: 'He loves to tease her but she never, never gives in to it. She's always willing to give and take, you know – it's very un-American actually. She just knows how to handle him, she knows when to act a certain way and she's a very good balance for him. It's not manipulative, though.'

And Jerry had quite a lot to put up with. Even before the 1982 summer spate of womanising there were several flings that she found out about. The daughter of an English newspaperman was one such interlude, and Jerry is reported to have telephoned her and told her, somewhat curtly, that she had found her raincoat in

Mick's flat on the Île de la Cité. The girl abandoned the raincoat rather than face Jerry's wrath.

Some of Mick's friends think that he was more smitten by Ogden Nash's granddaughter, Nenna Eberstadt, than anyone else. This affair must have made him feel his age – her mother, Isabel Eberstadt, had met Jagger with Jane Holzer in the early sixties. But the affair did not last long, and Mick's interest is said to have exceeded Nenna's. She went on to Oxford, where she got herself a first in English and a Pakistani boyfriend.

During the seventies a great many of the world's most visible heterae passed through Mick's bed. 'Mick's girls have always tended to come in two sorts. There are the international model and actress types, very glamorous, and the smart young English or American girls, most of whom are not at all glamorous. He's always found grand families as seductive as long legs.'

Mick was by now spending a great deal of time looking for new projects with which to become involved. He again considered several possible film deals. Some were with Donald Cammell, who had remained a friend since *Performance*. He spent some time in India, looking at possible locations for shooting *Kalki*, Gore Vidal's novel, which he said he was going to produce. At the beginning of the 1980s, after endless aborted schemes, he began working on a film. It was Werner Herzog's mad, grand *Fitzcarraldo*, telling the story of a man obsessed with the idea of building an opera house in the Amazonian jungle. Jagger was cast as the sidekick of Fitzcarraldo himself – who was to be played by Jason Robards. Illness smote Robards, and a war between Peru and Ecuador interfered with the filming. Other hazards included feuding local tribes and technical near-impossibilities. Jagger abandoned the project before finishing his part, and Herzog wrote his character out of the final version. Jagger's official excuse for quitting was that he had to prepare for the Stones' 1981 tour, but some observers suggested that he was motivated just as much by a feeling that the whole set-up was physically dangerous. Herzog talked about the making of *Fitzcarraldo* to Jonathan Cott, of *Rolling Stone*:

> I left his [Mick's] entire part out in my final script because I liked him so much as a performer in the film. He was so extraordinary I had the feeling that any kind of replacement would be an embarrassment. He's a great actor and nobody has seen that. I liked his attitude very much. In Iquitos, he had rented a car, a small Volkswagen; when we had some trouble getting people across town, he would chauffeur them for us. But that was only part of his general attitude. What I liked very much about him was that he knew the value of real work. And he's a professional in the very best sense of the word. The test on Mick was particularly strong, because, during the past fifteen years, he has lived quite a different life – a life where everything is organised by other people. But he adapted very quickly to the circumstances.

Of course whatever other schemes Mick had in mind, there was the work of the band, which entailed quite a lot of organisation on his part. Between 1978 and 1981 the Stones recorded in Paris, in Rotterdam, in Nassau and in New York. And there were major tours in 1978 and in 1981–2, when they covered Europe as well as North America. In 1977–8 the entire future of the band seemed to hang in the balance, as Keith awaited trial in Canada on charges of trafficking in heroin and possessing cocaine and heroin (if he had been found guilty of trafficking he might have faced life imprisonment). Finally two of the charges were dropped, and he only had to face the heroin possession rap. And even so he escaped lightly – he could well have been sent to prison, but instead he was given probation, ordered to continue an addiction cure and to play a concert in aid of the blind.

Despite their encroaching middle-age the band continued to produce impressive albums – *Some Girls* (June 1978), *Emotional*

230

Rescue (June 1980) and *Tattoo You* (August 1981). Each attracted widespread acclaim and snide criticism. And each reinforced the supreme position of the Rolling Stones. Some of the songs on these albums seemed to be retractions of earlier Stones' statements. 'Shattered' on *Some Girls* wearily questioned rock 'n' roll values:

> Work and work for love and sex
> Ain't you hungry for success, success, success, success,
> But does it matter (shattered)
> Does it matter?

'Respectable' on the same album could also be seen to admit that the Stones' world had changed: 'Well now we're respected in society, you ain't worried 'bout the things that used to be.' And 'Summer Romance' (*Emotional Rescue*) spelt it out:

> Just a few days and you'll be back in your school . . .
> And I'll be down the pub, I'll be playing pool and drinking . . .
> I'm a serious man, I got serious lusts.

Other songs dealt with the old concerns. 'Let Me Go' (*Emotional Rescue*) and 'Beast of Burden' (*Some Girls*) had lyrics that could easily have been written over a decade earlier. But it was remarkable that successful rock songs could now incorporate an awareness of ageing. Rock 'n' roll, which had seemed to be the most intolerantly youthful of youth cultures, had, by the late seventies, become the backbone of all popular culture. Against all expectations, it survived the 1970s and was not replaced by a revolutionary youth movement. The new styles that emerged were only sub-cults, within the same framework.

As the 1981 tour of the United States approached it seemed impossible that the Stones would be able to deliver once again the goods that they had been pumping out for so many years. The mytholithic process, which had for so long portrayed them as living

231

harder, faster, badder lives than anyone else ever knew how to, now conspired against them. Whether it was wasted, smacked-out Keith, or the knowing Mick who had seen everything, or Woodie who seemed to be coming along nicely in debauchery under the expert tutelage of Keith, or Bill, still scowling discontentedly after all these years, or even darling Charlie with his bald spot, it seemed that none of the Stones would be up to the tour. As it approached stories of Mick's training regime were leaked, along with hints of the extraordinary cost of the operation and the vast crowds expected. He ran between four and six miles every day, it was said, and also carried out weight training and dance exercises, under expert supervision.

The success of the tour had a significance that exceeded anything to do with music. Rock 'n' roll might still be the predominant form of popular music, but for Mick Jagger's own generation that was not enough. They needed the Stones to tour again to reaffirm that still, whatever anyone else thought, they carried their youth with them. The children of the sixties had grown up to the Stones and the Beatles. The Beatles were long defunct, but the Stones still rolled. Unwearied by age, they and their contemporaries remained adolescent while those a decade younger seemed to be condemned beyond their years. 'Rock 'n' roll' had passed out of favour and had come back. Groups had become bands and hit parades charts. The old wisdom that the Rolling Stones were Brian's creation, and that the role of Mick was overestimated, had been replaced by a new orthodoxy. Now it was Keith's genius that was said to sustain them. None of it mattered. As soon as Mick took control of the stage, it was obvious that nothing had really changed. And although the opening concert in Philadelphia creaked a little, the Stones picked up as they hit the road. They were older than they had been, and perhaps there was an edge, a gut, missing now. But nevertheless they justified themselves, and the self-image of their peers. Before the American tour began the Stones warmed up with a supposedly unannounced concert at a small (room for 300) club in Worcester, Massachussetts. Word spread and there was a riot (tepid by the old standards) for seats which resulted in eleven arrests. In New York a pair of tickets for the concert in Madison Square Garden, originally $40, changed hands along with $500. And in Seattle a sixteen-year-old girl was killed falling from a ramp. It was all just like the old days, after all. Only the takings were bigger. Prince Rupert Loewenstein and Jagger had done a deal with Jovan Inc., a massive scent manufacturing company, for sponsorship of the tour. Jovan's name appeared on every ticket sold, in return for $4 million. The tour grossed $50 million. By the time they hit Europe in the spring of 1982 the machine was functioning perfectly – and the Stones received more publicity, and more money, than ever before.

The European tour also started with a 'surprise' date at a small club, for an invited audience of friends and critics. There were then three concerts in Scotland, followed by a trek round the continent. They played on the same stage that they had used in the United States. It was a massive, 64 ft wide construction, with 80 ft ramps stretching out from either side. It was decorated with pale, whimsical Post-Modernist cars, records and guitars. And the performance was essentially unchanged since the American tour – there were twenty-six songs, mostly old favourites. Only the spontaneous gestures were different, such as the moment in Turin, where a Stones' concert (on 11 July) coincided with the World Cup soccer game between Italy and West Germany. Before the show Mick predicted that Italy would win, 2–1 or 3–1. He was proved right. During the concert the result came through – Italy had beaten the foe 3–1. And Mick came out for an encore wearing a blue football shirt with the number 20, the number worn by the soccer star Paolo Rossi.

Mick seemed by now to have his life very well worked out. He bought a château near Amboise and a flat in Central Park West as well as property on Mustique in the Caribbean. He still owned the house in Cheyne Walk, but let it 'to rich Americans', as he put it.

233

Jade began to spend most of her time with Mick and Jerry as her mother became involved on the sidelines of Nicaraguan politics. Mick had always been good with everyone's children. John Dunbar says that 'he was a better mother to Nicholas than Marianne ever was'. And Christopher Gibbs says: 'He's wonderful with children, very patient, very good and sweet. He really likes them and treats them like people.' And Mick told Cordell Marks, who interviewed him in October 1981: 'I think I'm a pretty good father. I have a nice affinity with children, not just my own. I like taking bunches of kids out for the day. Kids keep you young and they keep you laughing. Last time I went on holiday I took four kids to some beach somewhere or other. Yeah, that's including Jade. I let them run free to a certain extent and then get cross with them occasionally, especially when it's four little girls, because they're always bitching about what they're going to wear. I miss Jade a lot when I'm away. It means I can't keep a steady check on her progress.'

As Mick himself pointed out to Victor Bockris, who interviewed him in 1973, 'I am extremely lucky because wherever I go people want to meet me and they will contact me and I have access to just about anyone in the world.' In 1980 Victor himself orchestrated a meeting for Jagger. He was writing a book about William Burroughs, who had been asked to write an article about the Rolling Stones, which he wanted to do. 'He felt this affinity with the Stones, but he didn't really have anything in particular to say. So he thought it would be interesting to tape a conversation with Jagger and use that. So we invited him over to dinner and asked Warhol because he (Warhol) had taken us out to dinner on a couple of occasions and we wanted to reciprocate it.

'So Mick Jagger came down to the Bowery, where Bill lived, with Jerry Hall. He was very nice and sat down, but then there was this terrible misunderstanding because Bill had been given the impression by David Dalton, who had asked him to contribute this material, that Mick had particularly wanted Burroughs to write something about him. And Mick Jagger had been given to understand by the interviewee who arranged the thing that Burroughs had wanted to ask him about writing something. So they both had the opposite approach as to what was going on. So Mick sat down and said, "What is this about now, what do you want to ask me about?" and Bill said, "Well, I thought you wanted to ask me about something," and was kind of stand-offish. Everyone was embarrassed and there was a kind of static pause. And then Bill turned to me and said well, as I had arranged the whole thing, what was it about? So it was all embarrassing and no one knew what to say and then we were all sitting around, with dinner on the table and here was Jagger as if he was getting up to leave. So we tried very hard to have a conversation for about an hour. I thought it was very funny and ironic because here were Mick Jagger, Andy Warhol and Bill Burroughs – these great icons of the sixties – and they were all sitting together and it was so flat. Mick didn't think it was at all funny, though.

'Actually, there was an interesting sort of generation gap, because Bill tried to salvage the situation by asking Mick some questions, like, "How do you feel about the cultural revolution that's going on?" And Jagger said, "What cultural revolution? Is there one?" Mick obviously played a major role in changing things in the sixties by his lifestyle, but since he is a person who lives very much in the present, and doesn't think about the past much, he didn't see it was much of a cultural revolution going on, and there isn't. But Bill is in his late sixties and for him, in his lifetime, the world has changed radically. But still things were tense, and Bill started trying to ask questions that were intellectual, I suppose.

'Finally, I was just desperate to get the conversation going, and I said, "Well, Andy, you were shot by someone, and Bill shot someone, and Mick, did you ever shoot anyone?" Everyone looked horrified, but Mick kind of piped up at this because it interested him and he said, "Bill, you shot someone, who did you shoot?" Well, sort of anyone who knows about William Burroughs knows that he accidentally shot his wife and killed her, so I was a bit surprised. I don't know whether he didn't know, or whether he just forgot in the heat of the moment. So there was another ghastly pause and Bill really didn't want to go into this and start telling the whole story, so he just said, "I haven't shot anyone lately, Mick, I promise you that I have been on good behaviour." And shortly after that Mick called for his car to come and pick him up.'

It has been suggested that even when Mick is feeling comfortable he is not always very articulate. 'He communicates largely with grunts and groans – and by moving around a lot. He's not very good with words,' a close friend says.

Mick's friends in New York included Warhol and several of the Factory gang, especially Fred Hughes. He also saw a great deal of some of his business associates, including Earle McGrath, a record executive, and Ahmet Ertegun, as well as old friends who had settled in New York. These included an English girl, Marsia Trinder, who had made clothes for the Stones when they first came to America. She now began to make clothes for Jerry, and was responsible for several of Mick's baseball-inspired outfits on the 1981 tour. Marsia lived with Lenny Holzer (formerly married to Baby Jane) in the same building as Mick and Jerry in Central Park West. Other friends lived nearby, including Larry Rivers (the artist) with his wife Clarisse. Marsia Trinder's son, Chayter, was about four when he first met Mick. Jagger appeared in the doorway of the flat, doing a characteristic jumping leap. 'Chayter couldn't figure him out. He kept saying, "Is that a big child or a grown-up?" And Mick just kept bouncing around. Chayter still isn't quite sure what he is.'

Mick had learnt his lesson from the drug busts that had wasted so much of the Rolling Stones' time and money. By the end of the 1970s he emphasised, in almost every interview he gave, how clean-living he now was. The public relations effort was efficient, partly because it seemed credible. A man in his late thirties must lead a disciplined life in order to be able to leap around on stage for hours on end, night after night. Mick's friends would publicly

236

reiterate the same line – he never touched a thing. But for many of them 'he never takes drugs' tended to mean nothing more austere than 'no needles'. In New York Jagger has been seen to consume quite a lot of drugs. A girl who lives in that city acquired a narcotic-packed briefcase that had belonged to a recently dead relation. She gave a party and shared her hoard. Mick was one of those who attended, and he seemed happy enough to dig into the lucky dope dip more often than most of the guests. He is also seen, occasionally, the worse for drink. But his extraordinary self-control has always enabled him to diet, and to stop taking drugs and alcohol at will, so that he can quickly clean himself up and go into training before a tour.

1982 was an ace news season by any standards. First there was heinous landing of some scrap-metal merchants on an almost uninhabited rock in the South Atlantic, outraging every standard of international decency. Civilisation, democracy and the British Empire were threatened. England once again faced a mighty, ruthless enemy, and once again she refused to be intimidated. She assembled a mighty fleet, and every true patriot's heart beat faster with pride at the thought of bashing Argies. Finally our brave boys beat the dago hordes that had swept unchallenged from one corner of the Falklands to the other. Meanwhile history was made back home as, for the first time in history, a Pope visited the British Isles. John Paul II visited England, magnanimously in view of the dreary schismatic heresy that most Englishmen had practised, nominally at least, for the past three hundred years. And then, to compound the national rejoicing, the Princess of Wales gave birth to a son – the future King of England, Wales, Scotland, the Falkland Islands, Gibraltar and Northern Ireland. Joy knew no bounds, except in Northern Ireland where three quarters of a million Catholics took it personally that the family who governed them against their will should name their heir after the ancestral enemy of the Catholic population – King Bully, as he is familiarly known to one and all in those parts.

But just when our cup seemed to be in danger of running over –
we had had a decent summer to boot – England's calm was shattered
by the news that Mick Jagger's home life was disrupted once again.
The storm broke 5 November, when Nigel Dempster devoted an
entire page of the *Daily Mail* to the story, entitled 'Sangster is
Hallmarked and Mick don't get no Satisfaction'. The gist of it
was that Miss Hall had ditched Mick for Robert Sangster, multi-
millionaire racehorse owner and football pools heir. The two were
said to have planned a rendezvous in America, and Jerry was quoted
as saying, 'Where could I go after Mick? Robert can buy him out ten
times over.' Sangster had already eloped once before, with Susan
Peacock, wife of a former Australian Foreign Affairs Minister,
Andrew Peacock, at Christmas 1974. It was noted that Jerry claimed
to have an IQ of 162. Since Mick had been photographed night-
clubbing in New York the previous month with at least three different women, it seemed that everyone concerned had got what they
deserved. But the Jerry-go-round, as the world's press began to
describe it, was only just beginning. She was in Los Angeles staying
at the Beverley Wilshire. Sure enough, Sangster soon hotfooted in
from Melbourne and booked into the adjoining suite. From east
and west, from north and south, came the TV crews, the paparazzi,
the reporters and the gossip column stringers. Mick, meanwhile,
went off to Paris, talent-spotting. He had, after all, been in New
York for weeks on end. Mr Sangster's wife, Susan (ex Mrs Peacock), deciding that Melbourne was where the action wasn't, flew
into Heathrow, and then went on to the Sangster house, oddly
called The Nunnery, on the Isle of Man. Jerry then flew out of
Los Angeles, and was spotted arriving in New York. Sangster told
newspapers, 'It is true I have seen her [Jerry] here [Los Angeles].
But I have not left my wife.' And Jerry, clearly as unwilling as
anyone to see a good story die, said, 'Who knows what any of us
will be doing in the future?' But her next move had been predictable. She flew into Paris, where Mick met her at the airport. She
was seen running into his arms, and his first words, 'Where have

you been, then?' were reported by most of the world's newspapers. (Not surprisingly – it was a terrible affront to the notions of the power of the press that anyone, anywhere, did not know exactly where Jerry had been.) Next, Sangster left Los Angeles, stopping off at the bloodstock sales in Lexington, Kentucky, on the way to New York. Then it was reported from Paris that Mick had asked Jerry to marry him. The other man then travelled to Shannon airport whence he flew by private plane to the Isle of Man. Not to be outshone by the Jagger/Hall reunion, the Sangsters got themselves photographed having dinner at a restaurant in Douglas, Isle of Man. A friend of theirs was reported saying, 'It's their way of showing they are still together.' But, just when it seemed that everyone was back where they had started, and all four were being super lovey-dovey, publicly, with the right people, Jerry was reported to have flown back to America. And in Nigel Dempster's column, where we had first learnt of the drama, friends of Jerry's revealed that Mick had 'physically twisted her arm' as they drove away from the airport. And then, as suddenly as it had flared up, the story died down. The media could not continue to be so absorbed in Mick's domestic imbroglio for ever. There was another sex scandal that autumn: the intrigue of the poodle bitch sent to a stud kennel who appeared, judging by the look of her progeny, to have been involved in a spot of freelance nookie. And Keith and Mick had to get to work on the new album.

Although Mick and Jerry appeared to be more or less reconciled after the brouhaha had died down, none of Mick's friends held out much hope for the relationship. 'Mick isn't going to stand for being humiliated by her going off – he just won't ever forgive her,' one says. And others saw a pattern in the way in which Mick's *affaires* ended which seemed to be repeating itself. 'Mick gets bored with them and starts playing around, but he is affectionate and indecisive and can't make a break. But he makes their lives hell, and they go off with whoever comes along. Then Mick goes berserk with rage at anyone daring to cuckold him. So he makes them come back, but then treats them worse than before. It happened with Chrissie Shrimpton and with Marianne. Only Bianca got away. I'd give it a year, eighteen months.' The newspapers had made much, in their speculation about the affair, of the suggestion that the rift was caused because Jerry wanted to have a baby but Mick didn't. It seems an unlikely explanation, in view of Mick's love of children, and stated desire to have more. Marriage would seem to be a more likely bone of contention, if there was such a thing. Jagger has said consistently, ever since his divorce, that he would never marry again. The emotional and financial cost of his divorce from Bianca had been too high for him to risk repeating it.

For the next few months the Stones, and especially Mick, seemed unable to keep out of the press. There was the sub-plot of Keith's marriage plans. It was announced, over and over and over again, that he was about to marry his girlfriend of five years, Patti Hansen. There was the continuing drama over whether or not Mick could write the story of his own life. And just as the issues seemed to be resolving themselves the story got another shot in the arm. The Hell's Angels, it was revealed, had not forgiven Mick for trying to shift the blame for the unfortunate death of Meredith Hunter onto them. A committee of the United States Senate was investigating the activities of the Angels, and among the mass of evidence it received was the testimony of a former Angel identified during the hearing as 'Butch'. Butch was said to be the former president of the Cleveland Chapter. He informed the committee that even though the Angel who had been charged with the stabbing had been acquitted, the Angels had not overlooked Mick's perfidy. Butch, who was unfortunately himself serving a prison term for murder, said that the Hell's Angels had an 'open contract' out on Jagger, or any Rolling Stone. 'This has been discussed many times, killing the band,' he said. 'Anyone doing this would get in good grace with the California Angels.' He also made it known that since Altamont no good Angel ever listened to Rolling Stones music. The terrifying idea of being the object of an Angel's vendetta was lessened slightly as he went on to say that, due to circumstances beyond their control, the Angels had already goofed twice in attempts to dispatch Mick. In 1979, Butch said, they had tried to blow up a 'waterside mansion' where the Stones were staying, by planting plastic explosives under the house. But the best laid plans can go wrong. A raft on which the explosives and the assassiniferous Angels were heading for the house sprang a leak and sank. So that scheme had to be abandoned. The other attempt had been even more pathetic. An Angel, equipped with a gun and a silencer, had stalked around a hotel, methodically planning the murder that would take place when the Stones arrived. It was through no fault of the Angels that the band cancelled their reservation. But still, the Senate hearing was bad for the Angels' image. It confirmed the secret belief of many that the Hell's Angels were just a bunch of amateurs, full of enthusiasm, admittedly, and fine for beating the brains out of anyone who happened to be on the spot, but hopeless at anything that required planning. Mick, however, was taking no chances. He and Keith are both said to have stepped up their personal security arrangements as a result of Butch's revelations. They could not have been more upset than Sonny Barger, who, in an attempt to salvage the Angels' reputation, said that there was no hit list, and that the Hell's Angels and the Rolling Stones were the best of friends and often partied together. But this brave face-saving attempt was sabotaged by the Stones' spoilsport London office, who said that there had been no evidence of the Angels on the 1981–82 tour, partying or otherwise.

Fear for his own safety seems to be one of Mick's few weaknesses. It is something that has always worried him, and understandably the murder of his friend and New York neighbour John Lennon seems to have made matters worse. It was probably one of the factors that lead him to buy a house in Riverside Drive. It would be easier to guard than an apartment. Otherwise, apart from the constant striving not to spend money, he seems to have far fewer worries than most people. His contemporaries from Dartford

Grammar School are by now heads of departments in big schools, partners with firms of City solicitors, businessmen and redbrick university lecturers. They are middle-aged men, successful or otherwise, with the burdens and responsibilities of children, mortgages, career struggles and so on. Twenty-five years ago they and Jagger inhabited together the cut-throat, bitchy, sex-obsessed world of clever adolescents. Mick still does. The life of a rock superstar offers the freedom and the indulgent self-absorption of adolescence, without its anguish. Of his class at school Mick Jagger must be the only one whose present life would be envied by his fifteen-year-old self. The most dramatic difference between his life at fifteen and at forty, apart from the wealth, must be that in the pursuit of sex he is now, frequently, the quarry not the hunter. Many of his friendships involve some of the nastiness that characterised his teenage relationships. 'He's always having fights with people – all you hear is a stream of bitchiness. The fun for him is bitching about people, it's the fun of that sort of fag-hag life. He's always been a fag-hag. Loves being surrounded by them,' according to an old friend.

Mick continues to seem, as he always has done, happier and luckier than most people. Donald Cammell: 'Mick is coldblooded but instinctive. And in his own work his instincts are absolutely spot on and accurate most of the time. He's got a better batting average than anybody else in the league when it comes to the product. The strength behind him has always been commercial success, otherwise he wouldn't be the kind of performer he is or have the crowd he has emotionally. He can still wow the kids. But another thing is that he's unbelievably lucky. He never knew what it was to have to struggle for something. He talked about, they all used to talk about, what a hard time they had, you know, but it took him about a year and a half to come from absolutely nowhere, from being in school to being a superstar. I'm not saying what that means from a musical point of view, but from a personal point of view it meant that he had just been conditioned to a certain kind of adulation at such an early age, even when they were still comparatively young in their twenties, that they were totally imprinted with it. One thing is that he's stuck with a lot of courtiers that hardly anybody would want to have, and so a lot of his life is fucked up by that. But at the same time, again it's a question of mirrors. He loves seeing pictures of himself. He's a performer, he's a star, and his beauty has been his greatest joy. That's the most important thing for him, far, far and away more important than anything else. There would be – he'd have no hope if it wasn't. The greatest love in one's life can't compare with that thrill of performing . . . You see, I think all this thing about trying to find out the real person behind the artist is irrelevant. It simply isn't like that in real life, they're the same person, always breaking down into the different. It's the same person only they live in different mirrors. Mick is *par excellence* as a performance. Sometimes you get him on a good night and he's playing a character that's really interesting and sometimes it's *unbelievably . . .*'

Select Bibliography

Aftel, Mandy, *Death of a Rolling Stone* (Delilah Communications, 1982)

Carr, Roy, *The Rolling Stones: An Illustrated Record* (New English Library, 1977)

Charone, Barbara, *Keith Richards* (Futura, 1979)

Christian, Peter, 'It's Only Minnesanger . . .' (unpublished paper)

Dalton, David, *The Rolling Stones: The First Twenty Years* (Thames and Hudson, 1981)

Miles, *Mick Jagger in His Own Words* (Omnibus Press)

Sanchez, Tony, *Up and Down with the Rolling Stones* (William Morrow; Wild & Woolley, 1979)

Scaduto, Antony, *Everybody's Lucifer* (Mayflower, 1975)

Tremlett, George, *The Rolling Stones Story* (Futura, 1974)

Index

245

247